POLITICAL ECONOMY OF ENVIRONMENT

PROBLEMS OF METHOD

ENVIRONMENT AND SOCIAL SCIENCES
ENVIRONNEMENT ET SCIENCES SOCIALES

2

PARIS • MOUTON • THE HAGUE

MCMLXXII

POLITICAL ECONOMY OF ENVIRONMENT

PROBLEMS OF METHOD

Papers presented at the symposium
held at the Maison des Sciences de l'Homme, Paris
5-8 July, 1971

PARIS • MOUTON • THE HAGUE

MCMLXXII

Published in collaboration with

ÉCOLE PRATIQUE DES HAUTES ÉTUDES, VIe SECTION

Library of Congress Catalogue Card Number : 72-76340

Printed in France

Contents

Introduction

The growing concern with environment both on part of public opinion and government is forcing economists to take a new look at the state of their art.

Are we able to measure adequately social costs and human welfare? Can we take care of negative externalities in our calculations supposedly leading to rational choices? Is the failure of the economic profession to tackle in time the issue of environment to be credited to fortuitous circumstances, bad use of existing tools, lack of such tools or deeper theoretical weaknesses?

In other words, does the present insatisfaction arise out of lack of development of *economics of environment* — an extension and application of economics of choice or praxeology? Or are we facing a much deeper crisis which calls for a breakthrough at the level of *political economy of environment*, a social science aiming at revealing the complex interplay of all interests at stake, digging into the relationship between environmental disruption and the working of social systems and, last but not least, not hesitating to take a normative approach instead of pursuing the illusory goal of optimization? Such a breakthrough would lead to the complex of issues related with the organization of future-oriented decisions and people's participation therein, *i.e.*, to planning conceived as an institution and not as a set of techniques.

All these questions came to the fore or were present behind the scene, at the Paris symposium on which is based the present volume.

For obvious reasons, we could not expect that so many and so important problems would find a solution there. The Paris symposium was meant as a beginning of a timely discussion, a *tour d'horizon* of the methodological and theoretical problems looming behind the fashionable subject of environment, a confrontation of conflicting viewpoints.

Out of our discussions emerged a much clearer understanding of each other's approach and some consensus on priorities of research to be followed. It was also agreed that periodical meetings devoted to more specific problems of political economy of environment would be held. In this way, the Paris meetings was a follow-up of the Tokyo 1970 Symposium on "Environmental disruption: A challenge to social scientists", organized by the International Social Science Council. This continuity was emphasized by the fact that we held our symposium under the auspices of the Council and that Professor S. Tsuru, Chairman of the ISSC Study Committee on Environmental Disruption, chaired both meetings.

January 1972
Paris, École Pratique des Hautes Études

IGNACY SACHS

SHIGETO TSURU

In place of GNP

Les grandes personnes aiment les chiffres. Quand vous leur parlez d'un nouvel ami, elles ne vous questionnent jamais sur l'essentiel. Elles ne vous disent jamais : "Quel est le son de sa voix ? Quels sont les jeux qu'il préfère ? Est-ce qu'il collectionne les papillons ?" Elles vous demandent : "Quel âge a-t-il ? Combien a-t-il de frères ? Combien pèse-t-il ? Combien gagne son père ?" Alors seulement elles croient le connaître[...] *On ne voit bien qu'avec le cœur. L'essentiel est invisible pour les yeux.*

Antoine de Saint-Exupéry, Le petit prince.

1.

It was Edmund Burke who wrote two centuries ago that "the age of chivalry is gone ; that of sophisters, economists, and calculators has succeeded". He was essentially referring to that period of momentous transition from feudalism to capitalism which was epitomized succinctly by Sir Henry Maine as that of "from status to contract". The transition was hardly a conscious act of social engineering. It was, as historians have shown, and evolutionary social process wherein the seeds of transition were nurtured in the very dialectic of feudal societies.

It appears that we are, as far as advanced capitalist countries are concerned, confronted with another great transition in our socio-economic history, again not as a consequence of systematic planning by social engineers, rather as a cumulative effect of societal responses within the logic of existing institutional arrangements. We may say, paraphrasing Burke, that "the age of calculators is gone ; that of humanists is succeeding". Of course, "humanists" is a somewhat inadequate term here and would be better replaced by another, if such could be found or coined, to convey more precisely the meaning of what I intend to depict in this essay as characterizing the new age which is evolving.

That "the age of calculators is gone", however, seems to be certain. Not that there is no longer any place for "calculators" in our society; there may, in fact, be more of them in the near future. But what is certain is that what they produce, as calculators, will carry no more meaning than we assign to them in the full awareness of their specific relationship to human welfare and that numerical measures such as GNP will not automatically carry connotations as to the magnitude or extent of economic welfare. We shall have to question increasingly the meaningfulness of certain quantitative measures or indexes which in the past we have been conditioned to take for granted. Or rather, it would be better to say that we should turn around and address ourselves to any calculated measures with an attitude of complete innocence as to their specific welfare content.

In general terms, there are two reasons justifying this scepticism. One is the serious crack in the connecting links, which, in the past, could be assumed, between the calculated figure of national income (or GNP) and the relative magnitude of economic welfare. The other is what Marx referred to as "the development of the societal individual" [1] or the transformation of human labor made possible through technological progress such that it "no longer appears as enclosed in the process of production — man rather relates himself to the process of production as supervisor and regulator [...] and the great pillar of production and wealth is no longer the immediate labor performed by man himself, nor his labor time, but the appropriation of his own universal productivity, *i.e.,* his knowledge and his mastery of nature through his societal existence" [2]. This second point is related to the first inasmuch as "as soon as human labor, in its immediate form, has ceased to be the great source of wealth, labor time will cease, and must of necessity cease to be the measure of wealth, and the exchange value must of necessity cease to be the measure of use value" [3]. In other words, correspondence between the *physical* aspect and the *value* aspect in society's production becomes broken and the answers to welfare problems have to rely more and more on analysis of the concrete, physical content of any particular situation. In what follows we shall concentrate mainly on the first of these two points.

1. K. Marx, *Grundrisse der Kritik der politischen Ökonomie*, Berlin, Dietz Verlag, 1953, p. 593.
2. *Ibid.*, pp. 592-593.
3. *Ibid.*, p. 593.

2.

Economists' habit of equating the growth of GNP [4] with that of economic welfare used to be firmly enough grounded. There was a time, for one thing, when mass unemployment was a direct cause of severe suffering for millions of people and any measure that expanded effective demand, even including the nonsensical digging and refilling of holes in the ground, was regarded as a positive step towards increasing welfare so long as it brought about a net increase in employment. In fact, the close association of growth in GNP with that of economic welfare, in the minds of economists, developed in the period immediately following the Great Depression, thanks largely to the Keynesian revolution in economic thinking.

But aside from this short-run policy orientation of the GNP concept, there is a longer-range association, which could be predicated, between the size of GNP and the magnitude of economic welfare provided certain assumptions could be justified. The assumptions are of the type inherent in a mature exchange economy where practically all the economic goods are priced in the market. They are 1) that external effects, either positive or negative, are insignificant, 2) that the condition of consumer sovereignty obtains, and 3) that the failure of the reward system, for whatever reason, is insignificant.

True, even in the heyday of competitive capitalism these three assumptions could not be fully justified. Negative external effects were often serious enough, as is evidenced in the pollution damage caused to agriculture and forestry by the Ashio copper refining plant in Japan in the late 19th century. But in the era when the minimum requirements for the health of the workers were ignored in the interest of industrial prosperity, environmental disamenities were of secondary consideration. The doctrine of consumer sovereignty, too, one may say, was never more than a complacent rationalization by economists. In an address to manufacturers, John Ruskin perorated, more than one hundred years ago [5] :

> "You must remember always that your business, as manufacturers, is to *form the market* as much as to supply it [...] But whatever happens to you, this, at least, is certain, that the whole of your life will have been spent in corrupting public taste and encouraging public extravagance. Every preference you have won by gaudiness must have been based on the purchaser's vanity; every demand you have created by novelty has fostered in the consumer a habit of discontent; and when you retire into inactive life, you may, as a subject of consolation for your declining years, reflect that precisely according to the extent of your past operations, your life has been successful in retarding the arts, tarnishing the virtues, and confusing the manners of your country."

---

4. Here the term "GNP" is used interchangeably with "national income" or "national dividend".

5. Lecture delivered at Bradford in March 1859. See J. Ruskin, *The two paths*, London, Smith and Elder, 1859, pp. 109-110 (italics added).

Ruskin was no doubt a sensitive soul; but here is an insight — that "manufacturers form the market" — which could not easily be refuted, even in the days of laissez-faire market economy. As for the third assumption, it may be enough to make reference to the discriminating bias, due to inheritance, which gave a head-start to a select group of men, enabling them to capture a share in the national pie independently of their own efforts.

In spite of these deviations, however, we may say that, in the heyday of competitive capitalism, the presumption of a close association between magnitude of GNP and that of economic welfare was relatively free of seriously misleading connotations. But today matters are different in advanced capitalist societies. Not only is it true that technological progress has heightened the possibility of negative external effects of gigantic proportions, but at the same time the preference scale of consumers is gradually evolving in such a way that amenity rights of all kinds, not susceptible to quantification, are acquiring greater importance than before. It is especially important to remind ourselves at this point that nature, which is essentially a whole, made up of interrelated parts, best rewards those who respect this whole, and that as we make progress in the arts of controlling nature, the socio-economic system characterized by individualistic pursuit of profit maximization within the restricted horizon of "internality" is less likely to be capable of coping with the task of making the best use of nature's endowments. Here, the term "externality" is made to cover more and more of what, left out of the "internal" calculation, is yet of increasing importance from the welfare point of view.

As for the presumption of consumer sovereignty, Ruskin's indictment would surprise no one today. Galbraith, in particular, made a similar point forcibly, and in a more matter-of-fact way, by contrasting the "accepted sequence" of the unidirectional flow of instruction from consumer to market to producer with the "revised sequence" where "the producing firm reaches forward to control its markets and on beyond to manage the market behavior and shape the social attitude of those, ostensibly, that it serves" [6]. As regards the third assumption concerning the reward system, however, one could point to an improvement of a kind in recent decades on the grounds that inheritance and gift taxes are severer today in most capitalist countries than before and, in addition, opportunity for higher education and training are undeniably greater now than in the last century. The principle of equal pay for equal work is also becoming a reality. But a question has to be raised as to the meaningfulness of relating reward to the number of labor hours performed by each individual. We have already touched on this problem earlier and drawn attention to the fact that the degree of dependence, in the process of production, upon instruments incorporating man's "uni-

6. J.K. Galbraith, *The new industrial state*, Boston, Mass., Houghton Mifflin, 1967, p. 212.

versal productivity" is so large nowadays that human labor in its *immediate* form has ceased to be the great source of wealth, and labor time will cease to be the measure of wealth. We may be inexorably approaching the stage of social development where the precept of "to each according to his needs and from each according to his ability" will apply. More important still, this very development demands that we revise our thinking on the significance of emphasizing flows, rather than stocks, when we wish to obtain a measure of economic welfare.

In other words, the close association which once we could assume between magnitude of GNP and that of economic welfare has become tenuous in advanced capitalist countries as the impact of technological progress upon productive relations renders the old assumptions increasingly untenable. In view of this, we shall next focus directly upon those factors which play a part in actually expanding GNP and yet whose welfare significance is questionable.

3.

As stated earlier, the concept of GNP is predicated on the exchange of goods in the market, and is intended to cover those goods and services which are exchanged in the market. As a corollary of this, it may be added that the unit for measurement of GNP is money value as registered in the market. If one gram of opium, baneful as it may be, has the same market value as one kilogram of rice, these two items are considered equivalent in national income accounting. Welfare content is essentially concrete ; but when aggregated into national income or GNP, all goods and services acquire a single dimension, namely that of market valuation, and the quantitative expression obtained does not necessarily relate to concrete welfare content.

Stated alternatively, the concept of GNP is best applicable to a mature market economy, and its welfare significance depends essentially upon the performance of markets as an objective intermediary between final consumers and suppliers. A viable market is a market which can be sustained by the "money votes" of final consumers, who in turn part with such "money votes" in order to satisfy their wants and needs. But here is the rub. Man's needs in a society are often relative to institutional and other conditions of that society which may be contrived ; and man's wants are often artificially stimulated by suppliers of goods and services who, in extreme cases, are capable of actually embracing the market under their wings. In other words, among the "money votes" which consumers cast, and which thus enter as components into the GNP, there are some whose welfare significance are questionable ; and here we shall classify them into five different types :

1) "The cost of life" type
2) "Interference of income" type
3) "The institutionalization of waste" type
4) Depletion of social wealth
5) Inefficiency of dynamic adjustment.

"The cost of life"

We are all aware that, within our own consumption expenditure, there are certain items which fall into the category of necessary cost, which we prefer to remain as small as possible. Heating cost in a cold country would be the simplest example. High commuting cost without compensating advantages in environmental amenities, as we observe in a dense urban sprawl such as Tokyo, is another. But there are more sophisticated examples of cost-type consumption which induce citizens to part with their "money votes" on account of certain institutional and social developments. One example of this kind relates to the widespread use nowadays of expensive burglar alarms in America to cope with the mounting incidence of burglary in homes. A news item in *The New York Times*[7], with the headline " Booming burglar alarm industry finds that fear of crime pays " reported :

7. August 16, 1970. In this connection one cannot help recalling a discerning passage from writings of a "classical" economist a century ago, to wit : "A philosopher produces ideas, a poet poems, a clergyman sermons, a professor compendia, and so on. A criminal produces crimes. If we look a little closer at the connection between this latter branch of production and society as a whole, we shall rid ourselves of many prejudices. The criminal produces not only crimes, but also criminal law, and with this also the professor who gives lectures on criminal law, and in addition to this the inevitable compendium in which this same professor throws his lectures onto the general market as 'commodities'. This brings with it augmentation of national wealth, quite apart from the personal enjoyment which — as a competent witness, Herr Professor Roscher, tells us— the manuscript of the compendium brings to the originator himself. The criminal moreover produces the whole of the police and of criminal justice, constables, judges, hangmen, juries, etc.; and all these different lines of business, which form equally many categories of the social division of labor, develop different capacities of the human spirit, create new needs and new ways of satisfying them. Torture alone has given rise to the most ingenious mechanical inventions, and employed many honorable craftsmen in the production of its instruments [...] The effects of the criminal on the development of productive power can be shown in detail. Would locks ever have reached their present degree of excellence had there been no thieves? Would the making of bank-notes have reached its present perfection had there been no forgers? [...] Crime, through its constantly new methods of attack on property, constantly calls into being new methods of defense, and so is as productive as strikes for the invention of machines." Probably few economists today can identify the author of this passage. It is from K. Marx, *Theories of surplus value*, Moscow, Foreign Languages Publishing House, 1964, Vol. 1, pp. 375-376.

"Sales, they [manufacturers of burglar alarms] say, are a direct reflection of rising crime rates, and the projections are for a continuing steep upward trend. Burglary, or unlawful entry to commit a felony, was the single most frequently committed crime last year (1969), with 81 percent of the incidents listed as unsolved. Homes and apartments are prime targets. In Los Angeles, the city with the highest crime rate in the nation, the police reported 65 546 burglaries and attempts last year, against 36 256 in 1960. Single residences led the list with 21 968 burglaries, and apartments were second with 14 092 [...]
A typical home alarm system protects all exterior doors and windows with contact switches or other circuit interruptors. Entry when the system is not deactivated with a key or a switch usually sounds an alarm, or turns on the lights, or both. In some systems, it also alerts the installing company's central headquarters, which in turn calls the police [...] Such a system costs about $500 to install with a service charge of about $20 to $30 a month."

Whatever the explanation for the prevalence of this type of crime, citizens are more or less forced to take measures of self-protection on an individualistic basis. And the cost of burglar alarms for homes is a part of consumer expenditure, and thus constitutes a component of GNP. But it is clearly what might be called a "cost type" consumption, or a part of "the cost of life", and no one would dispute the fact that the smaller it is, the better.

True, it is often very difficult to draw a hard and fast line between cost-type consumption and end-object type. But there are fairly clear-cut cases of what used to be a luxury or a semi-luxury becoming a necessity in a dynamic situation. A good example, from Japan, would be the process of disappearance of public bath-houses. At present, about one-third of the population of Tokyo ward districts have no private baths in their homes, and there are upwards of 2 000 public bath-houses in the area. The break-even point fort a typical public bath-house calls for about 600 daily customers ; and yet it is reported that customers of many bath-houses have dropped to one-half of this level, owing to the steady increase of private baths at home. Thus, one after another, the public bath-houses are closing ; and casualties in recent years have been at a rate of twenty per year. Prices are periodically raised, but the loss of customers proves fatal for many. When a public bath-house disappears in a typical district, one third of the residents will have to choose between two alternatives : either go to a bath-house farther away or install a private bath at home. Private baths may be said to be a semi-luxury ; but in the circumstance they *become a necessity*. Furthermore, when one public bath-house disappears, the range of consumers' choice is narrowed.

A similar problem arises whenever a public establishment requiring a fair-sized number of customers to break even competes with private means of satisfying the same need on an individual basis. A bus line may be discontinued at a stage when there are still a large number of people for whom it is indispensable. When that happens, the purchase of motor-cycles or automobiles becomes a necessity and people may well consider such an expenditure as an added cost of life.

"Interference of income"

The term was used originally by the late Schumpeter who, in the light mood of cocktail conversation, jestingly disparaged the profession of American lawyers on whose services he had to depend when he went through the red tape of naturalization. Keynes, no doubt, would have sympathized with him for he, too, apparently felt the ubiquity of lawyers in the United States as essentially redundant. The story he told in his closing speech at the Bretton Woods Conference is quite well known [8].

The "interference of income" phenomenon might be defined as the generation of income by otherwise dispensable services, which are made indispensable through built-in institutional arrangements in the society concerned. There is usually a historical background explaining why a particular service acquires built-in indispensability in a particular society, and there is, of course, no opprobrium implied in singling out a particular profession as "income-interfering". As a matter of fact, an "income-interfering" profession in a particular society draws very often the best of brains in that society and its members distinguish themselves as outstanding citizens of the community. If lawyers serve as an example of "interference of income " in the United States, we may say that bankers and real estate dealers do so in Japan.

Here we may append a concrete example of the role of legal specialists citing a recent news item from the United States. With a headline : "Lawyers stand to reap substantial rewards in Penn Central case", *The Wall Street Journal* reported [9] :

> "To creditors, shareholders and bondholders of Penn Central Transportation Co., the railroad's decision to reorganize under the Federal Bankruptcy Act means plenty of uncertainty and woe. But for many members of the legal profession, it's nothing short of a bonanza [...] By the estimate of one attorney familiar with the intricacies of railroad reorganization, about 1 000 lawyers could eventually become involved, drawing fees totalling as much as $50 million. 'And that', the lawyer adds, 'could be a low figure' [...]
> In any event, some lawyers could well make an entire career out of the Penn Central mess. The late Russell Dearmont was appointed counsel to the trustee of the Missouri Pacific shortly after it entered reorganization proceedings in 1934. The case dragged on until 1956. Soon afterward, Mr. Dearmont was named a vice president of the road. He moved up to president in 1957."

---

8. Here is the relevant passage as reproduced in R.F. Harrod, *The life of John Maynard Keynes*, London, Macmillan, 1951, p. 583: "I have been known to complain that, to judge from results in this lawyer-ridden land, the *Mayflower*, when she sailed from Plymouth, must have been entirely filled with lawyers. When I first visited Mr. Morgenthau in Washington some three years ago accompanied only by my secretary, the boys in your Treasury curiously enquired of him — where is your lawyer? When it was explained that I had none — 'Who then does your thinking for you?' was the rejoinder."

9. July, 23, 1970.

The pattern of Mr. Dearmont's career is strikingly similar to that of many a banker in Japan.

"The institutionalization of waste"

Veblen wrote as early as in 1904 [10] :

"The absorption of goods and services by extra-industrial expenditures, expenditures which seen from the standpoint of industry, are pure waste, would have to go on in an increasing volume. If the wasteful expenditure slackens, the logical outcome should be a considerable perturbation of business and industry, followed by depression."

This is a prophetic statement ; but it is misleading to refer to these wasteful expenditures as "expenditures which, seen from the standpoint of industry, are pure waste". Business enterprises by nature abhor waste in the context of their own calculations. Whether a certain good or service is wasteful or not is not to be judged "from the standpoint of industry" but only from the standpoint of final consumers. What is at issue here, however, is not a moralistic assessment of extravagance or dissipation. Economists *qua* economists have nothing to say to a person who knowingly wastes something for his own enjoyment. But when waste is institutionalized in such a way that a less wasteful alternative, which may well be preferred by consumers, is deliberately withheld from the market, we are called upon to analyze the mechanism which makes this possible, and to draw out the necessary implications for economic welfare. Examples of built-in obsolescence, etc., are legion, as popularized by the writings of Vance Packard, and the mechanism wich encourages this type of GNP-inflating expenditure has been fully analyzed by Galbraith.

Depletion of social wealth

GNP is a flow in the same way as my monthly expenditure or daily food intake is a flow. Just as I can increase my monthly expenditure by drawing upon my past savings, we can make our GNP larger than otherwise would be the case by depleting our store of resources without replacing them.

It is true that there are certain resources used in the process of production that cannot be replaced. The earth's mineral deposits are of this

10. T. Veblen, *The theory of business enterprise*, New York, Mentor Book, 1904, p. 120.

type. So far as these resources are concerned, it would be meaningless to speak of replacing them, and the only alternative open to us is to find ways of economizing their use when the depletion process goes too far. There are, however, various other types of social wealth which, in different degrees and with differing time patterns, can be replaced after being used. Forestry and marine resources come immediately to mind in this respect, but we may also include here clean water, natural beauty and other environmental endowments, all of which, after all, provide the source of healthy and enjoyable life. By ignoring the need for conserving such amenities, a country can raise the growth rate of its GNP more rapidly than if it paid heed to them. The rapid growth of Japan's economy during the last decade provides a good example of this.

Inefficiency of dynamic adjustment

An economy in the modern world is always confronted with the need for dynamic adjustment in its use of resources. An example may be drawn from present-day Japan, where the area traditionally under rice cultivation is now patently in excess of needs and is likely to remain so in the foreseeable future although transfer of land to other uses is called for to the extent of at least 500 000 acres. In fact, as many as 830 000 acres of paddy field were left idle in 1970 and compensation was paid to farmers who cooperated in this reduction program. This year, an even larger area is likely to be involved in this program.

There is a pressing need for land both for industrial sites and for residential quarters. The need for additional factory sites by 1975, for example, is estimated to be about 250 000 acres, as calculated on the basis of the 10.6 percent per annum GNP growth rate during 1971-1975. The recent economic growth of Japan has seen a radical shift in the industrial structure — a shift from primary to secondary industries with greater and greater concentration in the heavy and engineering branches of manufacturing. Probable development in the near future is also in the same direction. If such is the case, we may expect that reallocation of land use from rice cultivation, for example, to factory sites, would be in order, and would continue to be so in the near future. This is one of the types of dynamic adjustment which economic rationality calls for. Actual development, however, has been otherwise, not because rice land on the whole is inconveniently situated from the standpoint of locating manufacturing plant, but for a number of reasons, among which the subsidy and compensation programs for farmers and the farmers' expectation (thus far justified) of continued rise in land prices have been major factors holding in check any large-scale reallocation program. As a matter of fact, the cost of reclaiming coastal bays is now definitely lower than the price demanded by farmers for nearby agricultural land for potential non-agricultural use. Thus the government, in cooperation with prefectural authorities, who generally welcome the establishment of new industries in their regions, has started a gigantic reclamation program along almost the entire coast of Japan's archipelago. The program for 1966-1970 involved the creation of new factory sites by reclamation to the tune of 37 000 acres ; and the new five-year program for 1971-1975 is three times the size of this, the cost of which is expected to run to three trillion yen. This sum is equivalent, on an annual basis, to one half of the total value added in the iron and steel industry and will no doubt contribute to the growth of GNP to that extent. It may be added that reclamation, both in the recent past and as planned in the near future, is taking place in the coastal bay areas, many of which are included within national parks or government-designated parks, and is damaging not only to natural beauty and to the recreational opportunities offered but is also, in some places, crippling fishing industries unique to the region. The most flagrant instance of a national park being sacrificed for industrial expansion is the reclamationn taking place in the Inland Sea. It is as if one were to spread the kitchen of one's house into the beautiful garden without providing for sewage facilities.

4.

The unusually rapid growth of Japan's GNP during the past fifteen years can be shown to have entailed all five of the GNP-inflating factors which have been mentioned in the preceding section. Those who are committed to "growthmanship", when pressed on this point, do admit that some of the growth components of GNP have been of doubtful character, from the welfare point of view, and that inefficiency in dynamic adjustment also existed. But, they point out, at least one thing is certain, namely that the aggregate supply capacity of the country is indicated faithfully enough by the GNP index, and they go on to stress that given that capacity, which keeps on growing, we can and should devise ways of improving our dynamic efficiency, and take measures to help restore consumer sovereignty to its rightful place.

Here is a problem which has been raised time and again in relation to the institutional motive force of economic activities under capitalism. An innocent GI was reported to have asked once : "If our economy can prosper by the production of 'the instruments of death' ; why could it not prosper better by the production of 'the instruments of life' ? " On a more sophisticated level, Keynes himself deplored the fact, in 1940, that it might well prove politically impossible, except in war time, to plan an expenditure program on a scale sufficient to confirm the validity of his new theory [11]. In other words, under given conditions of institutional arrangement, effective demand tends to flow into directions circumscribed by the influence and resistance exercised by dominant interest groups in the society. Take the example of the reclamation project referred to in the previous section. Here is an industry, already established, doing business on a scale of 600 billion yen a year, obviously concerned to continue in business. Pitched against them are individual citizens, large in number but unorganized, who may deeply deplore the loss of environmental amenities but have no effective way of registering their "money votes" in favor of conserving the beauty of nature, clean-water beaches, fishing facilities, etc. The only effective means they have at their disposal, at present, are political. Is economics incapable of translating the genuine preference of citizens in such matters as environmental amenities into terms comparable with those of market-valued goods and services so that it would somehow be possible to calculate the *net* positive welfare achieved? Must we visualize the situation as a confrontation between angels' and devil's advocates, neither of whom can concede to the other?

Attempts have been made in many quarters to compile some kind of a welfare index based on specific indicators, such as hospital beds, park areas, educational opportunities, sewage facilities, etc., but although each one of these is quantifiable, they are not commensurable in dollars and cents.

One need not dispute the usefulness of such a welfare index; but it certainly cannot take the place of GNP as an overall quantitative measure of economic welfare. A much more fruitful approach appears to me to be the ressuscitation of Irving Fisher's concepts of "capital" and "income" [12]. Attention was called to these concepts by Kenneth Boulding twenty years ago [13]. Nicholas Kaldor [14], too, found them useful in making a case for his proposal for "an expenditure tax". For Fisher, "income" consists solely of services as received by ultimate consumers, whether from their material or from their human environment which together might be called "social wealth" or "capital". Social wealth consists not only of producers' real capital such as plant and equipment but also of what are nowadays called "common property resources" as well as geological cap-

11. *New republic*, July 29, 1940.

12. I. Fisher, *The nature of capital and income*, New York/London, Macmillan, 1906. As a matter of fact, Fisher developed this set of ideas much earlier and published them in "What is capital", *Economic journal*, December 1896. The idea dawned on him, according to his son, "in the summer of 1894 as he drove from Lauterbrunnen toward Zermatt: 'It suddenly occurred to me while looking at a watering trough with its in-flow and out-flow, that the basic distinction needed to differentiate capital and income was substantially the same as the distinction between the water in that trough and the flow into or out of it'". See I.N. Fisher, *My father Irving Fisher*, New York, Comet Press, 1956, p. 123.

13. K. Boulding, "Income or welfare", *The review of economic studies* 17, 1949-1950, pp. 77-86.

14. N. Kaldor, *An expenditure tax*, London, Allen and Unwin, 1955, pp. 54-78.

ital and consumers' real capital. In this scheme, "production" is defined as an addition to this social wealth and "consumption" as a subtraction from it. Since "income" is essentially proportional to the stock of social wealth, "consumption" would have a negative effect on "income" while "production" a positive one. It is worth recording that Pigou, who took issue with Fisher over this problem, conceded that Fisher's conceptual scheme would be appropriate if one were interested in "comparative amounts of economic welfare which a community obtains over a long series of years" [15]. It is precisely for this purpose that I propose to make use of Fisherian concepts in place of GNP.

The statistical work involved here is, in the first instance, similar to that of compiling national wealth statistics. But it is not identical with the traditional estimation of national wealth. Although I do not propose to develop a full-scale methodology in this paper, we may take one component of national wealth, namely the stock of residential buildings, to illustrate the type of considerations we will have to introduce if we are to quantify social wealth as a welfare-related concept for the purpose of making historical comparisons.

The gross stock of residential buildings as a component of national wealth is usually estimated by 1) making tabulations of physical structures in terms of floor space, type of construction (such as wooden, reinforced concrete, etc.) and age, and 2) applying measures of valuation as if all the buildings were new. The net stock can be subsequently obtained by deducting an estimated value of depreciation for each type of structure. Measures of valuation do not usually reflect anything but the cost of construction and, therefore, are extremely limited as an index of welfare. If we are going to approximate the latter, we will probably have to take into account the following items :

a) Basic facilities for residential buildings such as provision of separate washrooms and kitchen ;

b) Environmental amenities such as exposure to sunshine, freedom from noise and air pollution, availability of playgrounds for children, etc. ;

c) Cost of commuting inclusive not only of transport cost but also of time cost involved ;

d) Shopping conveniences.

Not all these items, of course, are quantifiable ; but they are usually reflected in the rent paid or the property price itself or the price of residential land in a *relative* manner at *a given point in time.* Comparison over time of rents or property prices, even when deflated by a specific price index, does not, unfortunately, reveal the real changes over time as regards the various amenities cited above. Thus a basic difficulty of quantification

15. A.C. Pigou, *The economics of welfare*, London, Macmillan, 1932, p. 36.

remains. But some of the relative rent (or property price) differentials at a given point of time can be utilized to show historical changes in constant value terms. For example, a study by Ridker and Henning [16] — which showed that in the central city area of St. Louis (for the year of 1960) a reduction of sulfation level (by 0.25 mg/100 cm2/day) was correlated with a rise in the residential property value (of $ 83) — could be used as a basis for making historical comparison of welfare values of residential buildings. To the extent that relevant amenities themselves are quantifiable and are reflected in real estate prices at a given point of time in a manner permitting a statistically significant inference, we may say that a historical comparison of the type we seek is feasible. As for the cost of commuting, a more direct comparison over time is possible, although the compensating advantage of suburban living is difficult to quantify. On the whole, I believe that we need not despair of compiling a welfare-related index over time of at least some components of social wealth.

If we succeed in making quantitative comparisons of this sort as regards residential building for, let us say, two bench-mark years like 1925 and 1965, I suspect that the result will show a marked discrepancy between the stock approach suggested here and the flow approach typified by the use of GNP or national income. A rough order of the magnitude of such a discrepancy can be indicated in the case of Japan. Per capita real income in Japan rose by roughly four times between 1925 and 1965 and the proportion of expenditure on housing out of total household expenditure declined from 16.9 percent to 10.6 percent between these years. "Expenditures on housing" were divided, in both of these years, almost equally between those on "houses" and those on "fourniture and utensils". This means that expenditure on "houses" rose in real terms by 2.5 times between these years. On the other hand, the stock approach estimation shows that per capita floor space, to begin with, increased only by roughly [17] 15 percent over these years and that, according to one authority [18], the total stock of residential building in Japan increased from 9 934 billion yen in 1938 to 10 832 billion yen in 1960, in 1960 prices, that is by 9 percent (while the population increased by 32.2 percent over the same period). If we are to supplement these figures with considerations related to the relevant amenities, considerations which are admittedly impressionistic, it appears to me that the net change in the welfare stock

16. R.G. Ridker and J.A. Henning, "The determination of residential property values with special reference to air pollution", *The review of economics and statistics*, May 1967, pp. 246-257.

17. Statistical studies on this matter are extremely complicated, involving as they do such questions as urban vs rural, the household basis vs the per capita basis, the traditional style structure vs the western style structure, etc. Here it is sufficient if we obtain a rough measure of the change.

18. Professor K. Ohkawa. But the figures are still quite preliminary.

value of residential buildings in Japan over the forty years between the middle of the 1920's and the 1960's was, if at all, in a negative direction. Even if we err grossly on the optimistic side, the stock approach will give us at best a 15 percent rise, and this is to be compared with the 2.5 times rise in the flow approach.

Although the statistical scaffolding is as yet extremely inadequate, we can at least see that an alternative approach, within the Fisherian conceptual framework, is feasible in our attempt to obtain a measure of changes in economic welfare to replace the flow approach, which relies on GNP or national income figures.

PHILIPPE POMMIER

Projet de réponse à la contribution du Professeur Tsuru

Un entrepreneur ou des actionnaires cherchent dans la comptabilité d'entreprise, dans les grandeurs caractéristiques qu'elle fait ressortir (chiffre d'affaires, "cash flow", endettement, etc.) et dans la structure du bilan une mesure de l'état de santé de l'entreprise, un guide pour sa gestion. Mais ils ne prétendent pas y trouver un indicateur du bonheur ou du degré de satisfaction du personnel. S'ils s'interrogent sur ces problèmes ils auront recours à d'autres instruments de connaissance. Ceci ne veut pas dire que le bonheur du personnel n'interfère pas avec la santé d'une entreprise. Un mécontentement peut se traduire par des grèves ou des baisses de productivité qui apparaissent dans les résultats comptables de l'entreprise. Réciproquement, la "santé" de l'entreprise conditionne souvent la possibilité d'améliorer les conditions de travail et les salaires. De même la comptabilité d'entreprise n'est pas l'instrument de connaissance le mieux adapté à la définition de la stratégie de développement de la firme. Il faudra avoir recours à des études de marché, à des analyses de prospection technico-économiques... Cependant, une bonne comptabilité facilitera ces études ; une bonne gestion sera souvent une condition fondamentale pour la mise en œuvre de la stratégie choisie ; et le choix d'une bonne ou d'une mauvaise stratégie se répercutera certainement à long terme sur les résultats comptables de la gestion.

La comptabilité nationale est à l'échelle de la nation ce qu'est la comptabilité d'entreprise à son niveau : un bon guide pour la gestion courante. Elle ne prétend pas être un indicateur du bonheur ou du bien-être de la population. Elle ne peut pas être, en son état actuel, le seul instrument des choix stratégiques du développement.

Il est bien vrai que certains agrégats dégagés par la comptabilité nationale tels que le GNP ou le revenu national par habitant sont statistiquement fortement corrélés avec les principaux indicateurs généralement admis du développement ou du bien-être social : taux d'alphabétisation, nombre de lits d'hôpital, densité de téléphones, etc. Mais il serait dangereux de vouloir en faire une mesure du développement ou du bien-être social.

La communication du professeur Tsuru risque donc d'engager la réflexion dans de fausses routes en isolant arbitrairement des agrégats tels que le GNP de l'ensemble du schéma descriptif de l'économie que représente la comptabilité nationale. Il n'est pas difficile de démontrer que le GNP mesure mal ce qu'il ne prétend pas mesurer. On notera au passage que cette démonstration est d'autant plus facile que le mode de calcul des grandeurs de la comptabilité nationale est très précisément fixé. Sachant ce qu'il mesure, il devient possible de jouer avec les paradoxes et les perversions du GNP : si vous épousez votre femme de ménage, le GNP diminue même si le bonheur social augmente !

C'est l'utilisation du GNP comme indicateur du niveau de développement qui devrait être critiquée. Il est par exemple contestable de juger l'efficacité de la politique des pays en voie de développement en fonction de leur performance en taux de croissance du GNP. Et lorsque de ce jugement dépend l'octroi de crédits par les agences internationales d'aide au développement, il ne faut plus parler d'absurdité mais de volonté délibérée d'orienter la politique de ces pays dans des voies qui ne peuvent que les maintenir dans leur situation de dépendance et de sous-développement.

Si l'on veut se doter des instruments de mesure et de description de la réalité sociale nécessaires à la définition d'une politique de développement, deux voies sont possibles si l'on a reconnu que la comptabilité nationale telle qu'elle est actuellement pratiquée ne répond pas à cet objectif.

La première consiste à rechercher un moyen de mesurer le bien-être, de quantifier le développement. Dans cette perspective il semble nécessaire de bien marquer les limites et les différences de nature entre ces instruments à construire et la comptabilité nationale. La comptabilité nationale est un système de présentation de l'information très fortement intégré par l'utilisation d'une unité de mesure comme la valeur monétaire. Ce facteur d'intégration disparaît dans un système de statistiques sociales qui sera donc composé par la juxtaposition de plusieurs sous-systèmes plus ou moins articulés entre eux par l'utilisation d'un corps de nomenclatures commun. Il ne sera donc pas possible de dégager des indicateurs synthétiques du type GNP.

L'autre voie consisterait à garder l'hypothèse que la réalité sociale et le bien-être sont des conséquences de la structure économique. Il importe donc que les systèmes de mesure et de description fassent apparaître la réalité de la structure économique; cela veut dire qu'il faut profondément modifier la comptabilité nationale qui, dans une certaine mesure, masque cette réalité. Il faut écarter la notion de branche qui ne permet pas d'étudier les antagonismes entre différents modes de production, il faut faire éclater l'unité de l'agent "ménage" qui masque les différences de condition et les luttes entre les différents groupes ou classes qui constituent la société. Il faut analyser le pouvoir économique de ces groupes en étudiant la composition de leur patrimoine.

En résumé, une critique de la comptabilité nationale paraît bien nécessaire mais elle doit porter sur l'ensemble de sa structure et non superficiellement sur quelques agrégats mal interprétés.

CLAUDE MAESTRE

Outils de décision collective et qualité de la vie

Introduction

La "qualité de la vie". Ce bienfait que le développement économique devait apporter est devenu l'obsession pour ne pas dire le mirage des pays développés, peut-être leur luxe.

S'ils n'ont plus faim, les nantis se sentent malgré tout encore lésés. De nouveaux agresseurs ont surgi derrière les réalisations dont l'homme tirait sa fierté, et, pourri par une dure expérience quotidienne, il commence à remettre en question les données et les moyens du chemin jusqu'ici parcouru.

L'homme s'interroge. Quelles déficiences recellent les outils utilisés? Quelle part de lui-même qu'il sent blessée a été négligée? Vers quels horizons qu'il croyait auparavant heureux, et plus indiscernables que jamais aujourd'hui se dirige-t-il? Comment infléchir ce qui n'est pas inéluctable?

Les normes de l'économie classique, sur lesquelles se sont bâtis tous les développements et élaborées toutes les décisions, lui paraissent les premières contestables, et avec elles, les outils qui ont fourni les éléments de l'action. A quel stade se trouvent en France ces révisions? Celles-ci touchent à la fois les outils, les méthodes d'analyse et les structures. Avant d'aborder dans une étape plus lointaine les concepts, ce document abordera successivement les trois points ci-dessus énumérés.

L'outil de comptabilité nationale

La décision collective, dont la charge revient essentiellement au gouvernement, se concrétise dans l'acte budgétaire. La préparation de ce dernier se fonde essentiellement sur un outil, la comptabilité nationale.

Il ne saurait être question ici, ni d'en expliquer le fonctionnement qui sera supposé connu, ni d'aborder dans le détail et dans le fond ses déficiences reconnues. Il sera fait simplement état de quelques réflexions mettant en relief ses lacunes les plus apparentes.

1. *Considérations sur l'état et l'utilisation actuelle des comptes nationaux*

a) Valeur en tant que comptabilité *ex post*.

Les comptes nationaux ont été conçus dans le but de donner une image correcte de la situation économique du pays. Ils sont fondés sur les informations relatives aux flux marchands, et comme tels sont à même de refléter correctement une situation passée, tout en étant contingents, et de la valeur de ces informations, et des structures privées ou publiques susceptibles de les fournir.

Étant donné la dimension et la relative inertie des agrégats utilisés, les comptes nationaux peuvent servir de base pour des extrapolations à court terme permettant d'augurer des conséquences comptables de tel ou tel choix budgétaire sur l'économie nationale.

Moyennant une sophistication supplémentaire portant sur des agrégats en quantité physique (coefficients techniques, élasticité), et des hypothèses d'évolution relative en valeur, la comptabilité nationale a pu servir de fondement dans la préparation des plans de cinq ans.

b) Déficiences en tant qu'outil servant à la décision.

Sans mépriser pour autant les services rendus par les comptes nationaux en leur état actuel, il faut bien constater leur imperfection aussi bien dans le cadre de la décision budgétaire que dans celui de la planification.

— La nomenclature des comptes nationaux est une nomenclature de branche avec tout ce que cette notion comporte d'imprécision, de contingence par rapport aux structures existentes génératrices d'information, et de manque de souplesse pour prendre en charge l'évolution de la production en particulier sous l'influence de l'innovation.

Mais il y a plus grave, car la prise en charge quantitative d'éléments qui ne sont finalement que des moyens, conduit à privilégier implicitement ceux-ci par rapport aux services qu'ils seraient censés rendre.

Cette remarque est importante car elle rejoint la critique souvent faite aux budgets, d'être des budgets de moyen et non des budgets de programme.

— C'est ainsi que l'image donnée de l'économie par les comptes nationaux soit dans le cadre du budget, soit dans le cadre du plan, tend à se transformer en objectif. Ce fait est criticable sur deux plans: celui de la substitution de moyens aux objectifs comme on vient de le voir; celui de l'élimination dans la vision de l'état du pays et de la société qui l'habite, de tous éléments ne rentrant pas dans le cadre comptable. Or ce sont ces éléments qui, on le verra plus loin, touchent au plus près les problèmes de qualité de la vie. En fait, les comptes nationaux devraient être semble-t-il, beaucoup plus un outil de contrôle d'un cheminement qu'un instrument aidant à fixer les objectifs d'une collectivité.

Tout au plus pourrait-on admettre dans ce dernier cas sa valeur comme instrument servant aux tests de cohérence, ce dernier critère n'étant qu'un parmi d'autres, et pas forcément le plus important, pour de multiples raisons qui ne peuvent être commentées ici.

— Les concepts nationaux français, en l'état actuel des choses, donnent une description insuffisante des interventions de l'État, et ce fait limite fort, dans le cadre même de son utilisation au sein du budget, sa valeur d'instrument de décision.

Un outil digne de cette acception doit en effet permettre de saisir aussi directement que possible toute intervention du décideur et ses conséquences. Faute d'une adéquation suffisante entre l'instrument de préparation des décisions et les pouvoirs qui l'utilisent, toute intervention de ces derniers risque fort d'être mal préparée.

— Dans leur état présent, les comptes nationaux rendent compte très insuffisamment du comportement des agents économiques.

D'une part, en l'état actuel de leurs structures, ceux-ci sont saisis de façons très inégales; certains, telle la sidérurgie, sont correctement comptabilisés étant donné leur forte structuration et leur homogénéité, d'autres, telle la santé, sont approchés de façon tout à fait globale, imparfaite au travers d'une entité sans homogénéité.

D'autre part, et dans ce dernier cas en particulier, les grandeurs fournies sont des moyennes non assorties d'indications sur la dispersion des mesures.

Il faut signaler également que jusqu'à présent, les données fournies par la comptabilité nationale française n'étaient pas comparables à celles données par les comptes nationaux étrangers.

La mise au point récente, dans les deux cadres de l'ONU et des communautés européennes, d'une structure générale devrait permettre un alignement entraînant la comparabilité.

— Enfin, la description de la sphère non marchande de la vie collective est notoirement insuffisante. Ce dernier point touchant plus particulièrement au propos de ce document sera détaillé dans le chapitre suivant.

2. *Considérations sur les déficiences de la comptabilité nationale vis-à-vis de la "qualité de la vie"*

Pour bien comprendre les remarques qui vont être faites sur le cadre comptable national du point de vue de la qualité de la vie, il faut avoir présentes à l'esprit ses principales caractéristiques qui sont de faire ressortir:

Le processus de production marchande

La répartition et l'emploi des revenus issus de cette production

L'accumulation et le financement du capital physique

La valeur ajoutée au cours de la production

La rémunération des facteurs de cette production et l'investissement

Le rôle d'arbitre joué par les ménages entre la consommation et l'épargne

Le rôle de régulateur à court terme de l'activité économique joué par les administrations au moyen de la masse de leurs recettes et de leurs dépenses et par la nature des transferts qu'elles effectuent.

La critique des comptes nationaux peut, étant donné ces remarques, être faite à deux niveaux:
— Le premier de ces niveaux abordera les déficiences directes de la comptabilité nationale face à la prise en compte de la qualité de la vie, étant donné ses structures propres, variables, nomenclatures relatives.
— Le deuxième niveau tentera d'expliciter les déficiences par rapport aux hypothèses implicites faites par le cadre comptable.

Seront avancées ensuite quelques considérations sur l'évolution de ce cadre soit en lui-même, soit par mise au point de cheminements complémentaires.

a) Déficiences du premier niveau.

La comptabilité nationale n'embrasse que les relations à titre onéreux, c'est-à-dire qu'elle ne considère comme biens et services que ceux d'entre eux qui s'échangent ou peuvent s'échanger sur le marché.

Il en résulte, du point de vue de la qualité de la vie ou de son cadre, que:
— Les services rendus à titre gratuit ne figurent pas dans les flux positifs;
— Les nuisances produites ne figurent pas à titre de flux négatifs;
— Les prélèvements sur la nature ne figurent qu'au coût d'enlèvement.

1) Les services publics, auxquels revient de fait la responsabilité des éléments du cadre de vie susceptible d'en assurer la qualité au titre de la collectivité, ne figurent que par leurs recettes et leurs dépenses, et nullement par les services rendus.

En effet, l'investissement créateur figure bien dans le Produit Intérieur Brut (PIB), mais le flux de services en résultant les années suivantes ne se retrouve pas, car il ne donne pas lieu (ou ne donne lieu que partiellement) à des transactions marchandes (les écoles, les hôpitaux, par exemple).

Dans le PIB actuel, on s'enrichit en faisant des Tuileries un parking payant et de Notre Dame un immeuble de bureaux. De la même manière, la construction d'immeubles quels que soient les sites détruits, les normes, la vocation, contribue à accroître le PIB.

Ne figurent pas davantage évidemment les services individuels rendus à titre gratuit aux individus (travaux domestiques) ou à la collectivité (entretien ou aménagement de la propriété privée dans sa partie cadre public).

2) Les nuisances ne figurent pas comme flux négatifs, leur développement n'est pas budgétairement freiné. C'est là une sorte de prime donnée à l'incivisme.

La comptabilité nationale valide, sur le plan collectif, tous les calculs égoïstes puisque nulle part les pollutions ou les encombrements, ceux de la voie publique par exemple, ne sont considérés comme des pertes pour la collectivité.

Corollairement, la valeur des investissements réparateurs est sous-estimée du fait non seulement que les services rendus par le capital investi n'est pas comptabilisé, mais que ce service non saisi compense une nuisance.

3) Du fait de la seule comptabilisation au coût du prélèvement des ressources naturelles, il y a implicitement vision faussée de l'insertion de l'activité humaine dans le processus éco-biologique. Une comptabilité nationale fondée sur les seules transactions financières compte pour peu de choses dans la nature sinon pour sa seule utilité dans le processus de production.

D'autre part, ce même processus de production peut utiliser des ressources naturelles sans les payer, et donc sans qu'elles soient pour autant comptabilisées. Il en est ainsi de l'eau dans les centrales productrices d'énergie ou dans la sidérurgie, de l'air dans la plupart des phénomènes de combustion.

b) Déficiences du deuxième niveau.

Le calcul économique et chacune de ses expressions telles la comptabilité nationale, est fondé sur un corps d'hypothèses explicites. L'utilisation des outils de ce calcul peut être abstraite, et la contestation des hypothèses nulle. Leur image peut s'étendre à la réalité des choses et là encore la validité des fondements peut n'être pas outre mesure contredite. Quand le champ d'application touche de plus près à la réalité des êtres, il se revèle bien vite combien la technique utilisée repose sur des fondements irréalistes, le vécu manifestant ses exigences. Sans prétention d'exhaustivité et à titre de démonstration, ce document exposera sommairement trois types de déficiences du deuxième niveau:

— Déficience provenant de l'hypothèse implicite d'exactitude des données numériques;

— Déficience provenant de l'irréalisme des hypothèses faites sur le système des prix;

— Déficience provenant de l'hypothèse implicite de représentativité des utilités par les valeurs ajoutées.

1) Il est de fait que la quasi-totalité des calculs économiques sont effectués à partir de données non assorties de l'appréciation de leur marge d'erreur, et la comptabilité nationale n'échappe pas à cet état de fait.

Ceci est grave car les hommes sont fixés sur les chiffres, fascinés par leur magie, sans en voir la relativité et l'incertitude. Il est fort possible, comme l'avance O. Morgenstern, que le consensus créé autour du chiffre sans erreur soit essentiellement d'ordre politique, malheureusement, les conséquences de cette omission ne sont pas seulement d'ordre numérique, elles touchent à la vie d'une collectivité.

Que penser de la polarisation sur le PNB quand on découvre que les embouteillages le font croître par une consommation d'essence accrue et des montants de course en taxi augmentées!

Que penser des comparaisons sur les données du commerce extérieur quand on constate que les chiffres d'échange en brevets et licences entre deux pays A et B, varient dans un rapport de 1 à 7 suivant que la source d'information est A ou B!

Malheureusement, et tout particulièrement dans les milieux gouvernementaux, on ne fait pas de telles distinctions. Il faut reconnaître toutefois que la vulnérabilité des modèles économiques aux erreurs est variable. Mais qui peut préciser celle des comptes nationaux au regard de l'utilisation qui en est faite?

2) Le système de comptabilité nationale postule l'unité de signification de tous les prix. Or la chose est fort loin d'être vraie, car les prix parfaits reflètent les utilités marginales, ce qui est fort loin d'être réalisé pour de multiples raisons. Par exemple une situation de monopole engendrera fort probablement des prix supérieurs au coût marginal.

Une situation d'oligopole pourra engendrer une relative stabilité des prix, quelles que soient les variations de coût et de demande.

D'autre part, et de plus en plus, l'État intervient sur les prix par les taxes, les contrats, etc. Ceci est particulièrement flagrant dans le cas des prix agricoles.

On peut ajouter, et la chose est très importante, qu'il y a en général sous-évaluation des produits et services du secteur public. Enfin, et nous limiterons ici ces remarques sans prétention d'exhaustivité, les variations de prix ne peuvent refléter pour de multiples raisons les variations de qualité des produits.

3) Réduits à un chiffre dans le cadre des comptes nationaux, les grands agrégats ne donnent qu'une dimension des phénomènes qu'ils représentent: cette dimension est la valeur, celle-ci est due à leur caractéristique qui est d'avoir un prix. Celui-ci est alors insidieusement promu au rang d'unité de mesure des satisfactions, alors même que ces dernières ne s'additionnent pas pour une même personne et qu'elles sont différentes et non comparables pour des personnes différentes.

Les comptes nationaux effectuent donc par l'intermédiaire des prix des additions d'utilités non sommables!

Ne dit-on pas en outre de certaines choses essentielles de la vie qu'elles n'ont pas de prix!

En fait, l'acte d'achat est considéré comme un vote de ratification, la production des marchandises vendues étant approuvée par le corps électoral des clients.

Ceci peut être valable à la rigueur individuellement, ou au niveau des collectivités dont les membres éprouvent des besoins encore vitaux. Au stade des pays développés, cette optique est certainement fausse. Elle l'est encore plus si l'on envisage la conduite de l'économie par les technostructures chères à Galbraith!

3. *Évolution des comptes nationaux*

Il est bien certain qu'une évolution des comptes nationaux qui prendrait en charge les remèdes aux déficiences signalées plus haut (dont il faut rappeler qu'elles ne sont pas exhaustives) est difficilement envisageable à court terme.

On peut se demander d'ailleurs si elle est envisageable en dehors d'une évolution des concepts dont l'amorce commence à peine à poindre.

En tout état de cause, la comptabilité nationale évolue sur sa lancée dans trois axes qui seront successivement et sommairement abordés.

a) Rapprochement du cadre comptable international

b) Construction de comptes intermédiaires

c) Construction de comptes satellites.

a) Rapprochement du cadre comptable international.

Le rapprochement du cadre comptable international affecte les trois points suivants simplement énumérés:

— Du point de vue des secteurs:

. Classement des unités structurées en "secteurs institutionnels" selon leur fonction économique principale.

. Administration privée et administration publique constituent des secteurs institutionnels séparés.

. Séparation des entreprises d'assurances et des institutions de crédit.

— Du point de vue de la production des administrations.

On voit apparaître, dans le cadre comptable international, le concept de production non marchande des administrations. Cette production, mesurée conventionnellement par son coût, est consommée pour l'essentiel par les administrations publiques. Cette évolution dans la prise en compte des activités non marchandes devrait s'accompagner de progrès dans l'analyse des coûts.

En effet, cette production est considérée comme étant le fait de branches non marchandes des administrations dotées chacune de comptes de production et d'exploitation (enseignement, santé, recherche, administration générale).

— Du point de vue des comptes de patrimoine.

Des recherches sont en cours en ce domaine, aussi bien en France que dans le cadre de la Commission économique pour l'Europe des Nations Unies.

b) Construction des comptes intermédiaires.

De façon générale, le besoin s'est fait sentir de comptes intermédiaires entre les comptes nationaux et les agents économiques dont les unités disposent d'une structure comptable.

Ces comptes intermédiaires peuvent concerner les entreprises, les assurances par exemple.

Il est important de situer les comptes intermédiaires entre comptabilité nationale et comptes d'entreprise. Dans la mesure où ils sont des instruments de dialogue, ils doivent être proches des comptes des entreprises.

S'ils sont des instruments d'études, ils dépendent de l'objectif de celles-ci.

c) Construction des comptes satellites.

Alors que les comptes intermédiaires concernent des agents disposant d'un système comptable, les comptes satellites sont destinés à présenter les informations relatives à un domaine particulier sous une forme adaptée à ce domaine, c'est-à-dire faisant appel à des concepts et des classifications dont l'introduction dans le cadre central est difficile ou impossible.

On peut envisager de tels comptes dans les domaines du logement, des dépenses sociales, de la santé, de la recherche...

Certains comptes satellites peuvent correspondre au développement plus détaillé d'informations relatives à une activité déjà répertoriée dans le cadre central, telles que agriculture, commerce, transports.

Enfin, on peut envisager des systèmes satellites reposant sur une information quantitative autre que la valeur, rattachés au cadre central par l'intermédiaire des nomenclatures.

Ces comptes pourraient inclure la présentation d'indicateurs quantitatifs de la production non marchande, celle des administrations par exemple.

Les méthodes d'analyse

Depuis plusieurs dizaines d'années, et plus particulièrement depuis la dernière guerre mondiale, les méthodes d'analyse sont utilisées pour aider la préparation des décisions gouvernementales. Pour des raisons bien précises, leur domaine d'élection a été le domaine militaire, et dans une bien moindre mesure, certains champs d'activité tels les transports.

Voici quelques années, la généralisation de leur emploi a paru nécessaire, le besoin se faisant sentir d'une traduction plus efficace, et plus fidèle des politiques gouvernementales.

Cette généralisation n'a pas donné tous les résultats escomptés, et se pose aujourd'hui avec acuité le problème de la pertinence de l'usage des méthodes analytiques, particulièrement face à la montée des besoins d'ordre qualitatif.

1. *Considérations sur le Planning, Programming, Budgeting System (PPBS) et la Réalisation des Choix Budgétaires (RCB)*

Un chapitre consacré aux déficiences des méthodes d'analyse vis-à-vis de la prise en compte de la qualité de la vie ne pouvait pas ne pas commencer par quelques considérations et réflexions sur le PPBS et la RCB.

Ces démarches sont en effet nées d'un besoin accru de traduction efficace et fidèle d'une politique au travers du budget et de l'existence, pour ne pas dire la disponibilité (du moins croyait-on pouvoir employer ce mot), de multiples méthodes analytiques.

Le caractère appauvrissant des procédures budgétaires traditionnelles apparut en effet d'autant plus que croissaient, avec la quantité de services demandés à l'État, le caractère qualitatif de ceux-ci, et la complexité des choix à effectuer.

Il ne saurait être question de détailler ce que furent et ce que sont à l'heure actuelle les démarches en la matière, et pas davantage de tirer des bilans, une documentation abondante étant publiée sur le sujet.

Il paraît par contre opportun, en prenant deux des axes méthodologiques les plus expérimentés dans les cadres PPBS et RCB, d'en commenter les déficiences constatées ou pressenties vis-à-vis de la prise en compte de la qualité de la vie.

Ces axes sont les méthodes de coût-avantage et celles basées de près ou de loin sur l'utilisation de critères.

2. *Méthodes de coût-avantage*

Ces méthodes peuvent se classer en méthodes de coût-bénéfice et méthodes de coût-efficacité.

a) Méthodes de coût-bénéfice.

— Cette catégorie de technique implique évidemment non seulement la mesure monétaire des coûts, mais celle des bénéfices. Quand ces deux termes ne se définissent pas sur un marché par le jeu de l'offre et de la demande, le calcul impose des moyens de mesure détournés des éléments financiers.

Ces moyens impliquent des hypothèses dont la confirmation expérimentale est difficile puisque le domaine concerné est forcément hors mesures. (Voir par exemple les différentes méthodes censées permettre l'évaluation des services rendus par la forêt.)

— D'autre part, les résultats de ce type de méthode sont très contingents des hypothèses faites sur l'évolution des taux d'intérêt. Ceux-ci, quand ils sont liés à la vie monétaire, sont sujets à de nombreux aléas, d'autant plus imprévisibles que les termes envisagés sont plus lointains. Or il faut bien voir que nombre d'éléments naturels liés à la "qualité de la vie", tels que l'eau, l'air, la forêt, sont à évolution lente.

Cette même évolution lente les défavorisera si, étant pris en compte au titre d'un investissement les concernant de près ou de loin, ils font l'objet d'une étude de type coût-bénéfice basée sur un taux d'intérêt relativement élevé, privilégiant les investissements à court terme.

— Par ailleurs, au même titre que pour les études de type coût-efficacité abordées plus loin, le plus grand arbitraire règne dans la détermination objective des coûts et des bénéfices.

Les coûts directs présentent en général peu de problèmes, mais jusqu'où prendra-t-on en charge les coûts indirects, et pour quelle fraction de leur montant étant donné que celui-ci a de fortes chances d'être ventilable sur plusieurs programmes ?

Le même arbitraire règne dans les bénéfices, accru toutefois d'hypothèses faites sur l'avenir et du poids de ses incertitudes.

— Tous ces éléments font que les méthodes coût-bénéfice doivent être considérées, quand leur emploi touche à la qualité de la vie, beaucoup plus comme un cadre de réflexion que comme un instrument générateur de données brutes.

b) Méthodes de coût-efficacité.

Ces méthodes se rapprochent grandement des précédentes, à ceci près qu'elles prennent en charge, comme éléments de calculs et de comparaison, tous les termes autres que monétaires.

Si les difficultés propres à cette dernière variable sont certes éliminées, il en subsiste suffisamment pour que l'utilisation de cette méthodologie soit envisagée avec prudence.

— En effet, vis-à-vis des problèmes de qualité de la vie, problèmes au départ essentiellement qualitatifs, une démarche de type coût-avantage impose la quantification.

On pourra alors être tenté de privilégier, de manière parfaitement arbitraire, les données aisément quantifiables par rapport aux autres, ou d'attribuer à telle ou telle donnée quantitative une représentativité qu'elle n'a que partiellement au travers de nombreuses hypothèses implicites.

— D'autre part, l'efficacité ne se définit pas en soi, mais par rapport à des normes identifiées autour d'un objectif. C'est ainsi que les méthodes de coût-avantage sont parfaitement applicables à l'évaluation des systèmes d'arme.

Quand il s'agit de qualité de la vie, ces normes ne sont pas forcément repérables et identifiables *a priori*, et moins encore leur poids respectif.

Quelles normes en effet peut-on proposer pour préciser l'efficacité d'action visant à réduire le temps de transport ? Gain de temps certes, mais réduction de la tension nerveuse ? Amélioration du climat familial ? Présence accrue des parents auprès des enfants !

Quelles normes peut-on suggérer pour appréhender l'efficacité d'un accroissement sérieux des espaces verts ? Diminution de la pollution de l'air certes, mais équilibre biologique accru des individus ? Repos physique et psychique des hommes ?

— Au même titre que dans les méthodes de coût-bénéfice, se pose le problème de la prise en charge au travers d'une technique de la chaîne des coûts et effets indirects, extensibles à l'infini en soi, mais qu'il faut bien arrêter arbitrairement, la plupart du temps pour des raisons de mesurabilité, chaque programme n'étant pas considéré seul mais intégré dans un ensemble qu'il influence et qui l'influence.

— Pour cette raison, les méthodes de coût-efficacité, comme les méthodes de coût-avantage, doivent être considérées, quand il s'agit de qualité de la vie, beaucoup plus comme cadre de réflexion que comme générateur de données.

c) Problème des erreurs.

Une remarque générale sur les méthodes coût-avantage, la prise en compte des erreurs sur les variables et paramètres repères. Faute de pouvoir préciser ces erreurs, l'utilisation de ces méthodes devrait être assortie d'une large utilisation des tests de sensibilité permettant de préciser pour une problématique donnée, la marge d'erreur à l'intérieur de laquelle chacun des paramètres doit être précisé pour que les résultats d'ensemble présentent quelque validité

3) *Méthodes basées sur l'utilisation de critères*

Le plus souvent implicitement, mais parfois explicitement, l'utilisation de critères a été et est encore considérée comme un élément de méthode permettant de prendre en charge des éléments non quantifiables.

Ceci est exact dans une certaine mesure, et il n'est pour s'en rendre compte concrètement, que de constater combien leur détermination, leur choix, leur utilisation touchent au domaine politique.

Ils ne sauraient pour autant prétendre à la bonne représentativité des éléments de la qualité de la vie, ou plus exactement à la représentativité exclusive.

Il faut comprendre par là, non qu'ils donnent un schéma d'approche grossier, bien que correct des problèmes qualitatifs, mais que leur utilisation complétée par d'autres démarches qui seront discutées plus loin (indicateurs sociaux) peut s'avérer, dans le cas étudié par ce document, efficace et pertinente.

a) Remarques sur les critères eux-mêmes.

Il faudrait en tout premier lieu lever une ambiguïté fondamentale inhérente au terme qualité de la vie. Celle-ci n'existe pas *in abstracto*, elle est une chose ressentie, vécue par quelqu'un dans un certain cadre. C'est un problème à deux termes, la personne qui ressent, éprouve, apprécie, sur qui la collectivité et son gouvernement sont censés n'exercer aucune pression en tant que pouvoir, et le cadre dans lequel se déroule un vécu, cadre sur lequel par contre les autorités ont une responsabilité. C'est dans le domaine de cette responsabilité sur un environnement que peuvent être utilisés les critères dont il est question ici. Remarquons alors combien ces derniers sont contingents des "valeurs" vécues ou pensées de la société dans son état et ses préoccupations présentes.

Remarquons également combien les critères devraient représenter, ou plus exactement refléter, une véritable stratégie du développement de la vie en société.

En tout état de cause, et dans les formes méthodologiques actuelles, toute critériologie s'applique sur des éléments du futur. Éléments prévisionnels quand il s'agit de méthodes de type multicritères, éléments normatifs quand elle est utilisée au sein d'approche de type arbre de pertinence.

Plus le terme d'application est lointain, plus croissent les incertitudes relatives au cadre envisagé, et *a fortiori*, celles liées à la qualité de vie. En effet, comment pourrait-on prendre en compte ce qui touche aux réactions des individus à un environnement probable, indirectement anticipé au travers des critères? Ceci ne prétend en aucun cas être une critique absolue de l'utilisation de ces derniers. Il est nécessaire seulement d'en bien discerner les limites et par voie de conséquences, de percevoir les compléments méthodologiques et parfois même d'accepter les changements d'optique fondamentaux qui peuvent en résulter, dans le cadre de la prospective en particulier.

b) Remarques sur l'utilisation des critères.

Les critères sont toujours utilisés, quel que soit le cadre de leur emploi, au travers d'une combinatoire qui les critique par l'intermédiaire de pondérations.

Ces deux éléments, pondération et combinatoire, ne sont pas neutres, mais malheureusement, il est la plupart du temps fort difficile d'expliciter les hypothèses implicites qu'ils sous-tendent.

En outre, étant donné l'anticipation qui est à la base de toute critériologie, son utilisation accompagne, si même elle ne l'accroît pas, une focalisation qui limite fortement dans le temps et dans l'espace le champ des événements envisagés, prévus ou voulus.

Plus précisément, par exemple dans le cas des arbres de pertinence, est prise en compte une série d'enchaînements des actions pertinentes pour parvenir à un objectif. Ceci est parfaitement valable quand il s'agit d'un système fermé, ce qui n'est pas particulièrement le cas des éléments qui forment le cadre de vie. La critériologie devrait alors s'appliquer à toutes les actions possibles et à leurs conséquences repérées.

Sans doute dira-t-on que le développement de tous les enchaînements probables est impossible, mais justement, la prise de conscience de cette impossibilité est fondamentale pour juger à sa valeur, qui est grande comme outil de réflexion, mais contestable comme élément d'information, l'utilisation de toute méthode basée sur l'emploi des critères.

4. Les indicateurs sociaux

Depuis quelques années, s'accélèrent et se multiplient les études faites sur les indicateurs sociaux. Plusieurs raisons expliquent ce fait.

La finalité sociale directe ou indirecte des objectifs gouvernementaux est de plus en plus évidente pour les responsables, alors même que ceux-ci sentent bien, au moins intuitivement, combien il est impossible d'enfermer dans toute la méthodologie d'une planification et d'une programmation *a priori*, pour aussi sophistiquée qu'elle soit, toute la richesse, la complexité, les interdépendances, la fragilité du corps social.

La reconnaissance de cette déficience, implicite ou explicite, conduit à compléter la préparation des décisions *a priori* par des indicateurs donnant *ex post* des informations sur les résultats des actions envisagées, en particulier quand celles-ci concernent tout ce domaine de la vie en société, qui échappe à la quantification. Il ne peut être question de rentrer dans le détail des travaux concernant les différents types d'indicateurs. Il sera simplement procédé à deux remarques présentant un minimum de pertinence vis-à-vis de la perception de la qualité de la vie au travers des indicateurs sociaux.

1. *Problème de la lecture des indicateurs sociaux*

Quel que soit l'ensemble d'indicateurs considérés et leur vocation, il est assez évident que l'information potentielle totale est de loin supérieure à la somme des informations données par chaque indicateur.

C'est là un fait courant. Un pilote d'avion tire des renseignements non seulement de la lecture de chacun des cadrans de son tableau de bord, mais de la manière dont il les lit, telle donnée étant perçue avant telle autre et la valorisant.

Il effectue — le métier acquis l'y a préparé — une lecture intégrée suivant une certaine syntaxe. Cette syntaxe est liée à la machine et aux conditions dans lesquelles elle se trouve. Sans cette lecture ordonnée, le pilote n'aurait bien souvent que des indications essentiellement partielles le conduisant à des réactions inefficaces ou même dangereuses.

Ce problème de la lecture véritable d'informations multiples et complexes, est évidemment d'actualité dans les domaines à haute technicité exigeant une grande rapidité de réponse.

On trouve un aspect des choses quelque peu identique dans le domaine des indicateurs sociaux, à ceci près que les recherches en sont au stade de leur détermination, et que la question de leur lecture qui en est inséparable, est encore à peine abordée.

Peut-être l'un et l'autre ne pourront-ils être correctement résolus en première approximation qu'à partir d'une problématique suffisamment pertinente de la société.

En tout cas, il semble bien que la perception de la dimension qualité de vie par les responsables gouvernementaux, au travers des indicateurs sociaux, et en vue d'actions efficaces, ne soit possible que par l'intermédiaire d'une véritable lecture dont les mots et la syntaxe sont encore à découvrir.

2. *Recueil de l'information correspondant aux indicateurs sociaux*

Sans préjuger de la nature des indicateurs sociaux, mais en tablant simplement sur le fait que leur rôle est de signaler aux responsables l'état et l'évolution du corps social, on peut se poser la question de leur fidélité. En effet, interviennent au sein même de la vie et du fonctionnement de toute société des éléments engendrant un "bruit de fond" pouvant très bien absorber les signaux que tel ou tel indicateur social devrait collecter.

Le fait est évident dans tous les régimes très autoritaires. Dans les régimes dits démocratiques, les atteintes à la qualité de la vie peuvent très bien ne pas être signalées par les membres du corps social qui en sont les intervenants fondamentaux.

Il suffit pour cela que jouent, dans le fonctionnement du système, des éléments qui "désintéressent" les individus. Des accroissements de revenus, des changements de position hiérarchique, les honneurs, sont autant d'apport que chacun peut mettre en balance, avec telle ou telle donnée faisant partie de la qualité de la vie.

On perssent d'ailleurs par cet exemple qu'un système d'indicateurs sociaux, dont on attend bien évidemment un minimum de fidélité, ne peut être indépendant de l'éthique et du consensus du corps social dont il est censé refléter la situation et l'évolution.

La perception de la qualité de la vie sera donc relative et l'ensemble de la collectivité évoluant, les indicateurs devront dans leur définition suivre son mouvement.

5. Les structures

On a vu précédemment combien la comptabilité nationale, et corrélativement les procédures budgétaires auxquelles elle est intimement liée, sont imparfaites quand il s'agit de saisir non seulement la qualité de la vie, mais les éléments qui en constituent le cadre. On a vu également combien, par delà les espoirs qui avaient été fondés sur certaines d'entre elles, s'étaient révélées déficientes pour saisir ce "phénomène", les méthodes d'analyses utilisées dans les démarches de type PPBS ou RCB.

Il a été dit ensuite, combien la perception de l'insuffisance de l'appareillage méthodologique disponible pour la programmation *ex ante* vis-à-vis du problème de la qualité de la vie en société avait contribué à promouvoir le développement actuel des recherches sur les voies de contrôle possible *ex post* telle celle des indicateurs sociaux.

A ces constats doit être ajoutée la reconnaissance de la valeur des approches méthodologiques comme cadre de réflexion propre à aider la prise de conscience des responsables si ceux-ci se délivrent de la "magie" des chiffres. Enfin, il est impossible de méconnaître que commence à se créer dans les milieux de la recherche socio-économique une sorte de consensus au sein duquel serait admise l'existence de limites à la prise en charge méthodologique de la qualité de la vie. Ceci conduit à penser que la solution de cette prise en charge effective et efficace est avant tout d'ordre institutionnel et structurel, les méthodes s'intégrant au fonctionnement d'un ensemble comme cadre de réflexion exigeant tout autant qu'en fournisseur de données.

De telles perspectives conduisent à se poser, sur le plan structures, plusieurs questions:

a) Comment les structures actuelles peuvent-elles évoluer pour intégrer utilement, au titre de la réflexion et au titre des données, les démarches de type PPBS ou RCB et les méthodes qu'elles utilisent?

b) Comment doivent se modifier les structures actuelles pour utiliser efficacement l'information *ex post?*

c) Qu'entraîne, sur le plan structures, la reconnaissance implicite ou explicite, de l'impuissance de toute méthodologie à saisir "le phénomène" qualité de la vie?

1. *Intégration dans les structures des démarches de type PPBS*

Cette intégration met en relief la réhabilitation, au sein des structures d'administration gouvernementales, des quatre notions de "fin", "productivité", "responsabilité", "circulation" de l'information.

— Notion de "fins".
Les démarches de type PPBS ou RCB mettent l'accent sur les objectifs et le programme destinés à les réaliser, alors que les budgets classiques s'appuient sur les services ou structures. Ces dernières, de la place de finalité qu'elles occupaient, doivent redevenir des moyens. Un tel bouleversement d'attitude ne peut se faire rapidement et facilement. Il ne faut point s'étonner que les responsables de tels changements envisagent la poursuite de leurs efforts à des échéances de dix ou quinze ans.

— Notion de "productivité".
Cette notion, immédiate dans le secteur privé, ne s'est pas imposée aux administrations faute d'un marché coercitif débattant de leur production.

La diminution relative des ressources budgétaires aidant, cette notion de productivité devra retrouver sa place, exprimée, sinon en fonction de prix au moins retrouvée au sein d'arbitrages la prenant explicitement en compte par l'intermédiaire de facteurs divers.

— Notion de "responsabilité".
Pour de multiples raisons, n'existe, dans les administrations, pratiquement qu'une notion de responsabilité morale, hautement vécue par certains, paravant à l'installation, la sécurité ou la carrière pour beaucoup d'autres. Avec la responsabilité, doivent être réhabilités la sanction et le droit à l'erreur.

— Circulation de l'information.
Dans nombre d'administrations, l'information considérée comme source de pouvoir, est thésaurisée.

L'utilisation croissante de l'informatique, la multiplication des banques de données, la progression lente mais sûre des systèmes d'informations intégrées, exigeront la chute des barrières psychologiques ou structurelles à la circulation de l'information.

2. *Utilisation efficace de l'information* ex post

Cette efficacité exige *a priori* sur le plan structures que celles-ci remplissent deux conditions. Elles doivent être à même de détecter et de recevoir les "signaux" significatifs, même très faibles. Elles doivent être à même de réagir rapidement si les événements dont témoignent le signal l'exigent.

a) Réception des informations.

On a vu précédemment que des bruits de fond d'origines diverses pouvaient empêcher de percevoir les signaux diffusés par tel ou tel indicateur social.

Il est certain que la distance à l'événement signalé par un indicateur est un élément de ce bruit de fond. Le stockage anormal des fruits est perçu au niveau local; leur déversement sur les routes, au niveau central.

La détection et la réception doit donc se faire au plus près de l'événement, et ce également pour des raisons de délais de transmission.

Mais qui dit réception, dit réception par une structure active ayant par conséquent des pouvoirs. Une bonne réception implique donc une véritable décentralisation des pouvoirs.

b) Réaction aux informations.
La valeur d'une information est concrétisée par l'efficacité de l'action qui en résulte. Une grande finesse de détection et un temps de réponse élevés correspondent à une absurdité, ce d'autant plus que l'enchaînement des événements est plus rapide aujourd'hui qu'autrefois.

La rapidité de réaction implique, au même titre que la réception des informations, une véritable décentralisation des pouvoirs. La chose est parfaitement normale sur le plan qualité de la vie. Le terme principal de ce "phénomène" étant l'acteur, il importe au premier chef qu'il ait quelques degrés de liberté, et donc des pouvoirs, qu'il soit homme ou collectivité de quelque nature que ce soit.

3. *Conséquences structurelles d'une reconnaissance de l'imperfection des méthodologies par rapport à la qualité de la vie*

Il ne saurait être question ici de faire de longs commentaires dont le caractère spéculatif serait indéniable. Il paraît toutefois opportun de noter la nécessité de réfléchir tout particulièrement sur deux points:

a) Nécessité pour les structures qui prétendent contribuer à la qualité de la vie par delà l'utilisation de méthodes, de préciser en mettant à profit les leçons de l'expérience, les règles d'une véritable stratégie de leur action.

b) Nécessité pour ces mêmes structures, au sein de leur vie propre et de leur action tactique, d'une très grande flexibilité. Celle-ci ne serait jamais que le reflet d'une attitude au sein de laquelle serait admis concrètement l'imperfection de toute image *a priori* de la qualité de la vie.

6. Conclusion

La multiplication de tentatives n'ayant pas donné les résultats escomptés ajouté à une sorte de rumeur manifestant l'absence de pertinence des décisions prises sur la base du cadre économique classique par rapport à la qualité de la vie, font que s'introduit quelque humilité dans les recherches méthodologiques relatives à la préparation des décisions gouvernementales.

Ces recherches ne doivent pas le moins du monde, et pour autant se ralentir. Bien au contraire ; en particulier sur ce problème de l'intégration des méthodes dans les structures et institutions qui doivent profondément évoluer si l'on veut que soit de mieux en mieux assumée à l'avenir par les collectivités, leur responsabilité dans une vie ayant quelque qualité.

BIBLIOGRAPHIE

***
1969 "La comptabilité nationale française s'adapte à de nouveaux besoins", *Économie et statistique* 7.

***
1968 "Prise en compte dans la comptabilité nationale des services rendus à titre gratuit", *Études et conjoncture*, août.

Galbraith, J.K.
1968 *Le nouvel état industriel*. Paris, Gallimard.
1971 *Fraternité, finances et fantaisie*. Paris, Denoël.

Huet, P.
1971 "Présentation de la RCB en France", *Notes et études documentaires*, 3815-3816, septembre.

***
Rapport beige sur le PPBS. Bruxelles, Institut Administration - Université.

Maestre, C.J.
1971 *Politique scientifique gouvernementale et méthodes analytiques*. Paris, OECD.

Lévy-Lambert, H.
1971 *La rationalisation des choix budgétaires*. Paris, Presses Universitaires de France.

Morgenstern, O.
1971 "L'économie est-elle une science exacte?", *La recherche* 18.

Morrissens, M.L.
1971 "L'expérience américaine du PPBS", *Notes et études documentaires* 3815-3816, septembre.

Rieu, A.
1970 *Comptabilité nationale et qualité de la vie*, Université d'Aix-Marseille (thèse de doctorat).

Saint-Marc, P.
1971 *Socialisation de la nature*. Paris, Stock.

Schultze, C.L.
1968 *The politics and economics of public spending*. Washington, DC, Brookings Institute.

PAUL STREETEN

Cost-benefit and other problems of method *

A colleague of mine has a name for those whose heads are as soft as their hearts. He calls them goody-woollies. These goody-woollies have their fashions, and preserving the environment is currently a strong candidate for the top goody-woolly cause of the decade. As a reviewer of one of the flood of books on the subject pointed out, it has many of the ingredients beloved of women's magazines — animals, a strong medical interest and a readily identifiable villain. It performs the difficult feat of appealing to the most advanced sociologists and to those who detest change, to old women of both sexes and to the revolutionaries of unidentifiable sex, to the silent majority and the screaming minority, to the young swingers and the old danglers.

Economists have not been slow to jump on to the bandwagon. The smoke and sparks emitted by a factory chimney, which had been a curiosity in Pigou's *Economics of welfare*, now pervaded the atmosphere and set alight social cost-benefit analysis, which swept like a wildfire through articles, books, commissions and reports. Ministries in particular welcomed the opportunity to shift the burden of political choice on to a set of mathematical formulae. Peter Self, professor of Public Administration at the University of London, has borrowed Bentham's description of natural rights and applied it to some of the products of the growth industry of cost-benefit analysis: nonsense on stilts.

The problem

"Cost-benefit analysis is a practical way of assessing the desirability of projects, where it is important to take a long view (in the sense of looking at

*This article is an early version of a paper in a volume of essays in honour of Professor G.L.S. Shackle entitled *Uncertainty and expectations in economics*, edited by C. F. Carter and J.L. Ford and to be published in 1972 by Blackwells, Oxford.

I am grateful to Diane Elson and Nicolas Lethbridge for help in the preparation of this paper and to Wilfred Beckerman for stimulating discussions.

repercussions in the further, as well as the nearer, future) and a wide view (in the sense of allowing for side-effects of many kinds on many persons, industries, regions, etc.) *i.e.*, it implies the enumeration and evaluation of all the relevant costs and benefits". [1] A stream of future social benefits and of future social costs, properly adjusted for uncertainties, are discounted by a social rate of time preference and then compared.

Applied to the environment in underdeveloped countries, the problem is how to strike a balance between the benefits of raising the level of living of the mass of the people in poor countries, and its costs in terms of the deterioration of the environment. The basic criterion for deciding how much to spend on reducing the deterioration of the environment, *e.g.*, by choosing a more costly site for a dam, can be stated as follows. The deterioration should be reduced to the point where the costs of doing so are covered by the benefits from this reduction [2]. This formal statement — being a tautology — is immensely easier than its practical application. Two points of elaboration are in order. First, there are many aspects of a deteriorating environment, and these are spread over time. It is therefore important not to apply the analysis to one aspect in isolation. Intertemporal and interspatial interdependence must be allowed for, so that, for example, a programme designed to bring water does not later lead to excessive salination, or a programme to increase electricity supply to the excessive spread of schistosomiasis, or chemical pest control to the excessive killing of the destroyers of the pest. Second, priorities relating to the desirable objectives must be supplemented and modified by consideration of costs. Thus a high priority objective of environmental improvement which is very costly may have to give way to a lower priority one, which imposes lower costs.

Applied to, say, river development projects, the need is to identify options and to estimate the benefits and costs in the light of social priorities. Environmental safeguards, such as the preservation of fishing facilities, of farming land for existing tribes, the avoidance of canal-borne diseases, of aquatic weeds or of secondary poisoning of the killers of pests, are costly. These additional costs are acceptable if, but only if, the added benefits exceed them.

Plainly, planning the environment and balancing control of the environment against other objectives of policy, require a comprehensive analysis and calculation of the costs and benefits involved. After a brief discussion of "growth *versus* environment", the rest of this paper, except for the last two sections, is devoted to showing some of the limits and dangers of such calculations, particularly when applied to underdeveloped countries.

1. A.R. Prest and R. Turvey, "Cost-benefit analysis: A survey", *Surveys of economic theory*, vol. 3, London, Macmillan, 1966, p. 155.

2. *First report of the Royal Commission on Environmental Pollution*, London, 1971, p. 6 (4585 HMSO).

Growth versus environment

Some writers have presented to us a choice between preserving the environment and promoting economic growth. Growth, the argument goes, pollutes. As normally calculated, the growth of GNP does not allow for these social costs of growth. A more welfare-orientated policy would decelerate growth — some even argue for zero GNP growth — in order to preserve or restore a purer environment.

Many things are wrong with argument. The most basic objection to it is that growth, *properly composed and properly weighted,* can be complementary with environmental protection. Industrial anti-pollution devices and the technology that produces them are part of the GNP. And faster growth renders obsolescent more rapidly such polluting agents as the motor car. It is true that both pollution and the reduction of pollution are a function of the level of "income". The argument presented here depends upon the condition that the proportion of income devoted to anti-pollution devices or pollution-free innovations exceeds the proportion of income adding to pollution. If the appropriate social weights are attached to the components of income, measured "income growth" will show up as genuine growth only if the condition laid down in the previous sentence is met. On the other hand, there is almost certainly some trade-off between environmental objectives and growth in the short- and medium-long-run. Figures 1 and 2

Figure 1.

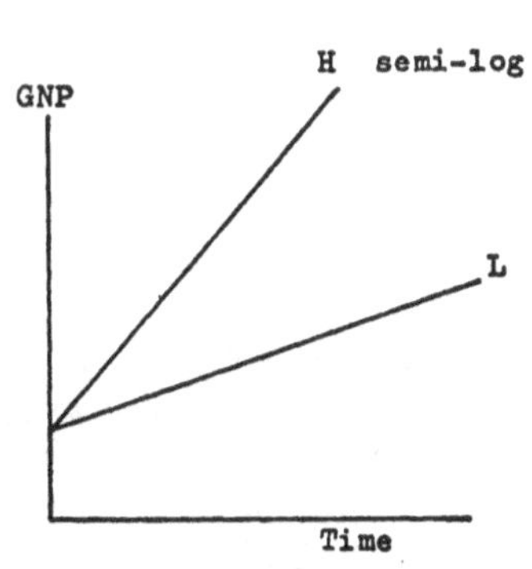

Figure 2.

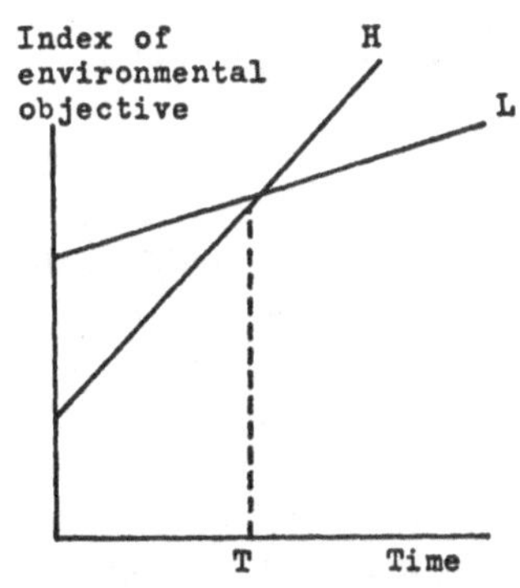

illustrate possible temporal growth paths of GNP and of something to be measured by an index of the preservation of the environment (or of reduced pollution). H is the high growth path, L the low growth path.

Until time T, the high growth strategy sacrifices the environment. But at T and forever after, high growth promotes a purer environment[3]. Which

3. The argument is adapted from an article by F. Stewart and P. Streeten, "Conflicts between output and employment objectives", *Oxford economic papers* 23 (2), 1971.

path is chosen will depend upon the rate of time discount for environmental purity, compared with that for GNP. Since the marginal utility of consumption declines with rising income, whereas the relative value attached to reducing pollution increases with rising income, the rate of time discount for the environment is likely to be lower than that for GNP. If this is so, those who lay much store by the environment ought to advocate a *higher*, not a lower, growth strategy than that dictated by optimising consumption over time. Only then can devices to protect the environment (a new growth industry) and the technology that evolves anti-pollution techniques, processes and products develop sufficiently rapidly.

Even this way of posing the problem greatly oversimplifies it. In fact, depending upon the relation between production and pollution and upon citizens' preferences, four choices are open. First we may abstain from producing as much as we otherwise would in order to reduce pollution. Second, we may devote resources that might have produced goods to produce products that combat pollution. Whether this means stepping up national product, slowing it down or changing its composition depends on conventions of national income accounting. Third, we may step up the production of ordinary goods, notwithstanding the fact that they aggravate pollution, to a degree that compensates for the growth of pollution. Finally, we might produce different products, not as attractive as those that would have been produced without regard to pollution, but with the compensating merit that they carry with them less pollution.

The use of mathematics

All cost-benefit analyses must use mathematics. Its scope and limitations depend on the problems treated. It is sometimes said that mathematics permits rigour, though possibly at the expense of relevance. In fact, much mathematical economics is vague, but for quite different reasons than those that give rise to vagueness in literary treatments. This is so because it is not made clear what real entities the mathematical symbols stand for, or, if it is made clear, the assumptions about the symbols do not apply to the concrete entities. While a, b and c lend themselves to rigorous manipulations, the identifications of a with an individual, b with a farm household and c with a firm, constitute large logical jumps. Rigour is lacking because the symbols are not identified or are ill-defined.

One danger of the use of mathematics is that it lulls its practitioners into a false sense of certainty. The temptation for the mathematical economist, and even more his mediocre disciple, is to mistake logic for economics or validity for truth, *i.e.*, the correct deduction of logical conclusions for the discovery of facts about the real world. For a minimax player it may be professionally comforting that the damage done by the computer in economics is less than in defence analysis. In both it can lead to disastrous decisions. According to the well-known principle of GIGO — garbage in, garbage out — results can be no better than assumptions. Mathematics is no substitute for thought or for values. Of course, all good mathematical social scientists know this.

Another well-known danger in mathematical decision-making is sub-optimisation. What is best for part of a system may not be best for the whole. The temptation is to proceed with those parts that can be treated mathematically and to neglect the rest. We then may do perfectly something that should not be done at all. Practitioners try to select the quantifiable, identify it with the important and happily proceed to sub-optimise. The result may be the worst of all possible worlds. As Kenneth Boulding has emphasized, rationality about a sub-system can be worse than sub-rationality about the whole system [4]. Decision-models, based on a set of explicit and quantified assumptions (the framework discussed in the next section), often cover such a sub-system, whereas decisions based on vague judgments and intuitions, with all their well-known faults, may take into account the whole system. This is particularly important in development studies in the light of the strong relationships between sub-systems and the lack of relationships within any given sub-system. It is also very important in arms control. It is the tendency to sub-optimisation that leads to the neglect of factors to which a mathematically less sophisticated but good policy-maker (admittedly an even scarcer resource than mathematical sophistication) would pay more attention.

Choosing the framework

Benefits are just benefits. There is normally no distinction between benefits that contribute to positive happiness, those that reduce misery that is inflicted by God or nature and those that reduce man-created misery. The blackmailer creates a nuisance, for the removal of which he extracts payment. Depending upon the assumptions and the terms of reference of the framework, the benefits derived from the removal of man-created nuisances count in the same way as the benefits that add to the net enjoyment of life. Social life is full of situations that can be comprehended only by the economics of blackmail: desires created by envy, by advertising, by habit formation, by the conspicuous consumption of others, by the prevailing income distribution; or needs generated by emissions of noise, dirty air or dirty water or just dirt. On the other hand, clearly not all man-created desires fall into the blackmail category. It is the purpose of education to generate desires for truth,

4. K.E. Boulding, "Economics as a moral science", *American economic review* 59 (1), 1969.

goodness and beauty, which can never be fully satisfied. Both the highest and the lowest wants are the result of want creation, of the generation of a void for whose filling someone can extract a charge that may count as a benefit. The point is that benefits cannot be aggregated without a series of value judgments in addition to the simple one that it is good that people should have more of what they want. The wants and their causes themselves must be subjected to a critical evaluation before we can apply a true cost-benefit calculus. If, as J.S. Mill thought, it is better to be Socrates dissatisfied than a satisfied pig, it may, in some cases, be better to widen the gap between "bads" and "goods". In other cases, the production of "anti-bads", to abate the nuisance caused by the generation of "bads", does not add to welfare.

Cost-benefit analysis must be conducted within a framework which selects certain relationships by putting them into equations, and involves moral, political and social considerations. This means that valuations enter; that they have to be selected, and then quantified. In locating an airport, for instance, such disparate considerations as surface travelling time, loss of agricultural land, differential impact of losses on rich and poor, the value to future generations of historic churches and houses, the loss of wildlife, as well as the more obvious capital construction costs and revenues collected, all have to be brought together. It is quite true that cost-benefit methods help to establish a logical framework for decision-making. The framework determines the outcome. It is bound to be less than fully comprehensive and by selecting some and leaving out other considerations biases the results.

Partial versus general equilibrium analysis

Formally, cost-benefit analysis can be made to fit all cases. In practice, it ceases to be usable for decisions that change what are normally taken as parameters of the system. This means that, if decisions affect the values of the variables in the rest of the economy, the partial equilibrium approach or the micro-approach, on which the analysis is based, breaks down and only a general equilibrium analysis will do. This sets severe limits to its application to underdeveloped countries.

Suppose that a river development project depends for its benefits not only on expenditure on investment and the external costs that became evident in the Aswan dam, but also on the incentives of farmers, in turn a function of the system of land tenure, and on their willingness and ability to adopt new methods of cultivation. These may be functions of the speed of modernization of the whole economy, itself partly dependent upon the river development project.

Conversion of political choice into technical

Cost-benefit analysis has a tendency to convert political, social and moral choices into pseudo-technical ones. Hence its psychological appeal to administrators, but also hence its logical flaw, evident to those trained in the analysis of choice. If two objectives conflict, say the requirements of industrial growth and the protection of the environment, someone will have to choose. The choice may be democratic or dictatorial or oligarchic, but choice it must be. It is possible to make the conflicting objectives commensurate by attaching numerical weights to them and then estimating how these weighted values are affected by different courses of action, allowing for interdependences, cross-effects and intertemporal connections. Different values can thus apparently be reduced to a single value: the maximisation of the numerical excess of "benefits" over "costs". But the clash has not disappeared. It has been concealed in the relative values (often highly arbitrary) attached to the objectives. The judgment is no more "objective". On the contrary, I would argue that policy makers should be fully aware of the choices and should not be confronted with fudged, predigested and prejudged pseudo-technical results. It is, for instance, formally possible to lump together the effects of a project on *a*) income distribution, *b*) the balance of payments and, *c*) the growth of industrial production. Shadow pricing of inputs and outputs can embrace all these objectives. But unless there is a clear and precise consensus upon the relative weights to be attached to these objectives (*e.g.*, to an extra dollar that goes to a rich and a poor man), a planner has a clearer picture by having the issues set out separately rather than being served with single figures that conceal the preferences. A decomposed set of indices will lead to better decisions than a composite index.

When exchange values are non-operational

One of the characteristics of cost-benefit analysis is that it attaches money values to choices that have never been and never will be subjected to the test of an exchange situation. In the first place, the money calculus cannot be applied if objectives are not commensurable; if we are not prepared to give up any amount of one thing for a little more of another. "Everything has its price" is just not true. If we regard human slavery or prostitution as incompatible with human dignity, or if we regard them as incompatible with certain inalienable human rights, the proof that these institutions come out well in a cost-benefit analysis is irrelevant. Secondly, even where there is commensurability, to attach values to choices that will never be put to a test is essentially arbitrary. Sensitivity analysis can determine what difference would be made by varying the values and, if we are lucky, certain variations will make little difference to the outcome. But others will be crucial. Interviews and hypothetical questions about what value we attach to time saved or beautiful flora and fauna preserved do not help much. We all know about the gap between words and deeds, particularly if we are not faced with the deeds. Thirdly, whenever ends are not given but explored, modified or discovered in the process of allocating resources, the model that confronts given competing ends with scarce means does not fit the facts.

The cost of information and uncertainty

A full cost-benefit analysis requires not only a carefully constructed analytical framework, but also a vast amount of quantitative data. The construction and gathering of this knowledge take time and skilled manpower, which is very scarce in underdeveloped countries. The costs of acquiring the information and knowledge to maximise net benefits must be weighed against the extra benefits to be derived from them. It may then be perfectly *rational* to stop short of being *perfectly* rational.

Allowances for uncertainty can be made in three ways: "1) in the assessment of annual levels of benefits and costs; 2) in the assumptions about length of life; and 3) in the discount rate. The first is most appropriate if the risk dispersion of outcomes (or inputs) is irregularly, rather than regularly, distributed with time. If the main risk is that there may be a sudden day of reckoning when benefits disappear or costs soar, the second type of adjustment is needed. The third correction, a premium on the discount rate, is appropriate where uncertainty is a strictly compounding function of time." [5]

Professor Shackle has rejected orthodox probability theory for situations that cannot be repeated many times. Even if chances of success and failure could be calculated actuarially, disastrous outcomes put an end to further "trials". Professor Shackle has proposed to replace probability distributions by his highly original concept of "potential surprise". Ignorance as to which of many possible events will occur is reflected as a low potential surprise value of each, not, unwarrantedly, as a low "probability" of each. He has substituted for mean value and dispersion his concepts of "focus gain" and "focus loss" — the most attractive and the most repellent outcomes, thus rejecting the addition of mutually incompatible hypotheses.

It might be argued that these innovations do not apply to public investment projects. Many of these will have only very small effects on average incomes per head of the population or on those of a particular group. It may therefore be thought that, where a probability distribution is known, actuarial risk can be applied. On the other hand, the kind of projects that we are concerned with will be sufficiently large and localised to have considerable effects on groups of people and the possibility of disastrous outcomes may

5. Prest and Turvey, *op. cit.*, p. 171.

be important. Focus values of the type proposed by Professor Shackle will then be more appropriate than adjustment to actuarial risk. Furthermore, in conditions of uncertainty, flexibility will be appropriate. Even though costs for any given outcome will be higher or benefits lower than they would have been, had this outcome been expected with certainty, costs will be lower or benefits higher if outcomes deviate from the expected values. No method that uses certainty equivalents can deal correctly with this phenomenon.

Implications for aid-giving

By looking at aid-giving in isolation, we have not taken into account the possible harmful effects on the environment in poor countries which are caused by the transfer of our technologies. I have tried to enumerate some of these in *Development in a divided world* [6]. The most important is the introduction of cheap and effective methods of reducing death rates, without a correspondingly cheap and effective technology to reduce birth rates. This has upset the population equilibrium and has vastly contributed to the difficulties of development. Other examples are the capital-intensive techniques of production which aggravate the unemployment problem, the transfer of Western institutions such as trade unions and modern social services, and most recently the new seed varieties. Not only have we isolated aid-giving from its total effects in recipient countries, but we have also isolated it from our other national policies which have an impact on development. Vast sums are spent on research and development which make the primary products obsolete, on whose exports developing countries depend; we prevent them from selling more manufactured products in our markets by cascading tariffs, rising with the stage of processing, and impose quotas on imports when they show signs of being successful; we encourage the immigration of scarce professionals whom these countries have trained, while shutting our frontiers to unskilled immigrants; we conduct our foreign policy in a manner which imposes added burdens on the poor countries. No cost-benefit analysis has yet embraced these highly relevant considerations.

The need for interdisciplinary studies

There are two good reasons for conducting interdisciplinary studies, one obvious, the other less so. The obvious reason for interdisciplinary work arises from the requirements of applied research. The solution of particular practical problems, such as urban congestion and slums, pollution, location, river

6. P. Streeten, pp. 77-77, in: D. Seers and L. Joy (eds.), *Development in a divided world*, London, Pelican, 1971.

development, nutrition, population control, labour utilization and many others, requires the contributions of different disciplines and their application to the specific issue. The prevalence of government planning at all levels has contributed to the cooperation between, and sometimes the integration of, different discipline. The planner has to draw on all relevant knowledge and skills, without being bound by conventional boundaries. This practical need to bring all relevant methods and data to bear on the solution of a specific problem does not affect the method used in the contributing discipline. It is because they are specialists in their fields that the different members have a contribution to make to an integrated solution.

There is, however, a second and deeper reason for interdisciplinary research [7]. The justification for having separate disciplines and for specializing in them is that between the variables encompassed by one discipline and those treated by another there are few interactions and the effects of any existing interaction are weak and damped. Only then are we justified in analysing problems in one field, without always and fully taking into account others. As Michael Lipton has argued in a stimulating and valuable article [8], the need for interdisciplinary studies does not arise because people in underdeveloped countries, particularly in subsistence households, perform many functions normally separated in rich countries, but because there is interdependence between variables normally analysed separately. "Lack of specialization among the people being studied in no way justifies lack of specialization among the students. A student of Michelangelo could well confine attention to his sculpture, while caring little for the architecture and painting in which Michelangelo also excelled." [9] The fact that functions in underdeveloped societies are less differentiated does, of course, have a bearing on the interdependence.

If interdependence between variables normally studied separately is strong, or, though weak, if reaction coefficients are large, or, even though small, if they change size for moves above a certain critical size, interdisciplinary studies are indicated. The situation can be illustrated diagrammatically.

Figure 3 illustrates the absence of interdependence between the variables X and Y. Figure 4 shows interdependence, but it is weak and damped, so that if one variable diverges from the stable equilibrium point S, the system will tend to return to it. Whether we are justified to neglect such interdependence will depend upon the size of the reaction coefficients (the comparative slopes of the lines) and on the time lags in the adjustment process. Figure 5 shows a cumulative process away from the unstable equilibrium at U. Clearly,

7. Some people object to terms like "multi-disciplinary" or "interdisciplinary". It is true that they sound somewhat pretentious and abstract. I have not been able to think of a better expression for this type of work.

8. M. Lipton, "Interdisciplinary studies in less developed countries", *Journal of development studies* 7 (1), 1970.

9. *Ibid.*, p. 6.

Figure 3.

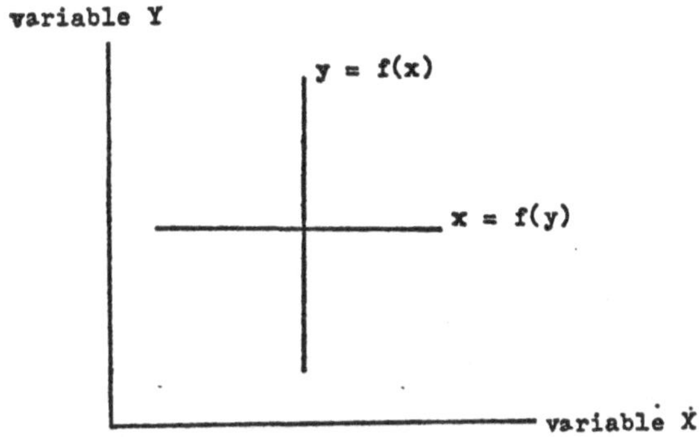

Non-interdependence

Figure 4.

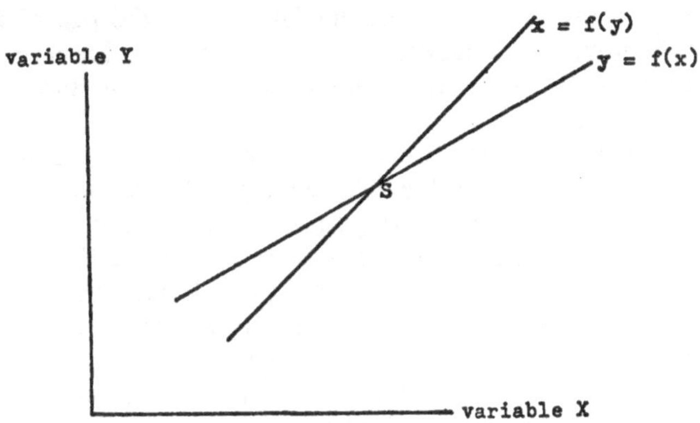

Damped interdependence

Figure 5.

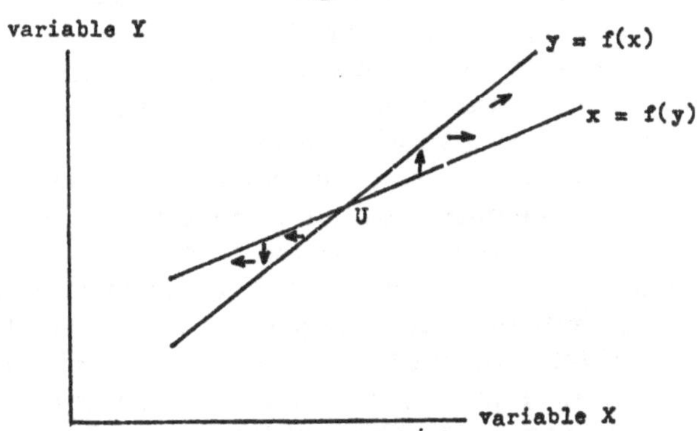

Explosive interdependence

Figure 6.

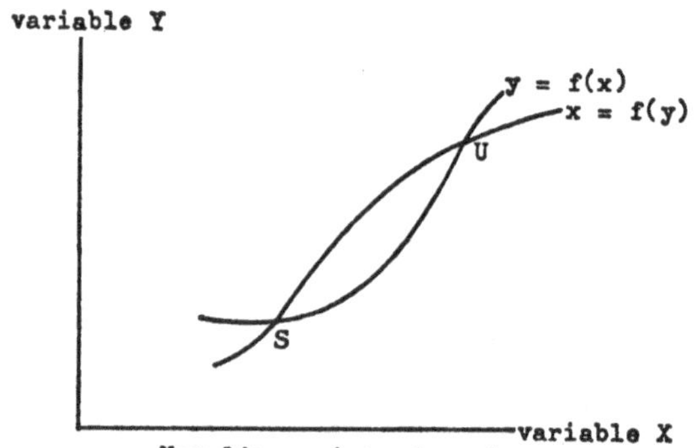

Non-linear interdependence

we must not neglect such interdependence in our studies. Figure 6 shows that stability and instability may be the function of the size of the move, so that for small moves, interdependence is damped and for large ones explosive. Theories of the large push or the critical minimum effort are based on such non-linear relationships.

There are numerous illustrations of such interdependence in the field of development studies. One is the relationship between income per head and population growth. High rates of population growth may be assumed to reduce income per head and higher income per head may be assumed, in certain conditions, to reduce population growth. Or take the relationship between the level of living of a deprived minority group, *e.g.*, a low caste or a racial minority and an index of prejudice against it. Prejudice will be a function of the level of living — the less educated, the less healthy, the stronger the grounds for prejudice — and the level of living will be a function of prejudice — the stronger prejudice, the stronger discrimination in jobs, education, *etc.* Or consider the relationship between productivity per man and the investment/income ratio. The higher productivity, the higher will tend to be the savings and hence the investment ratio, but the higher the investment ratio the more capital per man and hence the higher productivity. There is also interdependence between the quality of interdisciplinary studies and the quality of the scholars they attract. One can go on.

Strong interdependence, or weak interdependence with cumulation or weak interdependence without cumulation within certain limits but cumulation beyond these limits, constitute a case for interdisciplinary studies, where the variables under consideration belong to different conventional disciplines.

It is possible to draw two quite different conclusions from this. On the one hand, it may point to the need, not so much for interdisciplinary studies, as for a *new discipline.* I do not mean some kind of super-politics-economics-sociology, but a discipline that builds with concepts and models appropriate to the physical and social conditions of less developed societies. Alternatively, the framework of the established disciplines may continue to be used but some of the substance may be provided from outside these conventional fields. Thus the concept of a production function or of capital may be adapted from economics but we may operate with non-economic inputs such as educational or health levels or distance from towns in an agricultural production function, or we may widen the concept of capital to comprise national integration or improvements in the quality and attitudes of the labour force, if these "investments" raise the flow of production above what it would otherwise have been. In either case, we may in the process incidentally gain new insights into social phenomena in advanced industrial countries. Studies of the caste system may throw light on trade union behaviour; scrutiny of the capital/output ratio may change our view of the production function; a wider concept of capital may throw new light on incentives and management; a study of underdeveloped countries will improve our methods of dealing with underdeveloped regions in advanced countries. If this happens, it will be a bonus over and above what we had bargained for.

MATTHEW EDEL

Land values and the costs of urban congestion: Measurement and distribution *

1. Introduction

In a market economy, many costs imposed by congestion or urban areas may be capitalized as decreases in land values. Contamination of the environment and diminished mobility may reduce the demand for urban space. Since land in particular locations is a fixed factor, reduced demand results in diminished Ricardian site rents. This well-known phenomenon has been proposed as a basis for the measurement of the social cost of air pollution and other congestion phenomenon. Less well recognized is the corollary to capitalization of costs in rents : capital losses are imposed on the owners of properties whose site-rents are reduced. These losses may affect the distribution of wealth in an economy.

This article surveys the extent to which, in a "mixed" capitalist economy congestion costs will be capitalized in land values. In particular, two points will be demonstrated.

1. Land prices are an imperfect measure of the net social cost of congestion, and at best can give a rough order-of-magnitude approximation to these costs under stringent assumptions.

2. Land prices do capitalize enough of the costs of congestion that they can play a role in the distribution of these costs among different property owners.

* Material presented draws upon three ongoing intellectual investigations: research into the measurement and causes of land values by John R. Harris, Ronald Grieson, David Wheeler, and members of the urban economics workshop, MIT; studies of the history of the Boston area land market by the author along with Elliott Sclar, which are supported in part by the Ford Foundation under a grant for urban studies to MIT; and explorations of hierarchical stratification in the US economy by members of the Union for Radical Political Economics. Gratefully acknowledging his debt to the participants in all three studies, the author also accepts responsibility for the opinions presented and any misrepresentation of other investigators' opinions that may have occurred in this attempt at a synthesis.

The discrepancy between capitalized and total congestion costs, and the unequal distribution of the respective capital losses, may stem both from the same causes. These are the structure of demand specific to institutional economy systems, and institutional market imperfections and fiscal structures within these systems. In addition, the presence of positive economies of agglomeration, which are themselves affected by economic institutions, complicates the measurement of social cost. Thus the principal use of land value measurement may be in the study of distribution, rather than in the measurement of aggregate social welfare cost (either gross or net of positive agglomeration economies).

Some preliminary applications of these conclusions to the study of land values in United States metropolitan areas will also be presented in the following pages.

1. Comparisons of cities of different sizes indicate that on the average, economies of agglomeration outweigh costs associated with agglomeration for cities of a size up to at least half a million in population. For metropolitan areas of a somewhat larger size, the balance is more doubtful. For some larger cities, including metropolitan areas of several million inhabitants, rising land values again indicate a private net benefit to those taking part in the urban agglomeration. However, these benefits seem limited to cities with certain corporate headquarters functions. Thus particular corporate institutions appear to allow a market viability for cities of a size whose congestion costs would not be warranted otherwise. Since these institutions are centers of hierarchical distributions of control, the possibility emerges that congestion costs are being incurred for the maintenance of hierarchy.

2. Within cities, changes in land values due to successive economies and diseconomies of agglomeration and congestion may be shown to distribute wealth regressively among the classes of real estate owners, which in the United States include a majority of the total population.

2. Capitalization of environmental costs

Much of the evidence for the capitalization of urban congestion costs is based on cross-section comparisons of real estate values in different districts within metropolitan areas. Given the specific form of data collection in the United States, the nearest approximation to ground rents available on a geographic basis is often the census estimate of the value of single family houses. In order for this to serve as a proxy for site rent, variables representing housing age and size, and neighborhood amenity and quality variables such as school quality must be included as independent variables in regressions explaining house values. In addition, cross section estimates normally show strong evidence for increased values with accessibility to downtown routes and nearness to business centers. These evidences for economies of agglomeration require that accessibility factors be included also as background variables when tests for the costs of congestion are made. Positive correlation between amenity and low congestion, or between accessibility and high congestion within a metropolitan area may complicate the statistical analysis of congestion costs.

Notwithstanding these difficulties, cross-sectional studies have presented some convincing evidence that air pollution and other congestion phenomena do impose costs which are capitalized by the land market. Oates (1969) has tested the impact of local taxes on real estate values in New Jersey; *ceteris paribus* higher taxes are associated with lower property values. Taxes to offset congestion presumably are included among these taxes. While Oates shows that the negative effects of taxes for support of education may be offset by increased property values due to improved school attractiveness, the same is presumably not true when higher levels of taxation merely maintain *similar* levels of amenity in the face of differing congestion. The provision of adequate sewers might be one such service. Similar results have been generated for other metropolitan areas as by-products of cross-sectional studies of other influences on land value.

A deliberate attempt to measure the effect of air pollution levels on real estate values has been made by Ridker and Henning (1967) who regress house values by census tract in the Saint Louis metropolitan area on sulfation levels and a number of amenity and accessibility variables. Ridker and Henning present a number of alternative specifications for their estimating equations, in order to minimize the distorting statistical effects of multicollinearity among the explanatory variables. Their estimates of the effect of sulfate pollution vary with the assumptions, but all show a negative correlation between pollution and property values. What they consider the most convincing model gives an association between each 0.25 mg/100 cm^2/day of pollution and a reduction in house values of \$ 245. They conclude, "an estimate for the effect of air pollution on residential property values has been obtained that can be used with some confidence". Similar regressions have since been run using data from other cities, and a negative association has been found in these cases as well.

But what has the regression analysis actually estimated? Can the cross-section association of pollution and property values be used to estimate the social cost of pollution? Ridker is more cautious in his book on the subject than in the article co-authored with Henning, and well he might be. In the first place, this regression analysis — like many econometric estimates — can be interpreted in one of two ways. It may measure the costs imposed on households by pollution, estimated on the assumption that the prices households bid for land will rationally reflect the true cost and disutility of dirty air. Or it may measure the extent to which the market and the bid prices offered by families really capture these costs. One does not know which is being tested — the cost of pollution or the efficiency of the land market[1]. An insignificant relationship between pollution and property values might imply either that pollution is costless or that markets do not capitalize it. Ridker and Henning's results show that there are some costs which the market capitalizes, but these may underestimate total costs if the market does not capitalize all differentials.

A second problem arises when Ridker and Henning try to estimate the total impact of pollution on land prices for the metropolitan area as a whole. The authors write, "using the $ 245 figure and assuming the sulfation levels are reduced by 0.25 mg but in no case below 0.49 mg [...] the total increase in property values for the Saint Louis standard metropolitan statistical area could be as much as $ 82 790 000". But it would not necessarily be this great, even if the regression is properly estimated. If pollution in all districts of Saint Louis were reduced to the 0.49 mg "background" level, demand for space in the formerly most polluted neighborhoods would certainly increase. But this increase might come at the expense of demand in census tracts that formerly had a unique advantage in low pollution levels. The $ 82 790 000 estimate assumes that demand will increase in the newly cleaned areas to equal demand elsewhere now, without the balancing effect of demand reduction. It is therefore almost certainly an overestimate. Indeed there is no certainty that the total land value in Saint Louis would increase *at all* if pollution were removed. If the same population used the same total amount of land with and without pollution, but only reallocated its demand within the same area, there might be no net change in total values.

The argument is the same as that holding for the effect of improved commuter transportation on land values within a metropolitan area. Improved commuting increases the values of land on the city periphery, but reduces value by reducing demand and density of population in residential districts close to the business center. Total land values for the entire area may either rise or fall, depending on specific elasticities of demand for elasticity and space. The argument, first suggested by Haig (1926) and recently proved by Goldberg (1970) could be applied directly to the pollution case, treating pollution as a factor affecting land as a negative counterpart to accessibility. Indeed, it even suggests it is logically possible that removing (and hence equalizing) pollution might reduce total property values.

Notwithstanding the error in their prediction of property value changes, Ridker and Henning *may* be correct in their estimation of an $ 82 790 000 value

1. When independent estimates of marginal products and factor prices are available, they may be compared to estimate the degree to which markets are effective. Thus, the "rationality" of peasant farmers and the "exploitation" of factors of production have at times been tested. But if no independent estimate of pollution costs is available, the market valuation of these costs can only be used on the untested assumption that the market is indeed functioning well. (See Edel, 1970.)

for the removal of pollution. If the $ 245 that is now bid for the advantage of a less polluted house represents the average of the values that all consumers would place on clean air, then multiplying this by the number of households should give the total benefit of cleaner air. The difference between this figure and the lower change in property values would be a consumers' surplus accruing to the families whose housing costs fell. Total land price changes would then be an inadequate measure of the benefits of an air cleanup, although the comparison of prices between polluted and nonpolluted areas would allow a measure of the benefits.

Even this measure would however be inadequate to the extent that the value of clean air to the marginal household failed to represent the average value. Thus, there is no assurance that the Ridker and Henning estimate correctly measures total benefits that would result from a cleanup, both because it may ignore benefits the consumers do not take into account "rationally" or the market does not capitalize, and because marginal and average benefits may not be equal. At least, however, there is no systematic reason to think it may overstate benefits, as it definitely does overstate the land-value-change portion of benefits.

Figure 1. *Supply (S) and Demand (D) for building space*

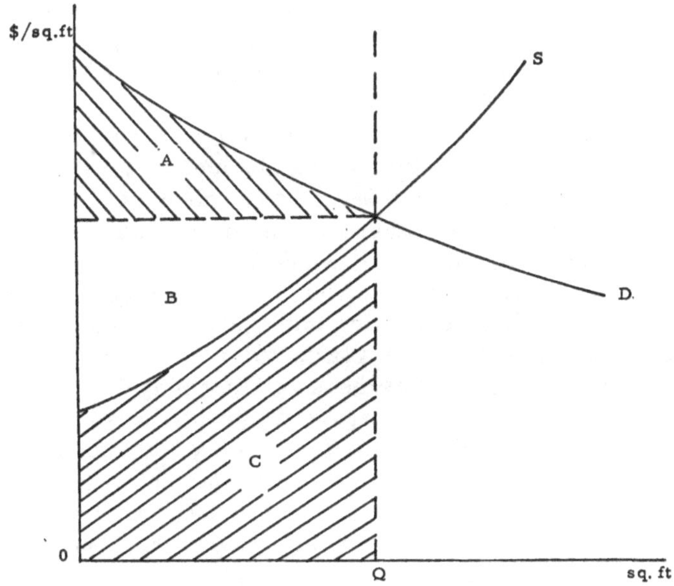

The distribution of total benefits into land rents and a consumer's surplus has been elucidated by Ronald Grieson (1971). Grieson argues that the demand for sites is best considered not as a bid for specific ground areas, but for usable building space in specified categories. The amount of usable space that can be provided within an area is not fixed, as is total land area, but is expansible, by construction of higher buildings. Expansion on this intensive margin takes place at increasing costs. Similarly, the supply of usable space may be expanded along an intensive margin by investment in transit facilities, also at an increasing cost. Therefore, in some submarket for space, such as the office-space or residential-space market of a city, there will be a supply curve such as that in Figure 1. The intersection of that curve with the demand curve for space determines the intensity of land use, and the rent for space. The equilibrium determined yields a consumers' surplus (A), as well as a total rent. This total rent itself, however, is divided into an area of building and transport facility costs (C) and a producers' surplus (B) [2]. This producer's surplus is what will be capitalized in ground values. The relation between areas A and B represents the division of benefits between consumers and landlords.

3. Land values and city size

Many of the same problems persist when the total costs of congestion for cities of various sizes are considered. While several of these costs have been measured on cross-metropolitan bases, the interpretation of these costs is unclear. Rents are higher in larger cities, but if these rents are the residuals received by a Ricardian landlord, they may measure the social benefit, not the cost, of urban residence. Commuting expenditures rise, but bring with them, in many cases, a wider variety of job markets. Werner Hirsch (1968) and others have surveyed the costs of government services. While the provision of some services show economies of scale over some range, for most the scale with minimum average cost comes below the size of population required for a town to qualify as a metropolitan area. Beyond some point, per capita public costs rise with city size. But interpretation depends on increasing quality of services, and no good index of this quality is available.

William Alonso has tried to cut the knot by arguing that higher wages (even corrected for measurable cost of living differentials) and continued immigration into large cities show their size is sustained by a market test. Firms' and consumers' location decisions show the advantages of agglomeration outweigh whatever costs may exist. Higher wages show the productivity in large cities is greater than elsewhere. This, of course, is not an attempt to estimate the *costs* of congestion as a separate phenomenon, and makes no claim that they are small. It is, however, a claim they are outweighed by the benefits of bigness. As a test, however, this is dubious. Higher wages *might* be a measure

2. If transit costs are included, they must be borne by the suppliers of rented space, as through a real property tax, for the figure as drawn to be correct. The distribution of producer's surplus will also vary with location within a market along standard Ricardian principles, if an extensive margin is involved. In equilibrium, the marginal cost of increasing density should equal the marginal cost of extensive expansion.

of the extra inducement needed to persuade labor to bear the extra commuting and pollution burdens of city life. Given a perfectly mobile labor force, wage differences for workers of equivalent skill would indeed have to cover the costs of urban living. Net migration to large cities may show that, for the individual, the wage differences are still greater than the congestion costs of city living, but (as Alonso himself mentions) it can be objected that individual or firm response is to an average, rather than a marginal, cost or benefit of urban location.

With no automatic measure provided by the labor market, a measure of net costs or benefits of agglomeration may still be sought in the land market. Very large cities do generally have higher property values than very small cities, which in turn have higher values than their rural hinterlands. This, too, has been used as a basis for arguing that a market test sustains large cities over small ones. Higher land values are certainly consistent with a hypothesis that the benefits of bigness exceed its associated costs of congestion. But they do not necessarily prove these net benefits exist. To demonstrate this, a model of costs, benefits and land prices in a metropolitan area must be discussed in some detail.

Assume that the average cost to each participant of suffering the burdens of congestion of cities of different sizes could be known. This cost would include the fiscal burden of providing transport, protective and other services through taxes; the cost of commuting; the psychic nuisance of noise and the physical damage of air pollution, and all other costs related to city size. It is at least plausible that such costs would increase more than proportionately with city size. In Figure 2 (p. 69), such a curve (AC) is assumed and drawn.

Similarly, an average benefit (AB) curve is assumed. This is drawn on the supposition that a larger city affords the resident individual or firm more opportunities of other residents with whom to interact than a smaller city; in addition to the accessibility of services with minimum scale requirements (*e.g.*, symphony orchestras or major league ballteams), and a saving on costs of intercity transport when business is transacted locally rather than at a distance. These economies of agglomeration have been made familiar to economists through discussions of New York by Haig in the nineteen-twenties, and Vernon in the nineteen-fifties.

On the assumption that the city is small in relation to the entire economy, so that the rest of the world may be taken as given, and on the assumption that firms and individuals respond to economic incentives, migrants would be attracted into a city as long as average benefits exceed average costs. Thus a city would grow until population reached the size N_e. If, however, land in the city is sold or rented in a market, the migrant would have to give up some of his average net gain from urban residence (the difference between average benefit and average cost) to secure a location in the city. Per capita rent in the city (AR) will thus be given by

$$AR = (AB - AC)(1 - \varepsilon)$$

where ε is the proportion of the benefit remaining to the resident individual or firm. The value of ε would depend on the supply and demand for space, as Figure 1. As migration approaches a perfect elasticity with respect to net benefits, and to the extent that supply of usable space in the city is inelastic (more expensive to expand at a cost by upward or outward expansion) the entire benefit per resident will be approximated by average land rent.

$$AR \simeq AB - AC$$

In such a case, and even if ε remains a large but still constant proportion, maximum per capita land rent or land value will be at population N_a, while rent would be reduced to zero at N_e. The somewhat surprising result is that a city would be expected to grow until rents were squeezed out completely, and that beyond a point, rents per person would decline with city size.

This, of course, is stated in per person terms, with the individual of firm responding to average benefits and costs. However, total benefits, total costs and total rents for different levels of population could also be calculated by multiplying average figures by population.

$$TB = N\ (AB) \qquad\qquad TC = N\ (AC)$$
$$TR = N\ (AB - AC) = TB - TC$$

From these total benefit and total cost curves, marginal benefit and marginal cost curves can be defined.

$$MC = \frac{dTC}{dN} \qquad\qquad MB = \frac{dTB}{dN}$$

The marginal cost curves derived from the average cost curves originally assumed are drawn in Figure 2. The distinction between marginal and average costs arises, conceptually, because each resident of the city imposes costs (or commuter delays, additional government burdens, pollution, etc.) on every other resident and also bears costs imposed on him by every other resident. Even if, in a city of any size at any time, all such costs are perfectly reciprocal, an upward slope of a curve relating AC to population will mean that a new migrant to the city imposes more costs on other people than they impose on him, the relationship being

$$MC = AC\ (1 + \varepsilon)$$

where ε is the elasticity of AC with respect to N. A similar relation holds for average benefits of agglomeration.

From the viewpoint of maximizing the total benefits generated by a city, the "optimal" population N is the population at which MC equals MB. But this population is also that at which total rents are also maximized. Since land value is the capitalized value of rent, a city will be of optimal population (assuming the rest of the world as given) as long as land value is maximized. Thus *if* ε is small, or constant for cities of different sizes, and *if* cities of different

Figure 2.

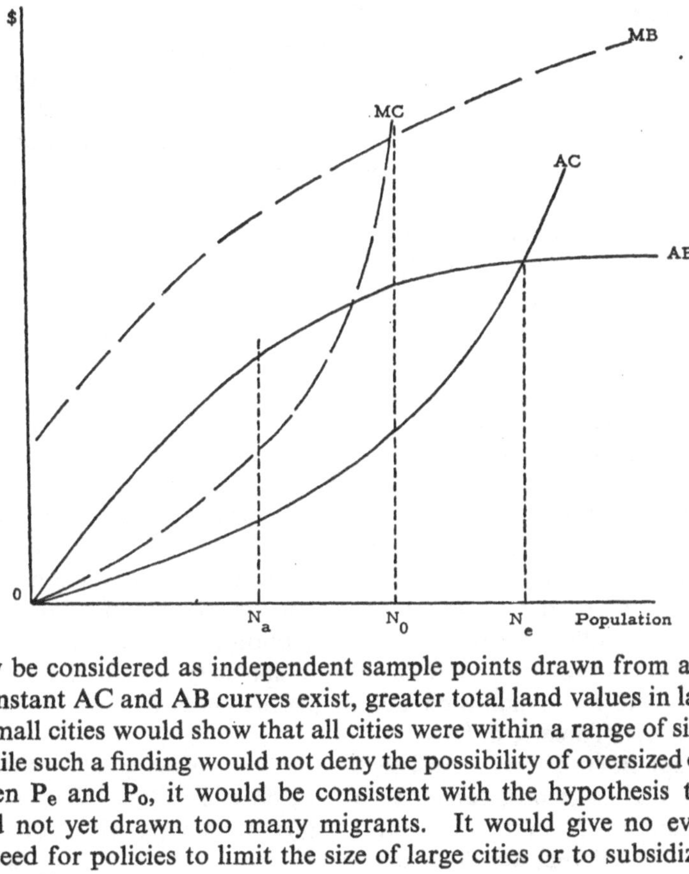

sizes may be considered as independent sample points drawn from a world in which constant AC and AB curves exist, greater total land values in large cities than in small cities would show that all cities were within a range of sizes below N_0. While such a finding would not deny the possibility of oversized cities with N between P_e and P_0, it would be consistent with the hypothesis that large cities had not yet drawn too many migrants. It would give no evidence of present need for policies to limit the size of large cities or to subsidize smaller "new towns".

Such a hypothesis seems at first to be substantiated by preliminary regression analyses of a cross section United States metropolitan area by John R. Harris and David Wheeler. They find that over the population of metropolitan areas with more than 50 000 inhabitants in 1960, total land value (TR) rose with city size. In a loglinear multiple regression analysis, holding several background variables constant, the elasticity of TR with respect to population was approximately unity. The largest city, New York, had by far the greatest total land value. However, these findings are not conclusive.

In the first place, a systematic relationship between N and ε could bias the results. If consumers' surplus were greater for users of land in large cities than in small, in proportion to ground rents, then economies of scale would be underestimated. Greater profits which some cross section studies have associated with larger cities might indicate this. Nonetheless, the higher wages in larger cities (which Alonso has argued indicate greater scale economies) may in fact merely be compensation to workers for receiving lower consumers' surplus in large cities than in small. Of course, for the purposes of the comparison, surplus per square foot rather than per worker or per dollar invested, is the relevant measure. This relationship is still in need of investigation, and has not yet been proven systematic, but the possibility of bias must be admitted. (The possibility of large random variations in ε is less admissible given the high values of the coefficient of determination obtained in the cross section regressions.)

Second, the estimated elasticity is merely the best fit when cities of all sizes are included in the sample, over the entire size range. However, when separate regressions are run for cities of different size ranges, elasticities may vary. If costs and benefits of agglomeration are as shown in Figure 2, elasticities would be greater than 1 in ranges up to size N_a, and then decline over subsequent ranges. This is borne out by estimates in ranges of size up to one million. The estimated elasticities are 1.45 for cities of 50 000-150 000 inhabitants, and 1.22 for cities of 150 000-250 000 inhabitants. Between one quarter of a million inhabitants and half a million inhabitants, the elasticity is only 0.91. From half a million to a million, it has fallen to 0.43 (not significantly different from zero at the 0.05 level). Thus it would appear that net economies of agglomeration are exhausted by a population of one million. However, above one million, the elasticity returns to approximately unity (0.99, significantly different from zero). That the economies of scale are greatest in the largest cities is clear from the reduction in elasticity to 0.56 if the five metropolitan areas of more than three million people are excluded from the sample. (See Appendix, Table 3, p. 85.)

These results might be consistent with the existence of similar average benefit and average cost functions for all cities if either of these functions contains an inflection point. But another possibility also presents itself. There may be different benefit functions for cities with different roles in society. If different cities do have different curves, then greater land values in a large city might arise from a more favorable curve, rather than closer approximation to its own maximum land value size. For example, in Figure 3, cities 1 and 2 have separate AR and MR curves (although sharing the same AC and MC curves). The population of city 1 is N_1, the "optimal" [3] population at which marginal costs and benefits of agglomeration are equal, while the population of city 2 is N_2, which exceeds its optimal population N_{02}. Although the land values of city 2 are less than they would be at size N_{02}, they are greater than land values in city 1 [4].

3. This is optimal if the number of cities is fixed and population of all urban areas together (migration from rural areas) is variable. If the number of cities is variable, but total urban population fixed, optimal size is that at which AB-AC is maximal (this is a smaller size).

4. If cities of different sizes are subsidized by a national government to a differential degree, land values may also provide a biased estimate of economics of agglomeration.

Figure 3.

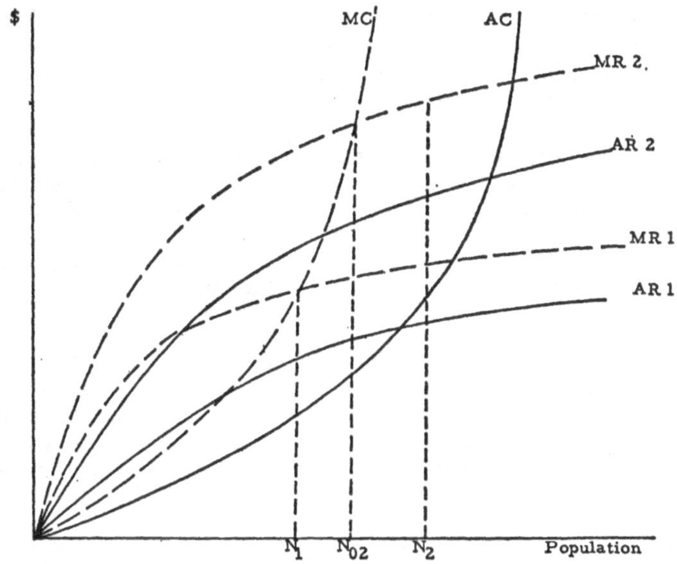

Economies of agglomeration could still be attributed to the entire range of cities *if* any city reaching size N_{02} could acquire a benefit function like that of city 2. But there is some reason to think that this is not the case. Cities do have unique functions, and often compete for the attainment of these functions. Selection as a national capital is one obvious example. Arnold Toynbee (1970) has recently examined factors which have determined the choice of capital cities by countries throughout history. Often the causes of selection are military or political, not economic. A city once selected, however, can take advantage of a wider variety of activities than other cities. It will have greater opportunity for economies of agglomeration. Similarly, historians of the United States have traced the political rivalry of different cities for railroad routes, and other government investments which created new business opportunities.

One recent discussion of city functions has posited a hierarchy of cities based on roles of different levels of control in large corporations. Stephen Hymer begins with a distinction made by Chandler and Redlich (1961) between "three levels of business administration, three horizons, three levels of task, and three levels of decision making [...]/and/policies". The lowest level, 3, is concerned with managing the day to day operations of the enterprise; level 2 is responsible for coordinating the field operations; level 1 is top management concerned with goal determination and planning for the lower levels. Hymer (1971) posits a "Law of increasing firm size", by which capitalist corporations have grown from local to national to multinational in scope, with levels 2 and 1 being separated from level 3 in the process.

Hymer suggests further that the application of location theory to the Chandler-Redlich scheme suggests a correspondence between the centralization of control within the corporation, and a hierarchy of control within the international or spatial economy :

"Location theory suggests that level 3 activities would spread themselves over the globe according to the pull of manpower, markets and raw materials. Level 2 activities, because of their need for white collar workers, communications systems, and information, tend to concentrate in large cities. Since their demands are similar, corporations from different industries tend to place their coordinating offices in the same city [...] Level 1 activities, the general offices, tend to be even more concentrated than level 2 activities, for they must be located close to the capital market, the media, and the government. Nearly every major corporation in the United States, for example, must have its general office (or a large proportion of its high level personnel) in or near the city of New York because of the need for direct personal contact at higher levels of decision making. Applying this scheme to the world economy, one would expect to find the highest offices of the multinational corporations concentrated in the world's major cities — New York, London, Paris, Bonn, Tokyo. These along with Moscow, and perhaps Peking, will be the major centers of high-level strategic planning."

According to Hymer, the hierarchy of city functions will be paralleled by a hierarchy of job structures, with a greater concentration of higher paid skills and occupations in higher power cities; a trickling down of new products between levels; and a relationship of dependency of regions with lower level cities upon those with more central cities. In terms of the theory of agglomeration, firms and individuals anxious to advance in the hierarchy will reap advantages from location at more central points. These cities, we might expect, would have different benefit curves (measuring benefits within the ground rules of the corporate economy) than cities lower in the hierarchy of power.

To test the possibility that different cities had different functions, and that these might reflect a separation of corporate functions, the cities in the Harris-Wheeler study were separated into corporate and non-corporate cities on the basis of the number of corporation head offices. An index was prepared of the number of divisional headquarters of large corporations (*Fortune's* two hundred largest industrials, and fifty largest in each of several non-industrial categories), weighted by the average business volume per division in each corporation. This index enters into the regression as an independent variable separate from population. The two are closely correlated only among the largest twenty cities when the sample is stratified. The relation between land values, divisional corporate activity and population for the two groups of cities proved to be somewhat different.

Curves of the relationship between population and total land values for the two groups of cities are presented in Figure 4. The curves are drawn freehand; however, several different variants of them have been estimated statistically on different specifications and for different subranges of city size. (Some of these regression results are discussed in an appendix, and other specifications will be presented in a forthcoming paper by Wheeler.)

Figure 4.

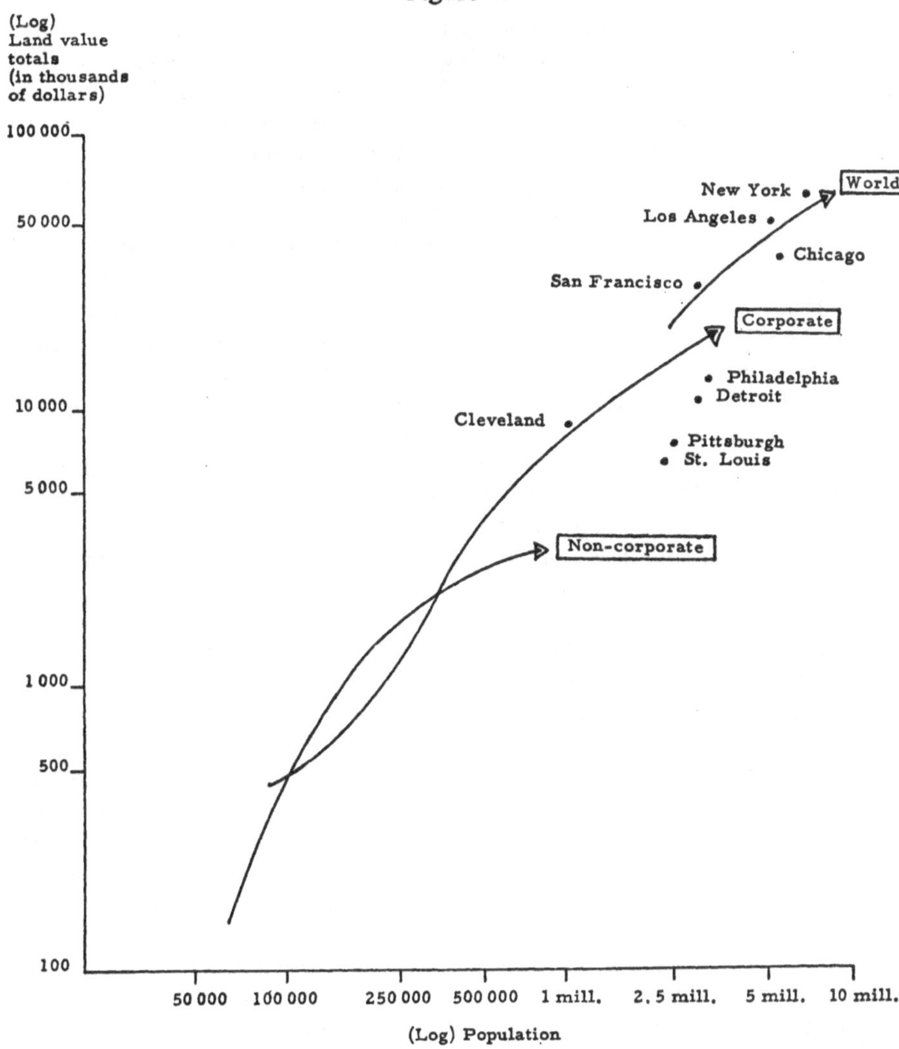

Source : SMSA data, 1960, from US Census.

The relationships found are that growth of land values in non-corporate cities is well exhausted by the time population reaches one million, and total land value reaches three billion dollars. There is considerable dispersion to land values at the upper end of this range, however, with a few essential non-industrial cities like Dallas, New Orleans, Atlanta and Miami showing somewhat higher land values (about five million dollars for metropolitan populations of about one million) but cities with an industrial base, such as Gary, have lower land values than the curve would predict, for sizes above 500 000 inhabitants.

For corporate cities, land values pass the three billion dollar mark at a population of half a million, and rise thereafter, slowing somewhat at a population above a million, but continuing to rise at a decreasing rate, to a value range of nine to thirteen billion dollars for a population of 2-2.5 million. Thereafter, the curve may be interpreted either as rising more rapidly again, or as dividing. Philadelphia and Detroit (with populations of about four million each) appear to lie on a continuation of the same curve. San Francisco (three million), Chicago and Los Angeles (about a million each) and New York (with a metropolitan population just under 10 000 000 at the 1960 census) lie above the curve. The land value for New York was approximately ninety billion dollars, about twice the asymptote to which the corporate city curve (excluding the largest four or six cities) appears to be approaching; many times the value for non-corporate cities. The assumption of a separate curve for the four cities — following Hymer's classification of a few top corporate cities as "world cities" is used in drawing Figure 4.

Assuming the specifications used are correct, the separation of non-corporate, corporate and (perhaps) world cities has several implications for the measurement and evaluation of urban congestion, and the factors which cause congestion costs. At the simplest level, it becomes possible to claim that for non-corporate cities there are no gains to agglomeration which outweigh congestion costs beyond a population of a million — or perhaps even half a million, for production centers such as Gary. A few of these cities seem therefore to be beyond the optimal size, although most cities which have not attained corporate functions do not appear to be "too big". For the corporate cities, assuming all but the "world-cities" share the same "average benefit" curves, none are visibly too large, although the absence of much value increase indicates that little is to be gained by directing further population to these cities, and that (if they share the same benefit curve) Detroit and Philadelphia may be too large already. For these cities, and others in this range (including Pittsburgh, Saint Louis, Cleveland, Baltimore, Minneapolis-Saint Paul, Houston, as well as Boston, which was not included in the regressions), the only chance of avoiding a decline of values with increasing population would appear to be a bid to take on "world-city" functions. Some of these cities, particularly Houston, are making such a bid; Baltimore and Saint Louis appear to have been casualties in competition with other cities earlier in their history. (Similarly, Dallas, Atlanta, Miami, and New Orleans appear to be able to hold their positions only if they do succeed in securing corporate-city ranking; Atlanta, at least, may have done so in the 1960's.)

For the world cities, whose functions may in each case be specifically unique, there does not appear to be any way of arguing from the graphs presented whether size advantages have yet outrun congestion. If New York is sufficiently different from Chicago, for example, it may be the case that removing from the city some of the low wage industries that have existed there since the period of European immigration and removing the part of the labor force engaged in those industries to some other location, would increase land values while reducing population.

All of this takes city function as given. However, Hymer's analysis suggests that the role of cities in the corporate hierarchy may be the result of a form of social organization not necessarily dictated by technology:

"The new technology, because it exercises interaction, implies greater interdependence, but not necessarily a hierarchical structure. Communicatons linkages could be arranged in the form of a grid in which each point was directly connected to many other points, permitting lateral communication as well as vertical communication [...] each point would become a center on its own; and the distinction between center and periphery would disappear. Such a grid is made *more* feasible by aeronautical and electronic revolutions which greatly reduce costs of communications. It is not technology which creates inequality; rather it is *organisation* that imposes a ritual asymmetry on the use of intrinsically symmetrical means of communications."

A similar argument has recently been advanced by Stephen Marglin (1970), who goes so far as to argue that the hierarchical structure of production within the factory itself is not necessary (and was not necessary when factories were first developed) for the technology of production. Rather it was adopted to facilitate control (and private profits) by manager-owners. Marglin argues that centralized control has a historical function of centralizing funds for investment and raising the rate of savings. With economic advancement, this function becomes less necessary; his argument would imply that perhaps even the economies of scale presumably reflected in the advantages of cities of half a million over smaller non-corporate cities might prove illusory. Hymer's position implies at least that any increase in congestion as cities surpass half a million or a million inhabitants, to become corporate or world-corporate cities, should be considered as a cost of hierarchical organization.

Whether this system is or is not able to generate benefits greater than its costs, it would be useful to know the costs it imposes. It is here, however, that the weakness of land value as an absolute measure of congestion costs reappears. The values in Figure 4 represent the excess of capitalized benefits over capitalized costs. Even assuming that all costs and benefits are capitalized, there is no way of identifying the costs and the benefits separately from the land values. To be sure, some specific factors which affect costs and benefits can be entered separately into a cross-section regression. For example, a term representing the ratio of 1900 population to 1960 population, when entered into the regression for the United States, was negative in most specifications. This may represent the greater problem of congestion resulting from antiquated street layouts, neighborhood externalities of slum formation, inadequate sewer facilities, and other disadvantages of older cities in adapting to greater size — although it may in part reflect a systematic underassessment of land and over-assessment of improvements for older buildings. But other congestion factors may prove to be too closely correlated with population size for independent entry into the regressions.

In this case, the best that can be done is to make alternative estimates, based on *a priori* reasoning about the shape of cost and benefit curves. These would allow a variety of estimates of the total congestion costs of cities of different sizes to be estimated. These would then allow the estimation of the total additional congestion cost of having, say, one New York in place of fifteen or twenty cities of the apparently optimal non-corporate size, or in place of six to ten smaller managerial centers. For one example of such estimates, suppose that in Figure 4, the curve of land values for non-corporate cities is generated by agglomeration economies alone up to the point at which per capita value is greatest (a size of 300 000 inhabitants, and a land value of 1.5 billion dollars). Presume that beyond that point, in the absence of congestion, per capita agglomeration economies (AB) would be constant. The gap between a total benefit curve projected from this point, and the observed land value curve would measure total congestion costs. Their value would be approximately half a billion dollars for a city of half a million, or two and a half billion for a city of a million inhabitants. On the assumption that benefits for non-corporate cities would remain at an asymptotic level of three billion dollars for non-corporate cities, and do not bend downward, the cost of congestion for New York would be sixty billion dollars. On these assumptions — selected, of course, from an infinitely large number of possible assumptions — the cost of operating New York instead of ten cities of one million inhabitants is forty-five billion dollars; the congestion involved in operating New York instead of twenty cities of half a million inhabitants is evaluated at fifty-five billion dollars.

One additional consideration which weakens faith in these speculative estimates is the possibility that some of the costs and benefits of agglomeration are not capitalized into land values. Even if ε is not different for cities of different sizes, so that net benefit figures are correct, estimates of costs alone may be too low. What is more, the possibility of systematic biases in ε may again be raised. Larger corporations, which will be concentrated in "world" and corporate cities may have higher profits than other businesses; some of the wage differentials observed between larger and smaller cities may be due to the sharing of some monopoly surplus with relatively advantaged sectors of the labor force in these corporations. Such a description of a dual structure of economic organization and labor markets has recently been suggested by a number of writers, including Robert Averitt (1968), Barry Bluestone (1970), David Gordon (1971), and Bennett Harrison (1972). Since some higher wages or profits may cover increased congestion costs or other bothers of bigness, while some are pure gain, to those participating in the corporate sector, identification of the congestion costs alone is further complicated. The existence of expense account privileges, consumption benefits of office space, and other wage or profit-like incomes in kind that are charged as costs on corporate records further complicates the analysis.

Nonetheless, despite the difficulty of identifying the actual costs of congestion, land values do seem to point to the existence of definite (if imprecise) relations between city size and net benefits of agglomeration, and to relations between city function (corporate or noncorporate) and these size-value relationships. Possibly greater non-capitalized net benefits for larger cities, since they are the result of corporate-sector institutions of the hierarchical economy, may not affect very much the shape of the total benefit curve for noncorporate cities. That these seem to have a peak in per capita value around 300 000 inhabitants and to exhaust total value increases by a population of one million (a range of sizes only slightly greater than that suggested for towns by "utopians" who have in the past speculated about ideal city size) suggests the possibility of identifying "optimal" city sizes by the market. The existence of cities of over one million inhabitants appears to be due to the existence of hierarchical managerial functions — and the evaluation of whether the associated costs of congestion are too great depends on the overall evaluation one makes of the benefits of hierarchy.

4. Intrametropolitan distribution of value changes

The previous section has suggested that large cities owe their existence to large institutions; the costs of increased congestion imposed by this agglomeration will be borne, to a considerable extent, from the revenues of these institutions. Whether these revenues represent monopoly profits or returns to a socially useful form of information management, they are used in part to pay higher rents for access to other organizations, in part to pay workers for bearing the costs of congestion, and in part to pay transport costs, local taxes and other direct congestion related expenses. To the extent that the advantages of large organizations stem from monopoly (or political) power, the costs may be shifted to suppliers and consumers outside the corporate sector, throughout the society, and abroad. In addition, competition among communities for corporate plants and offices often allows a shifting of some congestion costs away from corporations through tax concessions, particularly at lower levels of the hierarchy, where activities may be more mobile.

Within large metropolitan areas, the burden of congestion costs must also be distributed among firms and individuals. While, for the more mobile forms of labor, recompense for higher current costs is required where congestion costs are higher, this may not be as true for occupational categories which exist only in corporate cities. The bearing of some congestion costs may make the privilege of occupation in certain high wage corporate occupations less lucrative than it would be were corporate participation divorced from locational factors. (The literature of and by exurbanites, deploring some of their problems, would suggest that long distance commuting costs, at least, are not negligible; these costs, however, do not seem great enough to reverse the relative ranking of occupational returns.) However, many of the costs of congestion may be sufficiently specific to locations within a metropolitan area that they may be capitalized directly (and negatively) into property values. The distribution of the capital losses involved — and also of the capital gains occurring when agglomeration economies outweigh congestion costs — may affect the distribution of wealth among different classes of organizations and individuals.

There are good reasons to believe that in the form of metropolitan areas typical of the United States (and some other advanced capitalist countries), the distribution of these capital gains and losses is regressive. This hypothesis is difficult to prove conclusively, due to the difficulty of obtaining good data on the urban real estate market at sufficient levels of disaggregation. Nor, at best, can it provide a complete account of the distribution of all gains and losses from agglomeration, since not all of these are capitalized in property values. Nonetheless, some historical and statistical evidence, as well as theoretical considerations, do point in the direction of regressive distribution among metropolitan property owners.

The pattern of land value changes that occur with urbanization may be inferred from the comparison of cities of different sizes. As a city grows larger, over some range at least, its aggregate land values increase. If the city does not achieve corporate-city and then world-city status, however, the growth of values will eventually taper off at least relative to other cities. Even with total values advancing, the growth is a result of offsetting economies and diseconomies of size. There is no necessity for the effects of both to be felt evenly at all points within the city. Indeed, cross-section studies of land values and uses within a city typically show that values are highest in the center of a city, and descend toward the periphery. The gradient is not always monotonic, as Frieden (1964) shows. Changes in values at different points of time may be different at different locations.

Higher land values downtown are related to the advantages of accessibility to the center of gravity of business. Particularly in corporate cities, where face to face contact between representatives of different businesses, and within-building contact between many functionaries, is necessary, space in a central business district is at a premium. Port and railhead proximity may have, in the past, created a similar premium on central space for manufacturing and warehouse functions, but this has been less true since the rise of the truck as a primary means of freight transport. Housing space near business and industrial centers is also at a premium, since it allows a saving in commuting costs. Typically, this saving attracts the low paid employee, who is forced by income constraints to accept high density residence, in order to save on transport. Thus more central land is likely to be devoted to multifamily dwellings. Higher land values than in areas of single family homes may coexist with lower per apartment rents than in more peripheral areas. Higher income earners, who can afford automotive commuting, are more likely to consume more space, at lower per foot costs, on the periphery of cities, than are low income earners.

The pattern of density, income and land value gradients generated by these considerations — which has been described in theoretical terms by Alonso, Mills, Muth and others — is sometimes reinforced by a pattern of aging of structures, in a growing city. Since older buildings are located within former boundaries of the metropolis, toward the center, the conversion of these to lower income, higher density housing use reinforces the centrality of poverty. Some divergence of the results of filtering from the model predicted by commuting cost considerations may occur if the oldest buildings are preempted by a non-employed lowest income group, which despite a lack of commuting savings, is forced to live there by an inavailability of non-central dwellings of sufficiently low quality. Zoning, building codes, or racial segregation, which restrict the poor to the central areas, may reinforce the pattern.

A cross-sectional glimpse at a metropolis may show this overall pattern, but although land values may be highest in the center of the city, it does not follow that values must be growing most rapidly near the center. Indeed, this is often not the case. As cities grow, assuming they have an expanding corporate business sector, central business district land values may be expected to expand. As total population increases, assuming transportation technology at the time allows an extension of the radius of commuting, new land on the edge of the city will be urbanized. Capital gains in the development process are typically considerable, although at times they have been anticipated earlier by speculative holders. Between the business district and the fringe, where land is already in residential uses, land value increases generally occur at a lower rate, for a number of reasons, as long as transportation does not restrict the growing population to a constant area. Generally a linear approximation to a land value gradient becomes flatter over time (as Mills showed in Chicago). In some inner ring residential districts, land values may actually fall (relative to the cost of living or GNP deflator). There are several reasons for these differences, some of which involve the capitalization of congestion costs.

Real estate taxes are one important factor. Tax rates in metropolitan areas have increased over time, and in the United States they have risen particularly rapidly in recent years. To some extent, these increases are the result of rising demand for schooling and other services, and to a lower rate of technical progress or capital-labor substitution in government services than in industry. Many of these costs, however, can be attributed to the problems of coping with congestion. These include sanitation and some health and protection expenditures, as well as the provision of transport facilities for commuters. Generally, in the American city, a fragmentation of jurisdictions occurs, with separate taxbases for central cities and suburbs, and many of the costs of the metropolitan area's services borne disproportionately by the central city and inner ring or older mixed residential and industrial towns. Rising taxes to some extent drive businesses and higher income residents from the inner ring communities, lowering demand for property there; institutions that remain often are able to exact tax concessions, if they are not already incorporated as tax exempt non-profit institutions. (The interjurisdictional relations involved have been explored by Margolis (1957), Sclar (1971), Vincent (1969), Levy (1971) and others. That taxes are capitalized in property values is indicated by Oates.)

Second, the extension of transport systems disrupts neighborhoods, takes land off the tax rolls, and imposes externalities of safety hazards, noise and air pollution on inner city neighborhoods. Whether the figures presented by Ridker and Henning represent the full cost imposed by pollution, or not, they show that at least some externalities are capitalized as decreases in real estate prices.

Third, congestion increases the probability that aging or deterioration of one building will decrease the returns to new construction or maintenance of other properties. These externalities have been investigated by Davis and Whinston (1961) and by Rothenberg (1967) as contributing to slum formation The demand for land is reduced in these cases — sometimes even to the extent of abandonment — and real estate values are correspondingly reduced. Older neighborhoods, which are generally found in the inner ring of the metropolitan area, are clearly more prone to these slum effects than newer, outer ring areas.

Fourth, there exists some psychological opinion that congestion in and of itself creates some forms of social pathology. (See some of the articles in the collection by Duhl.) If this is true, the creation of these problems will fall most heavily upon the more congested or poorer neighborhoods, and these, as areas of cheaper housing, will also bear the burden of immigration of persons affected from other neighborhoods. The poorer communities must thus bear any resulting burdens, in terms of decreased safety or greater fiscal costs. This point is, however, controversial — there is a body of opinion that exempts high density land use from blame (*e.g.*, Jacobs). Where welfare costs, and other burdens of unemployment are borne by local taxpayers and distributed as neighborhood effects, there is little doubt that they fall most heavily on central city or inner ring dwellers. (Whether these problems are due to congestion, or to other aspects of a corporate-dominated labor market, as others assert, does not affect the net distribution of burdens of the maintenance of the corporate hierarchy *if* congestion itself is due to this hierarchy [5].)

5. The influence of segregation or the presence of racial minorities is sometimes added, in the popular press, as a factor in the reduction of land values in "ghetto" neighborhoods. Economists, however, have rejected the notion that minority residence lowers long run land values. If a group is the victim of segregation, which limits the area available for its settlement, this will tend to *raise* prices in minority occupied areas compared to what they could be otherwise. Studies by Laurenti (1960) and others have indeed found some evidence of higher real estate prices in the American "ghetto" than in comparable quality white neighborhoods. Of course at a moment of racial transition, "block busting and panic selling" have been known to lead to very brief short-run depression of values.

All of these factors, which may be considered as congestion-related, lower land values in the inner ring or older residential areas relative to more peripheral and newer suburbs. However, identification of the effects of congestion on distribution is complicated because other important factors operate to shift land values in a similar direction. First, the aging of buildings themselves affects the worth of their own parcels of land. (This effect encompasses the result of deterioration occurring not because of surrounding slums or lack of public services.) Second, subsidy for the construction of new housing, while it makes available some housing for the poor by "filtering", does so by reducing higher income demand for, and thus prices of older houses. Third, inner ring land prices are depressed by the competition of new suburban land made available by changes in transportation technology, or new highway investments. All of these factors taken together, whether their base is in congestion itself, or in the dynamics of investment and aging of structures and public facilities, create one overall tendency of property values : values at the periphery of cities rise relative to those in older, more central residential areas.

This has implications for the distribution of wealth because, in the United States, the majority of residential housing is owner occupied, and a considerable proportion even of rented apartments are in two or three family dwellings, in which the owner occupies one of the apartments [6]. For most of the owner occupiers and even small landlords, the one building is the biggest element in a relatively small investment portfolio. On the other hand, land at the point of subdivision on the urban fringe is more often held by persons with larger investment portfolios, while land in the central business districts is more generally held by corporations or institutions. Corporate ownership, in turn, is largely concentrated in the highest wealthy groups. (Lampman's study found that 1% of wealth holders held 76% of all corporate stock but only 12.5% of personally held real estate, and presumably a lower proportion of houses. Estimates by the Bureau of Internal Revenue for 1962 were that real estate formed more than half of the wealth of persons with assets of less than $ 40 000, but less than one third of the investments of persons with wealth greater than $100 000.) Among home owners, furthermore, those with lower incomes are more often found in the inner rings or as they are sometimes called, "gray areas", of metropolitan regions, where the pressure of taxes, neighborhood externalities, and highway externalities on land values is greatest.

The result of these factors is an investment pattern in which the wealthier earn more rapid capital gains within the land market than do the non-wealthy.

6. Exceptions include 1) luxury highrise apartments; 2) very old rental housing, close to the center of the city where slum formation has already driven rents to the point at which they barely cover costs (a pattern of ownership by large scale investors earning their profit through depreciation privileges in the tax laws emerges); 3) and neighborhoods about to be taken over by large institutions or for upper income housing near these institutions when the central business district expands in an already large corporate city. In this last case a conflict over control of land and potential capital gains arises between old residents and new investors and users. (See Edel, 1972.)

A similar effect often occurs through other investments: the wealthy own corporate stock while the middle and working class investor holds life insurance and pension fund assets. Taking all assets together, Lampman found the top one percent maintained their relative share of national wealth, except during the depression, despite inheritance fragmentation and despite a lower ratio of savings to wealth than that prevalent in the rest of the population, because their assets appreciated faster than the average rate. Lampman's study covers the period between 1920's and 1953; between 1956 and 1966, corporate stock continued to advance in value more rapidly than single family residential structures or the land used for these residences. Non-residential urban land rose in value more rapidly than residential land.

Statistics assembled on a national level do not allow a comparison of the rates of appreciation of houses owned by persons at different wealth levels. A study of the Boston metropolitan area, now under way, should allow some estimate of these differences. Table 1 shows the differential pattern of assessed land values in three neighborhoods of the city of Boston, and for the city as a whole, over almost a century. Charlestown and East Boston are neighborhoods of older and more dense settlement than is Brighton. The city itself contains both older and more recently developed and peripheral areas within its borders, as well as the central business district. Land value decreases are marked after the 1920's except for Brighton.

Comparison of land values between Boston and the surrounding high and low income suburbs is more difficult, because data from assessments will have to be adjusted for different assessment ratios, and land and building values are not reported separately in state compilations of town data. However, calculations using assessments of land and building together for each town have been made. If towns are grouped by the proportion of immigrants in each in 1930, increases are lower for the towns with more immigrants (see Table 2). Since the immigrants were, in general, a lower income group than were native-stock inhabitants, the calculation is some evidence of a regressive distribution of property value changes [7].

7. The figures must be taken as preliminary because they are biased by new construction as well as by assessment inadequacy, and because they separate land and buildings inaccurately. A more comprehensive investigation is being undertaken by the author and E. Sclar. Factors influencing the different rates of property appreciation and depreciation are also being studied. A study by Sclar shows that inner ring, higher density and lower income communities subsidize the transportation used by more suburban communities through their taxation; Orr (1968), Heinberg (1970) and Oates (1969), have presented evidence for tax capitalization in house values in the Boston area. These studies cover only the period of the 1950's, but we are attempting to replicate them using historical data, covering the past century of Boston area history. Preliminary findings indicate the present patterns are not new. The Boston case is not necessarily typical, in that the business activities of Boston were relatively stagnant in the first half of the twentieth century, and the fragmentation of the metropolitan area into suburban jurisdictions is extreme. Nonetheless, such evidence as is available on other large metropolitan areas, including Hoyt's study of Chicago land values (1933), indicates a similar pattern of relative land price changes.

Table 1. *Land value assessments in Boston (1 000's current $)*

	East Boston	Charlestown	Brighton	Whole City
1876	8 595	14 954	6 847	320 133
1893	9 273	16 641	11 109	433 694
1900	10 787	18 524	14 798	532 934
1914	18 258	13 659	22 139	722 736
1923	22 435	24 738	20 916	853 304
1935	15 522	19 715	31 654	759 124
1945	15 871	17 959	33 618	585 722
1950	13 195	14 248	34 485	579 599
1956	12 030	13 805	35 304	528 735
1960	11 870	13 729	34 305	479 889
1965	12 678	13 046	32 892	452 534

Table 2. *Change in assessed valuation by decades, Boston area*

Groups of towns with different proportions of immigrants, 1930*	Percentage change			
	1920-1930	1930-1940	1940-1950	1950-1960
City of Boston	30.8	- 25.5	4.9	- 6.0
High immigrant	60.7	- 6.1	16.7	24.0
Medium immigrant	82.9	- 2.5	11.2	52.4
Low immigrant	88.7	7.9	22.3	51.3
Towns, rural in 1930	59.6	2.6	28.5	23.1
USDL Consumer price index		- 11.2	72.6	23.5

* Immigrant proportions from 1930 census : high more than 40 % foreign born, low less than 30 %. In all counties, rural areas had less than 30 % foreign born; city of Boston had more than 40 %.

The pattern discussed here does not hold at all times. When population grows rapidly in a city relative to the capacity of commuter transportation, rents on older and apartment housing in the inner ring neighborhoods may be bid up. In a period of tight money, such as the late 1960's, this may lead to realized capital gains for lower income owners of rental housing. Persons with single family residences in these areas are faced with increases in the sale value of their houses, but may not be able to realize the capital gains for want of alternative residential sites to which they may move, and may be unable to borrow on their increased house values for other purposes because of the tightness of credit. If credit loosens, but transportation still does not permit an increase in the commuter radius, conversion to higher density construction will occur, with resulting capital gains on inner ring land. However, even in these circumstances, the ability of lower income home owners to capture the gains will depend on their ability to defend themselves from urban renewal programs, tax increases and "block-busting" harrassment, which may force them to sell at low prices to developers who eventually will reap the gains from rebuilding.

The possibility of such a successful defense indicates that it is not inevitable that the costs of congestion be borne disproportionately by the lower income or working class home owner. However, the record of city growth during most of the past century in American cities, and the models available that represent this normal pattern of growth indicate some such disproportion. Combined with the previous discussion of land values in cities with different sizes and functions, they lead to the following tentative conclusion:

Land values do not provide a perfect indicator of the magnitude of congestion costs. Insofar as they do capture both the costs and benefits of agglomeration, however, they show the existence of larger cities, with greater congestion problems, is related to the existence of corporate institutions whose headquarters must agglomerate. Some of these costs are passed on to consumers and suppliers of the corporate sector, who may or may not also benefit from possible economies (doubted by Hymer and Marglin) or more efficient production due to agglomeration. Of those costs and benefits not passed on, some accrue as producers' and consumers' surpluses to firms and residents in the corporate cities. A considerable portion accrues to land, however. These benefits and costs are distributed among land owners regressively with respect to wealth [8].

APPENDIX

This appendix presents some of the regression estimates made thus far in our tests of the hypothesis that urban land values are affected by the hierarchy of city functions, rather than just by city size alone. Further estimates have been run by David Wheeler, and will be presented in later papers. Simultaneous equation models have yet to be estimated.

Table 3 presents linear and loglinear estimates of the effects of population on total land values for both groups of cities, as well as for the mixed group. In the first column, total land values are regressed on population, with no background variables held constant. For cities below half a million population, the slope for non-corporate cities is slightly greater than that for corporate cities, although the proportion of variance explained by population is lower. (In the case of non-corporate cities, sample sizes were great enough that separate estimates could be made for subranges of size; only twelve corporate cities of less than half a million population were identified.) Between half a million and one million population land values grew more rapidly for corporate cities, but in neither case was the relationship significant, nor did population account for as much as ten percent of variance. Finally, for corporate cities above one million in size, the linear relationship between population and land value was the steepest of all, and highly significant.

The second pair of columns presents the results of regressions on a number of variables, including (in specification 1) terms representing the presence of railroads, port facilities, the value added in mineral production and in agriculture within the metropolitan area, the number of college students, the number of factories belonging to the two hundred largest industrial corporations, the ratio between 1900 and 1960 population. When these factors were included, the proportion of variance explained increased greatly (except in the case of

8. The extent to which these conclusions hold for countries other than the United States should be made the subject of further research.

corporate cities over one million inhabitants, for which the other variables are closely corre lated with population which alone explains .94 of variance). Slopes for non-corporate cities remained positive over the entire range up to one million inhabitants (although they decline over each successive range); for corporate cities the population term is negative (insignificantly so, to be sure) over the half million to one million range, while positive over other ranges.

In specification 2, corporate and non-corporate cities are combined, and the variable for corporate divisional and general headquarters is included as an additional explanatory factor. Taking this variable as independent of population (which involves ignoring the close correlation between the two for cities of over one million inhabitants), the population term is significant only up to half a million inhabitants, and becomes negative above one million. In a loglinear formulation (used in the last column) in which the variable for corporate headquarters is squared; the square of industrial value added is used instead of the number of corporate factories; and logarithms of population and other independent variables are used, the effect of the log of population on the log of land values does not become negative for values over a million, but otherwise the effect of population is similar to that in earlier specifications.

Table 3. *Linear estimates of effects of population on land value (Slope and significance levels)*

City size range	LV = a + bPOP		Linear specification		Logarithmic specification	
	b	R^2	b	R^2	b	R^2
Corporate cities			(Specification 1)*		(Specification 3)*	
50 000-500 000	3.99	.82	4.70	.98	1.06**	.98
500 000-1 mill.	2.23	.06	-1.42	.59	-1.13	.83
1 mill.-10 mill.	7.26**	.94	3.73**	.97	.89**	.95
Non-corporate cities			(Specification 1)*		(Specification 3)*	
50 000-150 000	5.18**	.40	5.19**	.69	1.46**	.59
150 000-225 000	4.75**	.30	4.72**	.70	1.18**	.61
225 000-500 000	4.59**	.34	3.69**	.75	.90**	.59
500 000-1 mill.	1.18	.08	1.72	.86	.63**	.95
All cities			(Specification 2)*		(Specification 3)*	
50 000-150 000	5.19**	.40	5.19**	.68	1.45**	.60
150 000-250 000	4.91**	.33	4.33**	.72	1.22**	.62
250 000-500 000	4.19**	.34	3.65**	.68	.91	.60
500 000-1 mill.	4.12**	.24	1.71	.69	.43	.55
1 mill.-3 mill.	6.97**	.73	-3.07	.97	.56	.93
3 mill.-10 mill.	7.21**	.95	-1.58	.99	.99**	.95

* Specifications : 1. LV = a + bPOP + cjVARj where VARj's include: ratio of 1900 to 1960 population, number of factories of top 200 corporations, number of students, and factors for agricultural, mining, port and rail influences.

2. Corporate divisional headquarters index added as an explanatory variable. Otherwise the same as 1.

3. Logarithmic form LLV = a + bLPOP + cjVARj where some VARjs' represented in logarithmic form and, in place of factories, manufacturing value added is used.

** = Significant at .05 level.

These regression results — and a number of other specifications tried — are consistent with the pattern estimated freehand in Figure 4, in that they show a general exhaustion of returns for non-corporate cities among a million inhabitants, and a new growth of corporate cities beyond that range — or at least past three million in size, with the growth explained to a large extent by the number of corporate headquarters associated with population, rather than population per se. Indeed, if population is excluded as an explanatory variable, the other variables used explained land values with $R^2 = .99$ for corporate cities of all sizes, $R^2 = .99$ for all cities over one million, and R^2 ranging from .38 to .85 for all cities and for non-corporate cities in different size ranges up to one million. These do not necessarily rule out the alternative hypothesis that size alone causes both the land value differentials and the changing functional mix of cities. Some urban economists, such as Wilbur Thompson (1965), have argued that cities assume new functions as a result of greater size. Some preliminary explorations using two stage least squares estimation, however, indicate better results are obtained from a specification that assumes city function affects size than are obtained from the assumption that size causes function. Further simultaneous estimations will be made in an attempt to test the possible hypotheses. For the time, we have merely proved that the hierarchy hypothesis is consistent with the data, and under some specifications, yields a slightly better explanation of differences than does the hypothesis that population agglomeration alone causes changes in values.

Among the alternative specifications tried, some of the non-linear estimates give evidence of the downward bending relationship between land values and population for non-corporate cities, and the linked relationship for corporate cities. For non-corporate cities (excluding Atlanta, Dallas, Miami and New Orleans), the use of an inverse term for population yielded:

TOTAL LAND VALUE = 771 -54 RAIL INDEX + 3.92 MINERAL VALUE INDEX
(1.75) (3.93)
+ 2.81 AGRICULTURAL VALUE ADDED INDEX + 4.62 PORT INDEX
(1.11) (2.71)
+ 26.80 NUMBER COLLEGE STUDENTS — 240 RATIO POPULATION (1900/1960)
(2.71) (1.05)
+ 47.79 FACTORIES OF CORPORATIONS — 70504 (1/POPULATION)
(6.65) (4.18)
($R^2 = .759$ N = 120)

Land values are measured in thousands of dollars, and population in thousands of inhabitants, and figures in parentheses are t-statistics. The figures show the significance of both the number of factories and the population in affecting land values positively, in this specification. Addition of the four excluded cities did not affect the order of magnitude or the sign of any term, but reduced the coefficient of determination and the t-statistic on the inverse of population. Addition of a term for the (small) numbers of corporate divisional headquarters on these non-corporate cities had no significant effect. A specification in which 1/POPULATION enters negatively yields an asymptotic curve, in which as population becomes infinitely large, land value converges to an upper bound. In the present case, estimating the asymptote using the median values of all other independent variables gives a limiting land value of 1.006 billion. This is about one-third the figure to which the curve for non-corporate cities in figure IV appears to converge. The discrepancy comes from higher values for the other independent variables for larger cities. A formulation in which the inverse of land values is replaced by the population and the square of population yields a positive sign on population and a negative sign on the square. If the cube of population is added, POPULATION and POPULATION^2 are positive, and POPULATION^3 is negative. In this last formulation R^2 rises to .88, but none of the three population terms is significant at the .05 level. Finally, when only the non-corporate cities of more than 225 000 population are included, the significance and R^2 rise for the inverse of population specification, and the asymptote calculated rises. There is thus some further evidence, besides the linear subgroup estimates, to support use of the curve of the shape drawn in Figure 4.

For corporate-cities, a specification including corporate divisional headquarters and POPULATION, POPULATION^2 and POPULATION^3 yields the best results, with the square of population entering negatively, indicating that the growth of land values is lowest in the middle ranges of size. The estimated equation is

$$\text{TOTAL LAND VALUE} = -524 \underset{(0.33)}{-23.64}\ \text{RAIL INDEX} \underset{(1.18)}{-13.70}\ \text{PORT INDEX}$$

$$\underset{(3.02)}{-4003.6}\ \text{RATIO POPULATION (1900/1960)} + \underset{(6.65)}{146.2}\ \text{NUMBER COLLEGE STUDENTS}$$

$$+ \underset{(2.00)}{6.14}\ \text{MINERAL VALUE ADDED INDEX} + \underset{(2.83)}{8.68}\ \text{AGRICULTURAL VALUE ADDED INDEX}$$

$$+ \underset{(7.04)}{94.30}\ \text{FACTORIES OF CORPORATIONS} + \underset{(3.60)}{54.13}\ \text{HEADQUARTERS INDEX}$$

$$+ \underset{(1.24)}{1.05}\ \text{POP} - \underset{(1.96)}{.322\text{E-}^{3}}\text{POP}^2 + \underset{(3.54)}{.519\text{E-}^{7}}\ \text{POP}^3 \qquad (R^2 = .996 \quad n = 41)$$

Further confirmation of diminishing net economies of agglomeration for corporate cities below the world city level occurs when the largest five cities are removed from this equation. The sign of POP^3 becomes *negative*, although all three population terms are insignificant. If the next smallest six cities with population between 1 and 3 million are also removed, the sign on POP^3 becomes positive again and all three population terms are significant at least at the .10 level. Some evidence for a range of slower growth among smaller corporate cities is offered by the negative sign of POP^2 in this specification. There thus may be three rather than only two ranges of growth for corporate cities (roughly in the ranges of population around 100 000-150 000) just under a million; and among the largest "world-cities". Interestingly, for the very small corporate cities a term for the distance to the nearest city of one million population has a negative sign, and is significant. This is the only subgroup of cities for which such a term is significant, and may indicate a viability for small corporate cities as satellites of some of the large cities, a possibility of some interest to those trying to formulate "new towns" policies in the United States.

REFERENCES

Alonso, W.

1965 *Location and land use.* Cambridge, Mass., Harvard University Press.

1970 "The mirage of new towns", *The public interest* 19, Spring.

Averitt, R.D.

1968 *The dual economy.* New York, W.W. Norton.

Bluestone, B.

1970 "The tripartite economy: Labor markets and the working poor", *Poverty and human resources* 6, July.

Chandler, A.D.; Redlich, F.

1961 "Recent developments in American business administration and their conceptualization", *Business history review,* Spring.

Davis, O.A.; Whinston, A.B.
1961 "The economics of urban renewal", *Law and contemporary problems* 26, Winter.

Duhl, L.J.
1963 *The urban condition.* New York, Basic Books.

Edel, M.
1970 "Innovative supply: A weak point in economic development theory", *Social science information* 9 (3), June.
1972 "Market, planning, or warfare : Recent land use conflicts in the United States", in: Edel, M.; Rothenberg, J. (eds.). *Readings in urban economics.* New York, Macmillan.

Frieden, B.
1964 *The future of old neighborhoods.* Cambridge, Mass., MIT Press.

Goldberg, M.
1970 "Transportation, urban land values and rents", *Land economics* 46 (2), May.

Gordon, D.M.
1971 *Class, productivity and the ghetto.* Cambridge, Mass., Harvard University (Ph. D thesis).

Grieson, R.E.
1971 *The economics of property taxes and land values.* Cambridge, Mass., MIT Department of Economics (working paper 72).

Haig, R.M.
1926 "Toward an understanding of the metropolis", *Quarterly journal of economics* 40, February and May.

Harris, J.R.; Wheeler, D.
1971 *Agglomeration economies : Theory and measurement.* Paper presented at the Urban Economics Conference, Keele, England, July.

Harrison, B.
1972 *Education, training and the urban ghetto.* Baltimore, Md., Johns Hopkins Press.

Heinberg, J.D.; Oates, W.E.
1970 "The incidence of differential property taxes on urban housing: A comment and some further evidence", *National tax journal* 23 (1), March.

Hirsch, W.Z.
1968 "The supply of urban public services", in: Perloff, H.S.; Wingo, L. (eds.). *Issues in urban economics.* Baltimore, Md., Resources for the Future and Johns Hopkins Press.

Hoyt, H.
1933 *One hundred years of land values in Chicago.* Chicago, Ill., University of Chicago Press.

Hymer, S.
1971 "The multinational corporation and the law of uneven development", in: Bhagwati, J.N. (ed.). *Economics and world order.* New York, World Law Fund.

Laurenti, L.
1960 *Property values and race*. Berkeley, Calif., University of California Press.

Levy, F.
1971 *Revenue sharing, the Tiebout hypothesis and the urban crisis*. Berkeley, Calif., University of California (working paper).

Marglin, S.
1970 *What do bosses do?* Cambridge, Mass., Harvard University (unpublished paper).

Margolis, J.
1957 "Municipal, fiscal structure in a metropolitan region", *Journal of political economy*, June.

Mills, E.S.
1967 "An aggregative model of resource allocation in a metropolitan area", *American economic review* 57 (2), May.
1969 "The value of urban land", in: Perloff, H.S. (ed.). *The quality of the urban environment*. Baltimore, Md., Resources for the Future and Johns Hopkins Press.

Muth, R.
1969 *Cities and housing*. Chicago, Ill., University of Chicago Press.

Oates, W.E.
1969 "The effect of property taxes and local public spending on property valuation" *Journal of political economy*, December.

Orr, L.L.
1968 "The incidence of differential property taxes on urban housing", *National tax journal* 21 (3), September.

Ridker, R.G.
1966 *The economics of air pollution*. New York, Praeger.

Ridker, R.G.; Henning, J.A.
1967 "The determinants of residential property values with special reference to air pollution", *Review of economics and statistics*, May.

Rothenberg, J.
1967 *Economic evaluation of urban renewal*. Washington, DC, Brookings Institution.

Sclar, E.D.
1971 *Effects of public receipts and expenditures policies on the greater Boston transportation system*. Medford, Mass., Tufts University (Ph. D thesis).

Thompson, W.R.
1965 *A preface to urban economics*. Baltimore, Md., Johns Hopkins Press.

Toynbee, A.
1970 *Cities on the move*. New York, Oxford University Press.

Vernon, R.
1966 *Metropolis 1985*. Cambridge, Mass., Harvard University Press.

Vincent, P.E.

1969 *Fiscal impacts of commuters on core cities with varying revenue structures.* Los Angeles, Calif., University of California, Institute of Governmental and Public Affairs (working paper).

Wheeler, D.

1971 *The corporate hierarchy and metropolitan area land values.* Paper presented at annual meeting, Econometric Society.

K. WILLIAM KAPP

Environmental disruption and social costs: A challenge to economics

Phenomena of environmental disruption[1] and social costs have suddenly been thrust into the center of political discussions; they raise not only practical issues of environmental control which are likely to occupy industrial societies far beyond the decade of the seventies but also fundamental theoretical problems with which economists will have to concern themselves. The present essay is designed to discuss this challenge to economic theorizing and, in a broader sense, to social inquiry in general. As a topic chosen for this memorial volume it bears a direct relationship to certain theoretical and practical issues which were in another but related context of interest to Jacques Stohler: the problem of "externalities".

The critique of economic theory advanced in the following pages may be received with certain misgivings: and yet it appears to me that lack of popularity of a critical thesis is not an appropriate criterion of judgment. The issues raised cannot be decided by appeal to prevailing opinions, popularity or even authority. Habits of thought and theoretical frameworks have a tendency to spread and perpetuate themselves far beyond the point at which they tend to become ill-adapted and in fact irrelevant for the treatment of new problems. Moreover, theoretical systems, not only in the social sciences, can always defend themselves by new assumptions and refinements which redefine the scope of the analysis and tend to narrow the admissible evidence with a view to reinforcing the conclusions and to making empirical evidence to the contrary appear to lie outside the analysis. This was the case when the orthodox cosmology of Ptolomey introduced always new epicycles to

1. *Environmental disruption* is a term which was first used interchangeably with the Japanese term *Kogai* at the International Symposium on Environmental Disruption in the Modern World, held under the auspices of the International Social Science Council (Paris) in Tokyo, March 8-14, 1970. As such, it is a term which is still in search of a precise definition. Provisionally it may be said to refer to the impairment beyond certain definable threshold levels of the aggregate of all external conditions and influences affecting the life and development of humain beings and human behaviour and hence of society.

"harmonize" theory with "facts" and observation. I believe something of this sort has happened to economic theory during the last decades. The theory has been made increasingly more abstract and formal at the price of a loss of relevance for the treatment of problems like environmental disruption and social costs which, however, are assuming increasing significance as output, productivity and population density grow under the impact of new technologies based upon the accelerated advance of science and research.

Environmental disruption and social costs have long been neglected or kept at the periphery of economic theory; they belong to the more disturbing elements of economic reality which economic theory since the classics had set out to analyze with the aid of the construct of a largely self-regulating equilibrium mechanism capable of harmonizing micro-economic decisions into a consistent and rational pattern. This theoretical system became a powerful argument in defense of economic liberalism. However, step by step it has been forced into the defensive while the core of its theoretical framework, namely neo-classical utility and price theory has maintained itself, if not in its original form, so at least in its various manifestations of modern welfare economics.

Environmental disruption and social costs of the character and scale now confronting modern industrial societies have created such critical conditions that it has become urgent to raise new questions about the adequacy and relevance of the old framework of analysis. Indeed the acute and potential dangers involved in the disruption of our natural and social environment for human health and well-being, discussed by dissenters for years and even decades, have suddenly attracted world wide and political attention. This political interest may act as a catalyst for a new and more appropriate treatment of these phenomena by economic theory and social inquiry. In this as in other cases "stubborn" facts, particularly if backed by political interest may prove stronger than theoretical constructs.

However, let us begin our discussion with an explicit warning against the current political rethoric about the need of protection of the environment and against the mistaken belief that the phenomena of environmental disruption exhaust the problem of social costs. When politicians appeal to a rebellious younger generation which has legitimate grievances about the quality of their society and the politics of their governments, by invitations to "wage war" on the disruption of nature, such appeals may be not much more than an attempt to restore a consensus evidently severely shaken by such issues as the undeclared war in Indochina, the unresolved consequences of slavery and racial discrimination, the pernicious effects of a secular inflation and the continued poverty in the midst of plenty. Indeed, the problem of environmental disruption may well be used as an issue designed to restore a failing political unity which threatens the "establishment" and society. The declaration of war on the disruption of the environment just as the earlier "war on poverty" may turn out to be not much more than a diversion of attention and a fixation on a problem which seems to be less controversial and easily subject to manipulation without interfering all too radically with customary ways of thinking and established methods of conducting business, modified only by a few *ad hoc* controls. The current advocacy of *ex post* remedies by offering incentives and disincentives via subsidies and taxes may turn out to be just as ineffective as the Sherman Anti-Trust Act. This legislation too was passed to pacify a wide-spread populist dissatisfaction with policies and practices of big business oligopolies but was actually incapable of stopping the trend towards administered prices and the "planning" of production and sales by large industrial concerns. It would not be surprising if the contemplated legislation against environmental disruption by under-estimating its significance achieves not much more than the passing on to consumers or to society as a whole the costs of "cleanliness" without really coming to terms with the serious problems raised by the current disruption of our environment [2].

For, there should be no mistake that the impairment of our environment and the damages and costs resulting therefrom constitute one of the most fundamental, dangerous and long-run issues which mankind has ever faced. While it cannot be our purpose to present at length the empirical evidence for this assertion, we do intend to elucidate some of the complex interdependencies which, under given institutional arrangements, lead to various forms of environmental disruption and social costs for which conventional economic theory can offer no solution.

These interdependencies and the causal chain which give rise to environmental disruption differ in kind and complexity from those with which economists have traditionally been concerned. To illustrate this thesis it is not sufficient to point to the obvious interrelationship of population growth and the concentration of population in urban agglomerations emerging under the impact of the increased productivity made possible by the development of science and technology, particularly during the last 50 years. Of course, science, new techniques, increased production, population growth, are all causally related and play in their interaction, and under the impact of our institutionalized framework of investment and production for profit, a decisive role in environmental disruption.

However, the process of causation is more complex. Thus, air and water pollution are not only the result of, and not proportionate to the volume of production and the emissions of residual waste products. They are also governed by the interaction of a whole series of variables which may react upon one another. Thus, waste products of various kinds may not only react upon each other, but also upon other elements in the environment and in this way give rise to additional toxological effects on plant, animal and human life with delayed cumulative consequences on human health. In

2. For a good discussion of these possibilities by two political scientists, *cf.* J.H. Schaar and S.S. Wolin, "Where we are now", *The New York review of books*, May 7, 1970, pp. 6-7.

addition, the actual rate of air and water pollution at any given time is governed by such intervening environmental variables as wind velocities and direction, topography, temperature inversions, stream flows and water temperatures.

Similarly, the actual radio-active contamination of closed or semi-closed water systems like rivers or lakes by atomic reactors is dependant, according to nuclear physicists, not simply on the volume of gaseous emissions or water effluents but on the rate of dilution and the physical build-up of concentrations from one or more reactors and the rate of reconcentration of radionuclides by biological systems (*e.g.*, fish) [3].

Or let us consider some of the problems which arise in connection with the disposal of garbage in congested urban areas. Of course, the volume of production, concentration of population and the amount of garbage collected are related and this relation can be expressed in quantitative terms. Thus, the City of Tokyo collected *ca* 5 000 tons of garbage per day in 1960, whereas today (1970) the volume of garbage collected and disposed of amounts to 10 000 tons daily. Even if the volume of garbage collected in 1980 should have doubled again — an assumption rather than a calculated rate of growth of garbage — the character of the problem will be different because by 1980 Tokyo will have run out of space to dump the garbage and will have to make increasing use of incinerators thereby adding to air pollution. In other words, it would be injustified to operate with constant output-garbage coefficients and linear correlations of national or regional output and the impairment of the environment.

The cumulative character and complexity of the sequence of events could be further illustrated by a variety of economic activities, including those of agriculture, where erosion, soil depletion and the use of chemicals constitute the most typical and spectacular examples of cumulative chains of causation. Thus, the ingestion by cows of plants affected by chemical pesticides gives rise to a contamination of milk products and human tissues. According to American biologists, most mother's milk in the United States contains so much DDT that it would be declared illegal in interstate commerce if it were sold as cows milk [4].

One final illustration may serve to conclude this discussion of the cumulative character and complexity of the causal sequence which gives rise to

3. P.F. Gustafson, "Nuclear power and thermal pollution", *Bulletin of the atomic scientist*, March 1970, p. 23; also R. Dubos, "The human landscape", *ibid.*, p. 36.

4. P.R. Ehrlich and A.H. Ehrlich, *Population, resources and environment*, San Francisco, Calif., 1971. For an analogous case of the effects of missions of mercury into waterways on fish which were then absorbed into human tissue, see Kin-ichi Yoshioka, *Natural and social scientific study of itai itai disease*, Tokyo, 1970, and Ui, Sonoda and Iijima, "Excerpts from environmental pollution control and public opinion", paper presented to the International Symposium on Environmental Disruption in the Modern World, International Social Science Council, Tokyo, March 8-14, 1970.

environmental disruption and social costs. Let us assume that as a result of the increasing air pollution the content of carbon-dioxide in the atmosphere increases by 100 per cent by the year 2000, thereby raising the heat-retaining properties of the atmosphere; let us further assume that as a result the average temperatures rise. Under these assumptions it is conceivable that the resulting climatic changes may lead to a partial melting of the arctic ice floes with the subsequent advent of a new Ice Age and/or a rise of the water level of the oceans by, let us say, 60 to 100 feet. This in turn could have the effect of submerging a substantial part of existing continental land areas [5]. In short, problems of environmental disruption confront the social scientist with an unusually complex set of interdependencies and delayed cumulative effects; any attempt to treat the quantitative and qualitative relationships by assuming constant rates of environmental disruption can only give rise to a simplistic and hence inadequate and false view of the problem, particularly as far as the formulation of criteria for action is concerned.

Before taking up the central issue under consideration it is relevant to emphasize that the term "environmental disruption", by stressing the ecological aspect may divert our attention from those social costs which find their expression in such phenomena as work injuries and accidents, rythms of work inimical to human health, crowded and inadequate housing conditions, damaging levels of noise, enforced and uncompensated adaptions to structural changes, workmen compensation systems rendered inadequate by inflation and, last but not least, monopolistic determination of real estate values and rents in congested urban areas, all of which can and do arise in contemporary industrial societies [6].

For this reason it should be understood that when we speak of environmental disruption we mean in effect the disruption of man's natural *and* social environment.

In the light of the foregoing discussion of the causal chain and complex

5. R.L. Heilbronner, "Ecological Armageddon", *The New York review of books*, April 23, 1970, p. 3; also H.J. Barnett, "Pressure of growth upon environment" in: H. Jarret (ed.), *Environmental quality in a growing economy*, Baltimore, Md., 1966, p. 16.

6. These social costs are everywhere borne by the economically and politically weaker elements of society. Seasonal and so-called "guest" workers, as well as minority groups bear the brunt of these social costs. But they are not alone. In France nearly 65 000 farmers are forced annually to abandon their activity and their residence and more than half of the admittedly redundant retailers had to give up their occupations during the last 15 years under the impact of the impersonal market forces set in motion by deliberate policies of growth and structural change. (J.P. Soisson, "Les retombées de la croissance", *Le Monde*, May 20, 1970.) These middle class victims of economic growth and structural change may reach physical and psychological threshholds of tolerance, making them an easy prey of street corner demagogues and the current trend toward racism, chauvinism and authoritarianism — something which the theory and models of economic growth are incapable of taking into consideration just as the advocates of deflationary wage policies and balanced budgets were unable to anticipate the "external" effects of unemployment rates of 20 to 30 per cent during the thirties and prior to the advent of fascism and " national socialism".

interdependencies which give rise to a disruption of man's natural and social environment, it becomes evident that the conventional framework and tools of economic theory are ill-adapted and in fact irrelevant for the analysis of the phenomena under discussion. Economic theory and its analytical tools have been shaped by the basic perspective according to which the task of economic analysis is confined to the explication of the logic of choice and the purely instrumental allocation of "given" scarce resources to "given" competing ends by individual economic units (producers and consumers). Partial equilibrium analysis has developed a logic of choice within the context of market transactions by firms and households and has defined optimal solutions of allocation in terms of a principle of marginal valuations under static conditions. In addition economic theory has made it an axiom of "positive" analysis to exclude from its purview any discussion of human needs, requirements and aspirations. In fact, ends are regarded as given, both in the static sense of the term and in the sense that they are to be accepted by economic theory as final data on the ground that any other procedure would necessarily sacrifice the scientific, *i.e.*, the "positive" character of the analysis. It is these preconceptions together with the concentration of the analysis on market transactions to which the theory was originally confined, which have shaped both the scope and the tools of the analysis. And neither the scope nor the tools of the analysis are adapted to the kind of interdependencies and complex causal sequences which give rise to environmental disruption and their social costs. These interdependencies have nothing to do with market transactions or exchanges of any kind; nor are they the result of choices unless one is prepared to argue that they are caused by the deliberate action of private firms which in full knowledge of the consequences decide to shift part of their costs to third persons or to society. Nobody affected by the negative consequences can be said to have voluntarily and in full knowledge agreed to bear these consequences.

In dealing with problems of environmental disruption and social costs we are confronted with direct technological non-market effects which in their cumulative character and consequences make the customary equilibrium approach of conventional economics irrelevant and antiquated. In view of the increasingly harmful character of certain capital inputs and technologies in modern industrial societies, increasing output and increasing population densities in urban agglomerations, economic growth as measured by GNP gives rise to increasing environmental disruption and social costs, unless the institutional framework and criteria of action are radically changed [7].

7. We have argued elsewhere that the damages and social costs tend to increase absolutely and relatively as output (and hence inputs) and therefore residual waste products and debris are dumped freely into the environment. *Cf.* K.W. Kapp, "Environmental disruption: General issues and methodological problems", paper submitted to the International Symposium on Environmental Disruption in the Modern World: A Challenge to Social Scientists, Tokyo, March 8-14, 1970, and printed in *Social science information* 9 (4), 1970.

From this point of view it is indeed correct to say that "economic growth renders many things obsolete and one of the things is economic theory" [8].

Environmental disruption cannot be explained adequately as a case of market-failure, unless the term is understood in the sense of the failure of the market system and of conventional economics to come to terms with interdependencies and complex causal chains which have long ceased to occupy a peripheral place in modern industrial societies and are bound to assume increasing significance as residual industrial waste products and debris are permitted to be discarded freely into the environment.

The foregoing considerations should dispose also of the belief that since the days of Alfred Marshall, the concept of externalities has offered an adequate tool for the treatment of problems raised by environmental disruption. We cannot concern ourselves here with a systematic exposition of the "empty box" character and the logical shortcomings of the concept of externalities as a cover-all concept. When Marshall introduced the concept of externalities he was concerned mainly with problems connected with his concept of the representative firm and the notion of constant costs as a result of certain cost reductions resulting not from decisions of the firm but originated outside the firm and were bestowed upon it by expanding markets, access to a trained working force, higher standards of health, education and culture, provided for by other firms or more particularly by public investments [9]. In short, the concept of external economies was designed by Marshall to harmonize increasing economies in a dynamic world with the static assumptions underlying the principle of decreasing returns. As such it introduced dynamic elements into partial static equilibrium analysis [10].

Attempts to use Marshall's concept of externalities to cover the "diseconomies" reflected in environmental disruption and social costs have been hampered by the reluctance of many theorists to break out of the narrow range and perspective of traditional price equilibrium analysis. Thus, they failed to concern themselves with empirical evidence and did not consider the nature of the causal chain of events which gives rise to environmental disruption and social costs. In short, economic theory continued to treat allocation, production, exchange and distribution as if they occurred in an essentially closed and autonomous "economic" sphere with only minor effects on man's

8. A. Coddington, "The economics of ecology", *New society*, April 9, 1970, p. 596.

9. Used in this sense, the concept of external economies is in fact an important one; it has its relevance in connection with all problems related to infrastructure investments designed to create the pre-conditions of production and development by increasing the capacity to create wealth. *Cf.* G. Myrdal. *Rich land and poor*, New York, 1966, pp. 89-90, and H.W. Singer, *International development: Growth and change*, New York, 1966.

10. For this attempt to introduce a dynamic concept into static analysis, Marshall was criticized by Stigler, who held that Marshall's external economies involved not only an abandonment of static analysis but could serve only the purposes of historical analysis. G.J. Stigler, *Production and distribution theories*, New York, 1941, pp. 68-76.

natural and social environment. The main body of economic theory including welfare economics has continued to concentrate its analysis on the voluntary and mutual reciprocal exchange relationships between micro-economic units (*i.e.*, between firms and consumers).

As long as economic theory continues on this methodological path there is no hope for an adequate analysis of environmental disruption and social costs. In the first place the so-called autonomous economic sphere is a fiction contradicted daily by the fact that choice and behaviour are not autonomous but are shaped by dominating units with a commercial interest in the content of such choices. Secondly, for the immediate problem under discussion, the effects of production and distribution on the environment and society are anything but negligible. To assume that they are or to believe that we can save the analytical framework and the theoretical conclusions derived from it by introducing such terms as external diseconomies with no empirical content creates the false impression that the theory has adequately incorporated the interdependencies at work. In short, simplifying assumptions and empty terms create the impression of adequacy but do not solve the problem. They will give us empty conclusions such as that rational allocation and optimal efficiency will be the outcome provided that important external diseconomies (and economies) are absent[11]. Neither the assumptions nor the concepts nor the conclusions can lay claim to any of the virtues of which neo-classical and "positive" economics have traditionally boasted. They are neither neutral nor objective; they are misleading and apologetic if not consciously so at any rate in effect. Such assumptions and concepts do not reveal but conceal what is actually happening. Moreover, they distract our attention from what is really important and what needs to be investigated. Thus they are preventing us from formulating the problem in an adequate fashion and hence from developing adequate criteria of action and appropriate methods of control.

In other words, the phenomena of environmental disruption and social costs demonstrate once again that the scope of economic analysis is seriously challenged. The really important problems of economic analysis understood as a political science of public affairs are not so much those which concern intra-firm and intra-industry relations — these can be safely left to business administration and the science of business management — but to those macro-economic cumulative and extra-market and extra-industry cause and effect relations which neo-classical economics in contrast to the classics, Marx and Veblen, has neglected or ignored. Let me add that there will be considerable need for quantification and exact treatment of the problems of environmental disruption and social costs. However, the interdependencies which give rise to these phenomena and which economic theory with its

11. W.J. Baumol. *Welfare economics and the theory of the state*, London, 1965, 2nd ed., p. 206.

closed models is incapable of analyzing are marked by a complexity and are governed by a plurality of factors for which we still have to develop the appropriate analytical including mathematical tools. Formal equilibrium analysis will not suffice. Indeed, in order to grasp the causal chain in operation it is necessary to include within the scope of economic analysis a whole series of factors and relationships in a somewhat similar manner in which the modern student of cancer — an equally complex phenomenon marked by the interaction of a plurality of factors and different systems — had to become familiar with very specific and novel patterns of interaction before he was able even to formulate the nature of the problem [12].

We have argued elsewhere that environmental disruption and social costs must be looked upon as the outcome of an interaction of several complex systems (economic, physical, meteorological, biological, etc.) in which a plurality of factors interplay through "feed-back" processes [13] — an interaction which is much more complex and much less explored and understood than the functioning of any of the various systems which the conventional social disciplines have ever studied [14].

In addition to this fundamental challenge there are a whole series of further questions which environmental disruption and social costs raise with respect to economic theorizing. Thus, environmental disruption and social costs put in question not only the scope of economic analysis but above all the efficiency of the market as a mechanism of steering and coordinating the decisions of the various micro-economic units or subsystems in the light of the indicators or signals provided by the price system. For, if neither enterpreneurial outlays nor enterpreneurial returns or, for that matter, prices in general are capable of registering the extra-market physical flows which disrupt our environment and affect our health, our lives and our material assets in a negative way, then the price indicators are not only imperfect and incomplete; they are misleading. If we use them nevertheless without finding ways and means by which to induce or force the subsystem to take the fullest possible account of the destructive extra-market effects, it must be clear that efficiency and optimality of the sub-system (viewed in the light of its own ends and objectives) will not give rise to any social efficiency and optimum of the macro-system as a whole. On the contrary, the rational pursuit by the subsystem of the objective of maximizing net advantage (profit, utility) will take place by sacrificing with impunity those values and objec-

12. "Le développement d'un cancer est gouverné par de multiples facteurs: la constitution génétique du virus, la constitution génétique de la cellule, l'équilibre hormonal, le régime alimentaire, l'âge, l'intervention éventuelle de cancérogènes physiques ou chimiques, l'efficacité des réactions immunitaires." A. Lwoff, "Les tumeurs de l'homme", *Le Monde*, May 27, 1970.

13. Dubos, *op. cit.*, p. 37.

14. For a preliminary discussion of these complexities *cf.* Kapp, "Environmental disruption: General issues and methodological problems", *op. cit.*

tives which, from the point of view of the macro-system may be highly important and in fact constitute the foundations of individual well-being and survival. In short, optimal solutions by micro-economic units will *not* give rise to social optima; on the contrary, they may and will coincide with a disruption of the natural and social environment. It is not sufficient to point out that this outcome is greatly facilitated by the fact that the resources and values at stake have no market values (some of them were in fact until recently free goods) or that what we need is better information and greater transparency. Even with complete transparency there is no guarantee that micro-units would not continue to maximize their net benefits without much regard to the damages caused thereby to society and hence to other individuals [15]. It is this inherent irrationality of the allocation process which must concern us if economic theory and national accounting is to become relevant as a tool of analysis and adequate as a basis for the formulation of effective and substantive criteria of environmental control.

Before concluding this essay let us turn briefly to the implications of environmental disruption and social costs for our system of national accounting as a measure of economic growth and development. This system also derives its content and logic from the traditional scope of economic analysis and its perception of the circular market flow of goods and money, measured in terms of market values, adjusted in more or less appropriate ways in the case of the use of durable consumer goods and the public sector. Now since market transactions between firms and households and the resulting flows are only part of the total flows and, moreover, do not measure those physical flows and effects which take place outside the market (*e.g.*, the disposal of residual waste and debris by firms and households into the environment from where they emanate in the form of physical nuisances and damages and reduce our well-being) GNP and its derivatives are inadequate as measures of economic growth. What is more they are becoming increasingly inadequate as the omitted environmental disruption and social costs rise absolutely and relatively. In other words, we may register persistently high growth rates but do not take account of almost catastrophic rates of environmental disruption (as evidenced by rising rates of water and air pollution, mounting rates of chronic bronchitis and other diseases, increasing levels of noise and odor nuisances, higher frequencies of accidents and work injuries, etc.). As in

15. Marx and Veblen saw this more clearly, I feel, than Pigou. Whereas Pigou saw the divergence between private and social net marginal product, but considered the negative effects as of secondary importance and therefore hoped to come to terms with such divergencies by incentives or disincentives Marx saw the inherent and fundamental character of the problem in his treatment of "general economies" which concludes with the well-known statement : "No matter how economical capitalist production may be in other respects, it is utterly prodigal with human life [...] Capitalism looses on one side for society what it gains on another for the individual capitalist", *Capital*, vol. 3, 1909, p. 104, and *The engineers and the price system*, New York, 1921, especially chapters 5 and 6.

the case of the failure of the price mechanism referred to above a policy of growth guided by inadequate and incomplete indicators of output and income will turn out upon closer analysis to have given rise to a pursuit of pseudo-growth "in which increases of consumption or investment are made possible not by the growth of net production but at the expense of running down our natural assets in the form of both resources and amenities"[16]. This "running down of natural assets" by the disposal into the environment of residual waste products and the resulting environmental disruption with its "flows" of disservices and damages to man and society differ from the traditional market flows. They are not exchanged in any meaningful sense of the word. They have no market value; they are forced upon the environment and through the intermediary of a deteriorating environment upon man. The heterogeneous character of the disrupting flows of damages and the complex interdependencies to which we have referred above preclude any measurement and evaluation in terms of a common denominator (unless a common denominator be formulated in substantive terms, *e.g.*, in terms of objective safety limits or critical zones of maximum permissible or tolerable levels of concentration for instance in the case of water and air pollution). It is this heterogeneous character of the disruptive extra-market flows in addition to the complex and novel character of the interdependencies which give rise to environmental disruption, which constitute the greatest challenge to economic theory.

To meet this challenge it will not be sufficient to assign monetary values or shadow-prices to human beings, their health or their lives. It requires even more than quantification and mathematics. It requires a willingness to take account of and evaluate the physical flows and effects in real terms — something economic theory has always been reluctant to do and is indeed ill-equipped to do without any interdisciplinary effort. Above all, we need a critical attitude towards one's own habits of thought and a willingness to formulate basic concepts in the light of a realistic appraisal of the nature and significance of environmental disruption and social costs and their fundamental character as a threat to man and society. More specifically, it requires a willingness to evaluate and a courage to criticize institutions, arrangements and policies in terms of whether or not they contribute to the satisfaction of actual substantive needs and requirements of human life. In other words, the theoretical and practical issues[17] raised by environmental disruption and

16. Coddington, *op. cit.*, p. 597. Coddington illustrates the inadequacies of the present system of national accounts by supplementing the well-known voluntary and reciprocal flows between firms and households diagrammatically by a set of additional flows of residual waste products from firms and households to the environment on the one hand and the corresponding flows of damages and disservices to firms and household on the other.

17. We have not dealt with the practical issues raised by environmental disruption, *cf.* however the author's earlier paper which stresses the need for a translation of minimun safety standards in terms of maximum tolerable levels of concentration into a corresponding input mix and input-output pattern, together with the recycling of residual waste materials

social costs are such as to compel economic theory to abandon its concentration on purely formal definitions of utility, efficiency and optimality unrelated to actual levels of satisfaction of human needs and requirements. Only in this way, we feel, will it be possible to come to terms with the dangerous acute and potential hazards to which the production and use of the products of modern civilization expose our natural and social environments and threaten man and society.

---

in contrast with the more general but less effective measures of subsidies and taxation à la Pigou. *Cf.* Kapp, "Environmental disruption: General issues and methodological problems", *op. cit.*

WILFRED BECKERMAN

Environmental policy and the challenge to economic theory*

It is with great reluctance that I feel obliged to take issue with Professor Kapp over the whole tone of his paper on "Environmental disruption and social costs: A challenge to economics"[1]. The economics profession in general, and those who are interested in environmental problems in particular, owe a great debt to Professor Kapp. It was he who first drew our attention to the widespread nature of external costs imposed by many productive activities and the way in which these impaired the environment, in his pioneering book on *The social costs of business enterprise*. This work was not duly appreciated at the time it was published because this was before concern with the environment became fashionable.

Nevertheless, I cannot accept without protest the general theme of Professor Kapp's paper in which he argues that "the phenomena of environmental disruption and social cost demonstrate once again that the scope of economic analysis is seriously challenged" (p. 842). According to Professor Kapp, the phenomena of environmental disruption involve complex causal chains and inter-relations which "differ in kind and complexity from those with which economists have traditionally been concerned". This will come as a great surprise to most economists who have tended to believe that the reason why economics was so "difficult" is that the variables involved are so numerous and inter-related, and that any model which pretended to be anything like an approximation to reality involved highly complex feedback effects, changes in coefficients according to the time lags postulated, and so on. But according to Kapp, "in the light of the foregoing discussion of the causal chain and complex interdependencies which give rise to a disruption of man's

*This article is a summary of the position taken by W. Beckerman in his discussion with K.W. Kapp.

1. K.W. Kapp, "Environmental disruption and social costs: A challenge to economics", *Kyklos* 23 (4), 1970, pp. 833-848.

natural and social environment, it becomes evident that the conventional framework and tools of economic theory are ill-adapted and are irrelevant for the analysis of the phenomena under discussion" (p. 839), or, again, "neither the scope nor the tools of the (economic) analysis are adapted to the kind of interdependencies and oomplex causal sequences which give rise to environmental disruption and their social costs", or again, "in dealing with problems of environmental disruption and social costs we are confronted with direct technological non-market effects which in their cumulative character and consequences make the customary equilibrium approach of conventional economics irrelevant and antiquated" (p. 840), and so on and so forth.

Now, I am generally suspicious of calls for completely new "rethinkings" of any science. I don't know of any science that has made progress by starting all over again from scratch, even though in many cases fundamental changes in the foundations have been made. But even these have been deliberately made in the light of improved knowledge arising out of the previous work. In general, appeals for "wider" considerations to be taken into account, or vague appeals to the limitations of the existing body of knowledge in any science to answer all the problems of the world have come, in my experience, from those who are not prepared to work away at improving those technical tools in their own subject that happen to be important for purposes of solving the problems that they claim to be interested in.

In this particular case, for example, I find the whole of Professor Kapp's condemnation of the limitations of what now constitutes the main body of economic theory to be much too vague. He does not give a single concrete example of a case where the "correct" policy with respect to any environmental issue is not the one which economic analysis would indicate. But if conventional economic analysis is so misleading why can't he provide a single case where it misleads?

The whole of his attack on economics, of which numerous representative quotations have been given above, is in the same general vague form amounting to little more than unsubstantiated assertions and adjectives like "misleading", "neither neutral nor objective", "apologetic", "narrow range and perspective", "ill-adapted", "irrelevant and antiquated", etc. But there is not one single positive example of what he is actually talking about.

Let us take an example, of which there are numerous counterparts in the real world, of a firm that disposes into a river some polluted effluent which imposes costs of water treatment downstream in order that the water may be used for some other potential consumer. If nothing is done about it the economist will come to the conclusion, on the basis of elementary economics, that there is "too much" polluting effluent flowing into the stream. Would Professor Kapp deny this and claim that the economic analysis lying behind this conclusion is ill-adapted and misleading? To go further, the economist will then consider what is the best means of reducing the pollution to a level that, in terms of welfare theory, would represent the optimum. In the course of doing so he will be faced with numerous extremely difficult theoretical and practical problems, such as the identification of the damage done by the effluent, the costs of reducing it, the effects of alternative instruments (such as taxes, subsidies, rights to pollute which find their price in some market, or direct regulation), the choice between private and public facilities, the income distribution aspects of any instruments, possible local effects on the pattern of output and employment and the appropriate shadow prices problems which may then have to be taken into account, and so on and so forth. Which of these particular parts of the economic analysis does Professor Kapp believe to be misleading and irrelevant or antiquated? He never comes down to explicit instances. And if none of the above is irrelevant, is it some *other* specific parts of the relevant analysis that cannot be handled by the conventional economics? If so, why does he not say what they are?

Academic work in any subject is largely at the frontiers of the subject where, by definition, there is considerable ignorance and the well-trodden paths leading up to the frontier do not necessarily provide much guidance as to the direction in which it is best to proceed. But some people have to work away at the frontiers, doing their little bit to add to knowledge and to meet the new problems that will always, and for ever, be encountered. Professor Kapp is like somebody who has decided that he does not like the rigours of working in such unrewarding regions, and so tells everybody else that they are wasting their time there, and that they had better all join him in going right back again to the beginning. He does not say what they will do when they get there, except that he does imply that they will then all start re-thinking everything from scratch. What this would mean, I have no idea. Does it mean that we would all start asking ourselves whether, in fact, demand curves do slope down from left to right — or does he accept this piece of economic theory? Does it mean that we abandon interest in the conditions governing the maximisation behaviour of the individual? Or does Professor Kapp accept that this might still be quite a useful notion?

In other words, how far back to the beginning of the subject do we actually have to go? Do I have to march back a hundred miles, shedding all my useless baggage of demand curves; profit maximisation; flow and stock concepts; national income analysis; welfare theory; international trade theory, the whole lot, like the fleeing remnants of some defeated and disorganised army? Or do I need to move back only a mile or two, abandoning some exposed positions that have turned out to be liabilities rather than assets (if I may continue to use this terminology) and pick up the battle again from securer positions? Professor Kapp provides no guidance at all; he says neither *a*) in what particular environmental issue economics gives a misleading answer, nor *b*) which particular pieces of the economics baggage that professional economists have accumulated over the years are useless in a general way — irrespective of their impact on environmental issues. He is like the panic-stricken soldier who, as soon as he finds that he cannot just pick off the enemy with ease, prefers to throw away all his weapons and urge his comrades to rush off in no specific direction with bare hands.

In fact, not only is it difficult to believe that all the accumulated techniques of economics are useless for dealing with environmental problems, but the reverse seems to be the case. I have yet to see any demonstration that what is wrong with environmental pollution is not that it is basically a matter of an external cost not borne by the polluter. And the whole concept of external economies and diseconomies has been developed by economists, as Professor Kapp knows better than most people. He refers vaguely to the well-known fact that the consequences of some externality may be catastrophic, on a world-wide scale. But this does not detract a bit from the economics-based proposition that if the polluter had been made to bear the full cost of these consequences it is highly likely that the consequences would have been far less severe and may well have been negligible.

Economics is also the science that has developed other concepts and analytical tools that are central to the problem of the environment, such as the social welfare function; divergencies between private and social costs and benefits arising out of externalities of one kind or another; the effects on optimum resource allocation of taxes, subsidies and so on; the problems of discounting future costs and benefits; and the treatment of risk; not to mention the underlying method of thinking about problems in terms of some optimisation model and the conditions that have to be satisfied for optimal behaviour.

Economics is basically the logic of choice, and economic theory has made a vast contribution to this logic — as has been increasingly discovered in all sorts of spheres of human activity in which the attempt to choose rationally between competing alternatives is made. The underlying methods that have been developed over the decades, including some of the recent distinguished contributions concerning the logic of public choice and its relation to the economics of political decision making, have reached a state of great generality, and to pretend that it cannot be of any use for purposes of making rational choices in the area of environmental policy is to make so astonishing a claim that the reader is entitled to expect at least rather more explicit substantiation and clarification than Professor Kapp has provided.

In fact, I do not recognise the economics that Professor Kapp is talking about at all. What is this economics in which there is only partial equilibrium analysis, or purely static models, or in which no attempt is made to provide any empirical content to the welfare aspects of any policies, and in which there is no recognition that economic welfare is not likely to be achieved by the automatic workings of the market mechanism? This is certainly not the economics that my students are taught. Perhaps Professor Kapp has missed something through dismissing contemporary economics too contemptuously? In the first place, he might have discovered that his use of the term "social costs" is misleading and antiquated, since he really means only those social costs that are external to the producer, as has been pointed out in an article in the *Economic journal* about five years ago[2]. Secondly, he might have discovered the powerful and disconcerting doubts about the fundamental significance of relative prices (which, amongst other things, underlie the usual economist's array of cost-benefit analysis and so on) which have been sown by the work of Piero Sraffa and others at Cambridge.

Furthermore, it should not be thought that Professor Kapp's attack on the role of conventional economics will help those who are greatly concerned with the deterioration in the environment; and that in defending economics I am somehow or other weakening the environmentalist case. The opposite is probably true. On the basis of some very elementary economics it is possible to refute the bogus arguments often presented by businessmen in opposition to measures to combat pollution. For example, they often argue that nothing will be gained by imposing a tax on some polluting product since the resulting costs will merely be passed on to the consumers. But some elementary economic theory can be used to demonstrate that the resulting change in the pattern of output will lead to a rise in real income. Will Professor Kapp whisper in the ears of the businessmen concerned that they shouldn't be fooled by this old-fashioned economics since "optimal solutions by micro-economic units will *not* give rise to social optima" (p. 844)? Alternatively, it is often argued that the country's competitive position in world trade, the level of employment, will suffer as a result of anti-pollution policies. Hitherto, application of some elementary economic theory has made it possible to refute what is nonsense in these claims or to extract the grain of truth that may be in them. But now the industrialists can retort that they no longer believe these economists' arguments, for the well-known Professor Kapp from Basle has said that economics is all bunk.

Of course, economics is not able to answer all the problems with which it is faced, and certainly not those in relatively new areas such as environmental policy. But professional economists have always been aware of the fact that economic welfare is not the whole of welfare, and that our knowledge of the extent and manner in which even *economic* welfare is achieved is very rudimentary. Professional economists are also well aware of the impossibility of drawing any welfare conclusions without falling back on value judgements, of the difficulties of even defining an unambiguous social welfare function, and of the problems of "second-best" solutions. It is only the layman who thinks we are under the illusion that there are simple answers to welfare questions. But we must go on trying, particularly since Professor Kapp has not suggested anything better to put in its place.

Towards the end of his introductory remarks at the conference, he antici-

2. D. W. Pearce and S. G. Sturmey, "Private and social costs: A note on terminology", *Economic journal* 76 (301), March 1966, pp. 152-158.

pated that I might make this point but believed he was refuting it in advance on the grounds that the man who, for example, criticises the performance of some violinist cannot be reproached on the grounds that he might not be able to play better himself. But this is not the point; he should be able to say which violinist *can* play better. A violin critic is hardly likely to go about saying that *nobody* knows how to play the violin properly so that the instrument should be scrapped! The economist knows that everything is relative when it comes to making choices. If I want to listen to music and the music critic tells me that some orchestra is no good, I expect him to be able to tell me which one is better. If I want some choice problem of an economic character to be solved (including environment choices) it is no good Professor Kapp saying that economics is no use for this purpose unless he is able to tell me what I can put in its place.

The problems that have arisen in the context of environmental pollution and that call for further work with the aid of the standard tools of economic analysis are numerous and it must suffice here to give a few examples in order to demonstrate the applicability of economic techniques. First, it is fairly obvious that some attempt must be made to arrive at some measure of the damage done by pollution of various kinds. This gives rise to very difficult problems of valuation of, for example, the health effects of certain kinds of pollution or the value of the loss of amenities of an intangible character, such as beautiful views, quiet countryside areas, rivers that do not stink, and so on. Work has only recently started on some of these topics, and some of it, such as the pioneering work of Marion Clawson on the value of recreational amenities, has provided stimulating suggestions for further developments.

It is true that the health problem looks as if it is more intractable, but even this conclusion depends on the fact that it is economic analysis that has added to our understanding of the nature of the choices that are relevant. Professor Kapp says that "it will not be sufficient to apply monetary values or shadow prices to human beings, their health or their lives. It requires even more than quantification and mathematics. It requires a willingness to take account of and evaluate (*sic*) the physical flows and effects in real terms — something that economic theory has always been reluctant to do and is indeed ill-equipped to do without any interdisciplinary effort" (p. 846). Now I don't quite understand what these "real terms" are. Does he mean that human life, bad smells, noisy urban areas, and so on have some "reality" which is lost when we convert them into some common numeraire, like monetary value, in order to trade off one against the other? What is this "reality" that is so ephemeral that it can vanish simply as a result of my thinking about it in a different way, or even simply as a result of my quietly writing down a monetary figure for it without telling anybody else? What is this reality that is something other than the degree of satisfaction or dis-satisfaction that these things give to human beings and to society and which, therefore, economists try to measure in ways that enable society to decide as between different degrees of one or the other? Is it some Hegelian "essence" of bad smells and the like, or is it some other deep philosophical concept which, nevertheless, we are all expected to grasp without Professor Kapp condescending to explain it to us?

In fact, some interesting economics work has begun even on the problems of evaluating the health effects of pollution. For example, starting from the basic economics principles of evaluating things according to their equivalence at the margin — *i.e.*, how much money one would accept in order to be indifferent between having the previous number of units of some "good" and one less unit — it has become clear that the valuation of health must depend on whether it is being valued from the point of view of society *including* the person so concerned or *excluding* him. In the extreme case of a person's life, for example, it makes no sense to ask him how much money he would accept, if he died, in order to be as well off as if he were still alive! But it does make sense to ask society how much it values the corresponding reduction in risk to the average individual. It is no use denying this on the grounds that this is typical of the narrowness of economic theory and of economists' over-simplified systems of thought, for the choice frequently has to be made between, say, spending more money on education or private consumption and spending more money on improved old-age facilities, or raising the number of first births in maternity homes, or better accident facilities in hospitals, more drugs, and so on. Are the sentimentalists prepared to devote all the world's resources to saving life, even if it means that the whole of the world's population would then be reduced to conditions of poverty that have been unparalleled in living memory in all the advanced countries of the world? Presumably not. But in that case what principles and what criteria govern the choice of how far to go? It is here that economics provides the necessary discipline. Choices have to be made and no means of making them that is superior to the methods being developed within the framework of conventional economics has yet been discovered.

Similarly, it is not enough to decry, as does Professor Kapp, the need to go beyond the normal national accounts definitions of national product in order to take account of other ingredients in the wider concept of welfare which economists are perfectly aware of. It is true that national accounts are inadequate, but they are inadequate in many senses. First, they are not even adequate for performing the tasks for which they are primarily designed — namely macroeconomic policy. The degree of error in the estimates, and the time lag in the preparation of estimates of national product on a short-period basis, is such that they can be very misleading about the pressure of demand in an economy and the short-run trends in that pressure. This would have been a legitimate complaint; but it is not the one that Professor Kapp made, and it is anyway not one that will come as news to national accounts practitioners who are hard at work trying to improve their estimates.

But to complain that national accounts fail to provide indicators of welfare in some wider sense is far less legitimate unless one is prepared to at least acknowledge the great conceptual difficulties that arise in trying to combine together, in any meaningful aggregate, indicators relating to the environment defined more broadly, especially when Professor Kapp says that we must not convert these into the only common numeraire discovered so far in this wicked world, namely their monetary value (as this is not "real"). In fact, of course, much work is going on in connection with the extension of national accounts concepts to embrace what are known as "social indicators" and some of the most interesting work in this area is being done by J.R.N. Stone and Ingvar Ohlsson, two of the people who have made the greatest contributions to the development of national accounts! It is precisely because traditional economic theory provides some of the valuable insights and analytical tools that are required to handle problems of aggregating numerous otherwise disparate items, such as apples and pears or clean water and air, that some of the most interesting work in this field is being done by economists.

Of course, there is also no doubt that there will be a lot of useless economics in the field of environmental problems, although one can never be sure, in advance, what work will pay off and what work will be wasted. On the applied side, some students of input-output techniques will apply their input-output tables, in a purely mechanical manner, to the flow of the world's materials and effluents and will calculate what the indirect second-round effects of changes in output by some industry will be on the pollution of some other industry, provided one makes not only the usual completely unfounded assumptions about the stability of the usual production coefficients but also a lot more even more heroic assumptions about the pollution content of different industries and the like. But there are some people who will wheel out their input-output tables whatever the problem put to them — be it growth, or import savings, or the economics of education or of disarmament, or deep sea fishing, or tourism, or what have you. They do this because it is easier to produce an impressive array of figures and "answers" on the basis of a set of outrageous assumptions, by using the beautiful technique of input-output analysis that is now in every textbook, than to actually do some real work finding out what the pollution impact really is in any one specific case, what the costs of reducing it are, and what — given all the technical and administrative constraints — are the best methods of dealing with it. Unlike Kapp, when faced with some difficulties at the frontiers of the subject they do not throw away all the tools of economics, they pick up the one which, it must be admitted, is the prettiest and makes the biggest bang, and use it wherever they can on any problem irrespective of whether it happens to be the tool for the job [3]. In the

3. This is not to suggest that the whole notion of input-output analysis was not one of the important inspirations in applied economics during this century, and that in the hands of the master himself, it cannot be a useful tool for analysing even environmental problems (see W. Leontieff's article in the *Review of economics and statistics* 52 (3), 1970, pp. 262-271). But the master cannot be held responsible for the excesses of some of his disciples.

same way, on the theoretical side, there is certain to be a crop of growth models about pollution, in which the usual models will be adapted to take account of externalities. Some of these will be illuminating but most of them will not. In most cases it is highly unlikely that the optimum policy to deal with any particular environmental problem will be sensitive — or even affected at all — by the sort of information, if any, that this sort of work will throw up. But this phenomena must be common to *any* science, and should not be used as an argument for the irrelevance of economics (not that Professor Kapp did use this argument).

In conclusion, therefore, there is little doubt that economics does not have any ready-made answers to even the narrowly economic aspects of environmental pollution, let alone to the much wider problems of the standard of life and so on. There is also little doubt that some of the economics work being done now on these problems will be useless, but this must not be taken to imply that economics is completely ill-adapted to make its own particular contribution to the problems of the environment; it just means that we are all fallible and that only a small proportion of any research pays off in the end, in any subject. So let us get on with the work in the knowledge that it is all very difficult, and that ready-made answers will not be discovered simply by changing our whole patterns of thought. It is only amateurs who believe that there must be simple solutions to any problem and that there is some magic key which will open all doors if only we will throw away our antiquated modes of thought and branch off along the new paths to which Professor Kapp is pointing — if in all directions!

K. WILLIAM KAPP

Social costs, neo-classical economics, environmental planning: A reply *

Professor Beckerman describes my book on *The social costs of private enterprise* (1950) as a pioneering work which was not duly appreciated at the time it was published "because this was before the concern with the environment became fashionable"; however, he takes issue with "the whole tone" of my recent paper "Environmental disruption and social costs: A challenge to economics" [1].

He feels that my challenge carries the critique too far because in his words, I want to start "from scratch" and favor a new beginning, a "rethinking" of economic theory; moreover I am criticized for the lack of examples; my use of the concept of social costs is said to be "antiquated and misleading"; with respect to the complexity of the causal chain and effects of pollution. Beckerman holds that economists have long been used to the treatment of conditions with numerous and interrelated variables; in addition, he states that economics does recognize complex feedback effects and operates with changes of coefficients according to postulated time lags. Moreover, economists have developed new analytical tools; above all the logic of choice and optimization has reached such a level of generality (and by implication of general validity) that it can be applied to the new problems arising in connection with the environmental crisis and can form the basis for evaluations in monetary terms and decisions required for its abatement or control. Thus, according to Beckerman, economists have been able to handle the admittedly difficult problems of aggregating numerous disparate items in terms of the common denominator of money and we would do well to apply the principles of welfare economics to the treatment of the new environmental problems which are upon us.

* This article is a reply to the preceding paper by W. Beckerman, "Environmental policy and the challenge to economic theory".

1. K.W. Kapp, "Environmental disruption and social costs: A challenge to economics" *Kyklos* 23 (4), 1970, pp. 833-848.

I would regret it if it was the tone of my paper rather than the content and scope of my criticism which provoked Beckerman's objections. Nothing is further from my mind than to disrupt a rational dialogue by the *tone* of my observations. For I know only too well that there is no other way of advancing our knowledge than dispassionate analysis and rational criticism. For this reason I shall refrain from taking notice of Beckerman's remarks *ad hominem*.

Due to limitations of time and space I shall not be able to deal explicitly with all the points raised by Beckerman, but I hope that my reply will cover at least implicitly most of his specific objections. The major emphasis of my reply will be on what I consider to be the central issue raised: namely the question of the adequacy of evaluating environmental goals and values in terms of the individual's willingness to pay or accept compensation.

Beckerman believes that my book was not duly appreciated because it was written before the discussion of the disruption of the environment by economic activities became popular [2]. I believe rather that what was not appreciated was the association of social costs and business enterprise and the confrontation of economic theory with my empirical data and observations — *i.e.*, the great variety of losses borne by third persons and society as a whole. The main thrust of my conclusions was a critique of the practices of business enterprise and of the scope of our inherited economic theory with its concepts of market rationality and optimality. My central thesis was and has remained that the maximization of net income by micro-economic units is likely to reduce the income (or utility) of other economic units and of society at large and that the conventional measurements of the performance of the economy are unsatisfactory and indeed misleading. To my mind, traditional theoretical inquiry was neither guided nor supported by empirical observations and available data. I tried to show that micro-economic analysis ignored important relationships between the economy (wrongly viewed as a closed system) and the physical and social environment and that these intrinsic relationships gave rise to negative consequences of the economic process. It was and is my contention that the nature and scope of economic theory is too narrow. This restriction has affected economic theory at its foundation: *i.e.*, at the stage of concept formation (*e.g.*, costs and returns), in the choice of criteria of valuation and aggregation (in terms of money and exchange values) and hence in the delimitation of the scope of the inquiry. Not only the dynamic interconnection of the economy with the physical and social environment and the impact which the disruption of the

2. Incidentally, *The social costs of private enterprise*, Cambridge, Mass., 1950, was widely reviewed and discussed also in the United States, and was translated into five foreign languages; a second enlarged and revised edition appeared under the title *Social costs of business enterprise*, London, 1963.

environment has upon the producer (worker) and consumer but also the relationship between human wants and needs and their actual satisfaction have remained outside the scope and preoccupation of economic theory. Human wants and preferences (all subjective concepts), are treated as "given" and the analytical apparatus is designed to develop an instrumental logic of choice and allocation under these given conditions within a closed system.

This traditional restriction of economic analysis is not only contrary to the empirical facts of the interdependence of the economy with the environment but also protects the analysis and its conclusions against its critics who present evidence of the negative impact of economic activities on human health and human development. In fact, the whole procedure "alienates" economic analysis from what I consider to be one of its most important objectives, namely the appraisal of the substantive rationality (Max Weber) of the use of society's scarce resources. Critics of the traditional approach from Marx and Veblen to Myrdal and more recently H. Albert and W.A. Weisskopf have pointed out that the restriction of the analysis is the result of specific analytical preconceptions as well as hidden value premises. In short, the critics have argued that the restriction of economic analysis reflects a subtle dogmatism on the part of its practitioners [3].

In the light of this critical analysis it would appear that the formal logic of choice and optimization in terms of market costs and market returns is somewhat less generally accepted and more vulnerable than Beckerman seems to assume. In fact, the formal logic of choice reveals its limitations in the light of a substantive concept of rationality which considers the actual degree of satisfaction of human needs and human requirements. As to Beckerman's suggestion that I want to start "from scratch", it seems to me that Beckerman fails to see that my critique is not quite as novel as he implies and that in fact both my book and my article must be seen within the context of a body of critical analysis which has been advanced over the last decades. I shall deal with this point by outlining a whole pattern of reaction of an entrenched community of scholars against its critics. One reaction is

3. I shall not pursue these lines of thought here which could be extended to show that what has happened is nothing less than that economic analysis and welfare economics in particular have permitted their value premises to determine not only their hypotheses but their notions of the nature and essential characteristics of the economic process. Their perspective of what constitutes rational choice under given conditions in a closed system has formed their ontology. *Cf.* H. Albert, "Die Problematik der ökonomischen Perspektive", *Zeitschrift für die gesamte Staatswissenschaft* 117, 1961, p. 438 *sq.* On the problem of "alienation" and economics in the sense of a dehumanization of economic analysis, see the important analysis by W.A. Weisskopf, *Alienation and economics*, New York, 1971, and my observations in "Zum Problem der Enthumanisierung der 'reinen Theorie' und der gesellschaftlichen Realität", *Kyklos* 20 (1), 1967, pp. 307-330.

to ignore them by a conspiracy of silence by all those who have "invested" in the established body of doctrine and thus may be said to have a "vested interest" in it, to use a favorite term of Veblen. This period can last quite a long time.

However, when the accumulation of new empirical observations and data contradicting the conventional body of knowledge can no longer be passed over in silence, the relevance of the new evidence is likely to be questioned. After all, it comes from outside the realm of the traditional discourse; thus it may be said to be "non-economic" or "meta-economic" in character. The critics are considered as outsiders — sociologists or political scientists perhaps — who are not sufficiently familiar with what are admissible and relevant criteria with which to confront the conclusions derived from the closed model. At a later stage old concepts and assumptions will be refined in order to cope with the disturbing evidence within the traditional framework. This phase may be illustrated by the reaction of traditional astronomy prior to and during the Copernican revolution; the Ptolemaic astronomy accounted for discrepancies between its predictions and empirical observations by manipulating an ever increasing number of epicycles within its explanatory system. In short, it is the method of scholasticism — another of the devices of dogmatism.

Closely related to this phase are efforts to force the new evidence and data into old concepts despite the fact that the latter were originally designed to take account of different phenomena than those referred to by the critics. In other words, older concepts and new phenomena are reinterpreted in such a manner as to convince the community of scholars that no new approach is required and that in fact new data and facts can be and indeed have always been taken care of. The current discussion of the environmental issue has reached this stage and Beckerman is certainly not alone in this endeavor to show that the conventional wisdom is quite capable of dealing with the phenomena of environmental disruption in its own fashion. Environmental problems are being forced today into the conceptual box of externalities first developed by Alfred Marshal. In my estimation this concept was not designed for and is not adequate to deal with the full range and pervasive character of the environmental and social repercussions set in motion by economic activities of producers or the goods produced and sold by them to consumers. I agree with those who have criticized the use of the concept of externalities as empty and incompatible with the logical structure of the static equilibrium theory.

At the same time the linguistics of the critics will be rejected and found wanting in precision and determinateness. Their terms and concepts will be found to be "too wide", "confusing", "misleading" and after a while even "antiquated". Since Beckerman has raised objections of this sort against the use of the term social costs and feels that I "may have missed something", I shall deal with the problem of concept formation in order to elucidate a few fundamental points. Of course, conceptual precision is desirable and terms and concepts should not be misleading. Objections raised against terms and concepts should be met. However, let us not overlook that new ideas and concepts do not emerge immediately with the intellectual precision which may be desirable. In fact at an early stage of analysis some degree of openness of concepts may be actually useful. Ideas and concepts need to be elaborated and become more precise only as the analysis of substantive problems proceeds[4].

However, it is a logical error to make concepts more precise and determinate than warranted by the empirical data to which they refer. Myrdal has reminded us that statistical convenience and measurement must *not* be permitted to set limits to concept formations and thus to exclude relevant elements. This has happened in the case of many economic concepts such as capital and investment. Furthermore, an element of inescapable indeterminacy may remain either due to the lack of homogeneity of the facts or of people's valuations or due to a lack of accurate knowledge about causal interrelationships. This applies to social costs as well as to such concepts as unemployment, underdevelopment, monopoly, etc. In short "to define the concept more precisely than is justifiable is logically faulty" [5]. Finally, concepts in the social sciences are not the product of measurement as in physics where concepts are, as a rule, the by-product of observations and actual measurements. Social concepts are, as a rule, constructs, or abstractions or deliberate accentuations. As such they should define the empirical instances to which they refer. Our concepts are chosen and constructed for specific purposes; their relevance and usefulness are to be judged in terms of their effectiveness as instruments designed to grasp social facts even if some of these facts lie outside the scope of the traditional boundaries erected arbitrarily by the discipline. They reflect our perspective and thus help us to perceive novel and hitherto neglected aspects of reality. In this sense they may and indeed will reflect our value premises; the important thing is that these value premises be stated openly and are not hidden as in many endeavors to define concepts in an alleged "value free" manner, which conceal the hidden value premises of the investigator. The concept of social costs does not leave the reader in any doubt in this respect [6].

4. C. Wright Mills, *The sociological imagination*, New York, 1959, p. 125.

5. G. Myrdal, "Value loaded concepts", in: H. Hegelland (ed.), *Money, growth and methodology*, Lund, 1961, p. 285.

6. Beckerman's summary judgement that the term social costs is misleading and antiquated may be evidence of the fact that he holds different views about concept formation or he may have misread the article he quoted, which is directed against Pigou's use of the term "social costs", this article points out correctly that my use of the term is identical to what the authors call "uncompensated social costs", a term not quite unsimilar to my own suggestion to speak of "unpaid costs". The predilection to render the term social costs innocuous by using it to designate the total costs reminds one of an earlier episode in the history of economic analysis when some neo-classical economists tended to identify market prices as

In conclusion let me say that it is quite understandable that many economists defend the traditional perspective, assumptions, concepts and the narrow scope of micro-economic analysis. But this cannot last indefinitely, particularly if we remain committed to the notion that scientific inquiry has to do with a confrontation of theories and empirical observations. When empirical data and new facts become incompatible with, or can no longer be accounted for by established theories, the time has come for the formulation of new concepts, new modes of thought and procedures. This is the time of "scientific revolutions". In the history of science and in the history of the social sciences there have been radical reformulations of concepts as well as new modes of thought and new procedures [7]. However, they did not start from the beginning. Who would want to assert that Copernicus, Newton, Einstein or for that matter Marx, Walras, Veblen or Keynes started from a *tabula rasa*. But they faced the crisis of their disciplines by doing more than merely refining old concepts or forcing new data into old molds. I believe that economics faces such a crisis today largely as a result of the environmental disruption but also because of its inability to come to terms with the development problem in less developed countries and because of the failure of Keynesian and monetary methods to maintain economic stability and prevent inflation.

Beckerman complains that I cite no examples. In the following I shall show that his own propositions which reflect the procedures and normative conclusions of welfare economics provide examples and illustrations of what I am criticizing. For Beckerman, together with others, assumes that no fundamental revision of economics is required in order to come to terms with the environmental crisis. While he admits that there are still numerous unsolved theoretical and practical problems raised by pollution and its abatement, he is convinced that welfare economics is equipped for dealing with the problem of pollution policy. In fact he feels that there is nothing to take its place as if this — if it were true — proved the adequacy of what we are offered. According to Beckerman, the disposal of pollutants imposes external costs in the form of water treatment downstream and "the economist will come to the conclusion, on the basis of elementary economics, that there is too much polluting effluent flowing into the stream [...] [8]. The economist

"social value" in the sense of value to society. Schumpeter set an end to this apologetic reinterpretation of terms and concepts. *Cf.* J.A. Schumpeter, "On the concept of social value", *Quarterly journal of economics*, 23, 1909, p. 213-232.

7. T.S. Kuhn, *The structure of scientific revolutions*, Chicago, Ill. - London, 1962. *Cf.* also, by the same author "Logic of discovery or psychology of research" and "Reflections on my critics", in: I. Lakatos and A. Musgrave (eds.), *Criticism and the growth of knowledge*, Cambridge, Mass., 1970, pp. 1-23 and pp. 231-278.

8. Beckerman oversimplifies the problem when he suggests that economists can arrive at the conclusion that there is "too much" pollution. Elementary economics teaches nothing about pollution nor about the negative effects of pollution or the benefits of abatement.

will then consider what is the best means of reducing the pollution to a level that, in terms of welfare theory, would represent the optimum." Beckerman and others are convinced that the standard tools and procedures of economics and the logic and criteria of choice including the aggregation of numerous (environmental) disparate items in terms of money and willingness to pay can be used as criteria "for evaluating things according to their equivalence at the margin — *i.e.*, how much money one would accept in order to be indifferent between having the previous number of units of some 'good' and one less unit". In short it is believed that economists are on solid grounds and have the basic approach to a solution, if not the final answer, to the determination and evaluation of environmental values (including goals and preferences) and the formulation of the appropriate instruments of control and environmental planning.

Beckerman's open acceptance of the compensation principle (willingness to pay or accept money) as a criteria of evaluation has at least the merit of leaving no doubt about the common denominator to be used for the evaluation of environmental costs and benefits in contrast to statements which speak of "balancing" advantages of each activity and the physical and aesthetic discomfort created thereby or suggest, in general terms, that the improvement (of the quality of the environment) must be worth the costs of abatement without specifying how the "worth" of the improvement is to be valuated [9].

It is my contention that this treatment of the pollution problem within the conceptual framework of the formal theory of choice is logically defective and operationally ineffective. While it may be possible to express the costs of abatement and anti-pollution measures in monetary terms, I fail to see how the "worth" of the improvement can be evaluated adequately in monetary terms by the willingness of an individual or a group of individuals to pay for environmental amenities or to accept compensation for tolerating environmental disamenities such as polluted air or water. There are, as far as I can see, three distinct reasons which speak against the use of the compensation principle (apart from the practical difficulties of establishing the willingness to pay).

First, what a person or firm is willing to pay for clean air or recreation facilities or to accept as compensation for tolerating injuries to his health caused by pollution depends upon their income or their *ability* to pay. If incomes are unequally distributed (as they are), and if this inequality of distribution results among other things from unequal exchanges between unequal economic units in dominating and dominated positions (as it does), the resulting ability and willingness to pay are as arbitrary as the price and wage structure of which they are the outcome [10]. The problematical character of such attempts to

9. *Cf. Annual report of the Council of Economic Advisers* (to the President of the United States), Washington, DC, 1971, pp. 114-122.

10. Beckerman himself admits that it makes no sense to evaluate the life of a person by asking him "how much money he would accept, if he died, in order to be as well off as if he were still alive" (*sic*). To my mind methods of individual self-evaluation of life and

evaluate environmental goals becomes evident when it is suggested to determine the losses caused by the pollution of a lake in terms of the additional transportation costs of people seeking recreation facilities to reach the nearest lake not yet polluted, or to measure the value of improved environmental facilities (such as recreational facilities, parks, a marina for pleasure boats or a public park in a poor section of a large city) in terms of the willingness and hence ability to pay as reflected in money spent for admission or for the purchase of fishing and recreation equipment [11], or in terms of the hypothetical hourly income of those seeking recreation. In all these cases, the use of willingness to pay as the criterion of quantifying and evaluating the quality of the environment has the insidious effect of reinterpreting original human needs and requirements into a desire for money and of evaluating the relative importance of such needs in terms of criteria which reflect the existing inequalities and distortions in the price, wage and income structure. "The basically questionable point of departure consists in the fact that original physical needs for rest, clean air, non-polluted water and health as well as the inviolability of the individual are being reinterpreted in an untenable way as desires or preferences for money income [...]. These fundamental human requirements must not be articulated, nor are they to be satisfied through the market mechanism. Their reinterpretation and (evaluation) in terms of a desire for money within the context of the price system falsifies the original need and at the same time the core of the problem of decision-making. Health, opportunities for recreation in parks, clean water or aesthetically satisfying environmental conditions are objectives which today are not pursued primarily with regard to their actual contributions to GNP. In many instances, it will be possible to realize these goals only by actually foregoing a short and medium term increase of GNP in its present statistical computation." [12] The logical and practical result of using willingness to pay as a criterion would be that public parks or clean air in the ghetto sections of a large city would yield a lower benefit-cost-ratio than the marina for top management personnel. A mode of reasoning which leads to or indirectly supports such an outcome reveals its hidden, basically unequalitarian value judgments inherent in

health (*e.g.*, discounting future earnings, legal compensation claimed or received in liability cases, willingness to pay for insurances, etc.) make not much more sense. See C. Senior, *A model for quantifying risk: A cost effectiveness study of industrial safety*, Nuffield, 1971, pp. 8-9 (mimeo).

11. On the ground that "a logical basis for determining the probable recreation benefits to be derived from the proposed improvement is the concept that the value of these benefits bears a reasonable percentage relationship to the amount of money voluntarily invested by boat owners to obtain them", *cf.* US Secretary of the Army, 89th Congress, Second Session IIB, Cross Village Harbour, Mich. - Washington, DC, 1966, p. 31, quoted from D. Weiss, *Infrastrukturplanung*, Berlin, Deutsches Institut für Entwicklungspolitik, jan. 1971.

12. *Ibid.*, pp. 68-70.

the compensation principle as a criterion of evaluating the "worth" of environmental goals [13].

Second, apart from income inequalities which undermine the validity of the compensation principle there is the individual's inability to ascertain the full range of short and long run benefits of environmental improvements or, for that matter, of the full impact of environmental disruption upon his health and his well-being. It is today generally recognized that environmental pollution and the disruption of the environment are the results of a complex interaction of the economic system with physical and biological systems which have their own specific regularities. Moreover, pollutants from different sources act upon one another and what counts are not only the effects of particular effluents and toxic materials but the total toxological situation. The causation and the effects of pollution are far from being transparent to the individual. Those who have studied these complex causal relationships know that environmental disruption can easily become cumulative with pervasive and disproportionate effects per unit of additional pollutants [14]. To ask the individual what he is willing to pay for the improvement of the quality of the environment or what amount of compensation he is willing to accept to tolerate current or even higher levels of pollution constitutes therefore an inadequate and ineffective and indeed a highly problematical basis for evaluating judgments concerning the "amount" of value of alternative environmental goals. The practical consequences of making the content and extent of the control of environmental quality dependent upon individual willingness to pay could at best lead to piecemeal measures and an ineffective formal

13. Actually, welfare economists would probably shy away from the logic of their procedures by falling back upon their own personal value judgments, in which case society may again be poorly served in so far as these personal valuations may diverge from those which society may place upon environmental values through the political process. For in this case we would be faced with personal idiosyncrasies and potentially arbitrary judgments which would enter through the back door into the evaluation process. For economists and technocrats would then prepare environmental projects and policies which reflect market valuations "corrected" by their own views and values. Such projects and policies prepared by experts would still have to be ratified by political decision-makers. Some of the latter would like nothing better than this procedure which would enable them to present their decisions as being based upon the advice of "experts". In fact this is exactly the model of policy making by experts which J. Habermas has criticised; see his *Technik und Wissenschaft als Ideologie*, Frankfurt, 1968, p. 125 (*cf.* also H.P. Widmaier and O. Roloff, "Zur Kritik der quantitativen Wirtschaftspolitik", in: E. Dürr, *Neue Ansätze der Wirtschaftspolitik*, Berlin, 1971).

14. It is hardly convincing to argue, as Beckerman does, that economics is capable of dealing with these complex causal interrelationships and interdependencies because it has long dealt with economic systems with numerous and interrelated variables. Nor is the more recent recognition of feedback effects and time lags, or for that matter of multipliers and accelerators in traditional macro-economics of any help. Economists who do not study the causal chain which gives rise to pollution and its impact on human health are ill-equipped to deal with the elaboration of environmental plans and projects and to judge their effectiveness and relative worth.

sub-optimization if it does not become the pretext for endless delays or a policy of doing too little too late.

The third reason which speaks against the compensation principle is to be found in the fact that it does not lead to the systematic search (by R and D expenditures) for alternative non or less polluting technologies [15]. To suggest that environmental improvements are economically worthwhile only if the "worth" of the improvement (as measured by the compensation principle) exceeds or equals the cost of the improvement says nothing about the techniques to be employed or to be developed. It sidetracks this important issue and leaves it to the pollutor to develop anti-pollution techniques only in accordance with his private cost benefit calculations. This has not been adequate in the past and may turn out to have disastrous consequences with disproportionately increasing environmental disruption.

In conclusion, let me make explicit the basic elements of the approach I have used in dealing with the admittedly difficult problem of evaluation. Negatively speaking I feel the environmental issue forces us to abandon the traditional assertion that values and value judgments are beyond scientific inquiry and have to be accepted as given. In economic discourse this has meant that we have accepted individual valuations, prices and income as given. Instead I suggest that it is possible and necessary to follow an empirical or pragmatic approach to the study of value. Such an approach is based upon a critical analysis of the consequences of accepting criteria such as market values and an examination of the question of whether monetary values are appropriate for the evaluation of the characteristics of the environment. In the case under consideration the evaluative judgment must correspond to these characteristics as they affect human health and human life without arbitrarily excluding anybody (whether due to the fact that he is unaware of the consequences of pollution or is unable to pay or even prefers a polluted environment to the maintenance of minimum environmental standards). I have endeavored to show that monetary criteria (willingness to pay, compensation principle, etc.) are in this sense not appropriate because they do not evaluate the characteristics which define the quality of the environment and its potentially negative impact on human health, human well-being and human survival. This has nothing to do with Hegelian essences (as Beckerman seems to fear) but with the nature and quality of the environment, *i.e.*, its characteristics. Therefore the "amount" of its value needs to be quantified and evaluated in terms of criteria that express or measure its effects on human health. These can only be environmental standards for all concerned without exclusion. Such standards are not beyond reach; in fact they are available or could be developed. They will have to be objective or objectified criteria reflecting our current knowledge and are subject, at the same time, to change in the light of new knowledge and new experiences.

15. This is not to say that the pollution problem will be solved simply by the introduction of different technologies.

To repeat, the basic issue under discussion is not whether evaluations, *i.e.*, judgments as to the presence and "amount" of environmental values can be made in terms of willingness to pay but whether these criteria are cognitively responsible [16]. I have tried to show that monetary criteria are not cognitively responsible. The use of monetary criteria would have the effect of making environmental planning ineffective and would give rise at best to a piecemeal approach which will not overcome the sub-optimization which has characterized the outcome of the market system in the past. Today and with respect to the current debate of environmental policies they seem to be rather an expression of an attempt to force the not so new facts of environmental disruption once more into existing theoretical frameworks and conceptual boxes which have served our discipline as instruments to play down the significance of the phenomena of unpaid social costs by making them appear more harmless than they are.

This is not the place to set forth an alternative approach to the evaluation of environmental goals and environmental planning. Nevertheless, since Beckerman insists that the critic must show that there is a better instrument than that which he criticizes — a view which I do not share — I shall formulate a few generalizations in the hope that these sketchy observations may suffice to indicate at least the general direction in which a more effective approach to evaluating environmental values and environmental planning may lead us. Above all it would be necessary to recognize the systems character of the environmental problem and to admit that environmental relations differ radically and in kind from market relationships. Furthermore, the elaboration and acceptance of environmental goals call for a collective or social choice with a direct participation and expression of preferences by all members of society, even those outside the market and without reference to effective demand. Lastly, we need systematic cost effectiveness studies for alternative goals and projects together with the appropriate implementation, rules and procedures. This is merely another way of saying that economic theory will have to draw the consequences from the fact that formal rationality concept leave out of account a whole series of fundamental human needs, of which environmental requirements have been recognized rather late. In order to satisfy these human needs and to arrive at a substantive rationality in the utilization of society's scarce resources, these requirements will have been defined as objectively as our present knowledge permits and evaluated

16. Pepper speaks of evaluative criteria in discourse as becoming "responsible" by their attachment to the evaluative criteria which operate outside of discourse. Where this attachment does not hold or cannot be made out the evaluative criterion is cognitively irresponsible, *i.e.*, it is not true to the empirical fact of the matter. Quantitative standards must be correlated in an appropriate way with the defining characteristics of the (qualitative) definitions. C. Pepper, *The sources of value*, Berkeley, Calif., 1958, pp. 277-279.

by means of a deliberate collective, *i.e.*, political decision in comparison to other public goals to be pursued. This means that we shall have to face the task of introducing to an increasing degree politically formulated norms into the socio-economic process. In short we face the task of operating with objective substantive and socially acceptable criteria which have been politically sanctioned. This formulation of goals will be appropriate and necessary in all those instances in which the market fails to generate an effective demand and does not maintain environmental standards but actually contributes to their degradation.

IGNACY SACHS

Approaches to a political economy of environment

The environmental revolution constitutes a challenge to the social sciences in general [1], and to economic theory in particular. Up to now, economists failed to respond to it, and pioneering books such as Kapp's *Social costs of private enterprise* did not generate the discussion they deserved [2]. Coddington goes as far as to plead guilty for the failure of the economists as a profession, to integrate a major characteristic of recent technological progress into their theoretical thinking: the provision of opportunities for shifting costs from the producer onto society. According to him, the main body of economic thought is ill-adapted to coming to terms with the ecological viewpoint and, therefore, "it may even be the case that the greatest service economists can render posterity is to remain silent" [3].

This paper will take a slightly less pessimistic view. It will be argued that a *political economy* of environment, as distinct from an *economics* of environment might be constructed, provided we recognize the need for far-reaching revisions of large chunks of theory. For obvious reasons, it cannot be done in one paper, not at this juncture. Our aim is much less ambitious: to identify some of the problem-areas and to suggest a few priorities for further study. Before we turn, however, to this task, it may prove useful to clear the ground by attempting a brief classification of the main ideological trends discernible in environmental discussions. Social science production is never quite free from ideological bias and this is particularly true with respect to writings on envi-

1. See S. Tsuru (ed.), *Environmental disruption: A challenge to social scientists*, Tokyo, 1970 (Proceedings of International Symposium organized under the auspices of the International Social Science Council, Tokyo, March 8-14, 1970).

2. K.W. Kapp, *The social costs of private enterprise*, Oxford, 1950. The far-reaching implications of this book were underlined by J. Weiller in a review note, published in *Revue d'histoire économique et sociale* 29, 1951, pp. 414-417.

3. A. Coddington, "The economics of ecology", *New society* 393, April 9, 1970, pp. 595-597.

ronment, as any response in this field will perforce involve the collective action of large populations [4].

The motives behind the concern

Disregarding shades, and minor differences of emphasis, the bulk of literature on environment (mostly in USA) can be classified, for our purposes, into six groups.

1. The *diversionists* come first, as far as publicity is concerned. This is understandable since they enjoy the support of several establishments. In their view, environmental disruption — the reverse side of the scientific and technological revolution — is taking such alarming proportions that it should become a major and constant concern for citizens, at the expense of other political preoccupations nowadays considered less important. People are called upon to organize themselves in order to protect the ecosystem. But the action they are expected to take is to be of a purely conservationist nature ; no links whatsoever are established between environmental disruption and the working of the socio-political system. Young people in particular are exhorted to devote their exclusive attention to environment in the hope that they may thus be diverted from other burning international or social issues and that, at the same time, they will stop short of digging too deeply into the socio-political context of environmental disruption.

The writers who, in good faith, produce piles of gloomy books, pamphlets and articles on the alarming state of the biosphere and the imminent disaster facing humanity in this way become involved, whether they realize it or not, in a campaign of political mystifications. For those, however, responsible for having launched it, environment, as such, matters very little indeed [5]. It is just an issue which can be easily played up and lends itself to exploitation as a safety-valve, because many people are disturbed by the worsening quality of their lives.

2. The attitude of *big business* towards environmental concern is ambivalent. While some industrialists fear an increase in costs, threatening their competitivity [6], others, on the contrary, approach the matter from a more positive angle. Anti-pollution for them is likely to become an important market and, possibly, an additional pretext for the spending of public funds in such a way as to increase private profits.

4. See G. Vickers, *Value systems and social process*, Harmondsworth, 1970, pp. 181-183.

5. Were this a legitimate concern, it should reflect itself in the appropriation of public funds for environmental action.

6. See, *i.a.*, R.S. Diamond, "What business thinks about its environment", in: *The environment : A national mission for the seventies*, New York, 1970, pp. 55-64 (reprinted from *Fortune*).

As one of them has put it in an article entitled "Social-sector industries: The challenge of our conscience" (*sic*): "It is interesting to reflect that perhaps in the years ahead great careers and even fortunes will accrue to those who devote their efforts to societal — *not* production — problems. Air and water and noise and landscape pollution control; housing; recreation; education; transportation; public facilities requirements — these and other social needs present a market measured in the trillions of dollars and human survival."[7]

Seen in this perspective, the index of advertisers in the *Scientific American* special issue on Biosphere [8] makes very interesting reading indeed.

3. For the *neo-malthusians* busy keeping the underdeveloped countries from industrializing, environmental concern is an excellent pretext, as they may now claim that, not only food, but also all other resources of the spaceship Earth are supposedly in short supply, to such an extent that the Earth may even prove incapable of supporting on a sustained basis a population as large as the present one [9]. Such an approach is being consistently developed by Paul R. Ehrlich among others. In a best selling pamphlet [10] he enjoins Americans to write letters to politicians, insisting, *i.a.*, on the following points: population is far outstripping food production, more than half of the world is hungry and many are dying of starvation; not all countries can be industrialized; DCs cannot feed UDCs. In more scholarly papers he does not hesitate to ask for the stopping of aid to underdeveloped countries, unless a substantial share of the same is spent on population control: "We will have to recognize the fact that most countries can never industrialize and that giving them industrialization aid is wasteful." [11] In the same vein the Paddock brothers suggested [12] that the concept of "triage" borrowed from military medicine should be applied to aid policies. Underdeveloped countries which lag hopelessly behind in the population — food game should not be assisted, as the resources allocated to them will be wasted. They should be instead permitted to starve to death, in order to concentrate resources on better cases. The Paddocks had India in mind, but it seems that their recommendation will be first applied on a mass scale in East Pakistan, where millions of people are almost certain to die next

7. D. Carley, in: H.W. Helfrich, Jr. (ed.), *Agenda for survival: The environmental cr isis* New Haven, Conn., 1970, p. 98 (2nd ed.).

8. *Scientific American* 223 (3), September 1970.

9. L.G. Cole, "Playing Russian roulette with biogeochemical cycles", in: Helfrich (ed.), *op. cit.*, p. 14. See also the findings of the System Dynamic Laboratory of MIT summarized by G. Leach in *The observer*, June 27, 1971, and J. Forrester, *The world dynamics*, Boston, Mass., 1971.

10. P.R. Ehrlich, *The population bomb*, New York, 1970, pp. 177-178 (13th ed.).

11. P.R. Ehrlich, "Famine 1975: Fact or fallacy?", in: Helfrich (ed.), *op. cit.*, p. 64.

12. W. and P. Paddock, *Famine — 1975! America's decision: Who will survive?*, Boston, Mass., 1967.

year in the midst of world's indifference [13]. The fullest presentation of Ehrlich's views is contained, however, in his well-known book *Population, resources, environment* [14]. The DCs are asked to "de-develop" and at the same time to share their income with the UDCs. As for the UDCs, while they wait for the de-development of the DCs, they should content themselves with a "semi-development". In a passage of his book, which brings back memories of colonial theories, he explains what "semi-development" means to him:

"As examples of semi-development, Kenya and Tanzania might be semi-developed as combination agrarian-recreation areas. They, and some other African nations, can supply the world with a priceless asset: a window on the past when vast herds of nonhuman animals roamed the face of the Earth. They could also provide one of the many living stockpiles of organic diversity, stockpiles which may prove of immense value as mankind attempts to replenish the deteriorated ecosystems of the planet. These and similar areas could serve as rest-and-rehabilitation centers for people from the more frantic industrialized parts of the planet. They would also serve as guarantors of cultural diversity, as areas specifically reserved to permit peoples to maintain their traditional ways of life [...] We need to create a demand for what Aborigines, Eskimos, Kenyans and Honduras can supply, what might be called cultural resources. These priceless resources are in short supply, they are dwindling rapidly, and they are nonrenewable. A way must be found to permit these people access to more of the fruits of industrial societies without attempting to industrialize the entire world."[15]

In short, alleging the need to protect the UDCs from the mistakes of over-development and the limited resources of the spaceship earth, Ehrlich manipulates the concepts of cultural pluralism in such a way as to propose an international division of labour closely resembling relationship between public and animals in a zoo. Once more, his conclusions have little to do with environment as such, merely used by him to sell, in brand new packaging, an unsophisticated version of colonialist paternalism.

4. Let us turn to those who really mean environment when they speak about it. In most developed countries, environmental concern materializes in some kind of *institutionalism*. Even people who are not prepared to go deeply into the social and political roots of environmental disruption, but content themselves with a more phenomenological approach to this matter, insist on the need to create special environmental agencies, and on the enacting of legislation to make their action at all possible.

Although the scope and the type of collective action proposed varies from case to case all the institutionalists have at least one thing in common: they all emphasize the inadequacy of the individualistic approach and the urgency of

13. See the provisional estimations in the unpublished paper by D. Thorner and K. H. Iman, *The menace of famine in Bangla Desh.*

14. P.R. and A.H. Ehrlich, *Population, resources, environment: Issues in human ecology,* San Francisco, Calif., 1970.

15. *Ibid.*, p. 313.

building into the capitalist societies more social controls on private enterprise as well as on public services very much in line with Galbraith's criticism of the affluent society [16].

5. The last two trends are both *radical*, and they define themselves in opposition to one or more of the trends described above. Strangely enough the radicals split into two diametrically opposed positions.

Several authors consider environmental concern as a non-issue or a false issue for the workers and the masses of poor people. The arguments invoked vary in kind. It is thus claimed that preoccupation with environment is a typically middle or upper class problem. Poor people do not care about the pollution of Florida or Monte Carlo beaches because they never go there. "Conservation is an essentially conservative issue." [17] The motives of the "diversionists" are forcefully exposed and the new version of solidarism wrapped in environmental concern rejected. At the same time, it is feared that environmental quality management will be financed out of resources which could be better used in a genuine war against poverty. Poor people will bear a substantial part of the cost of such operations. Moreover, they would be the first victims of the policies devised to slow down the rate of growth in order to improve the quality of life (whose life?) [18].

The radicals' refusal to play the environmental game of the rich people finds its counterpart in UDCs' fear that environmental concern will be used

16. See J.K. Galbraith, *The affluent society*, London, 1958, and in particular ch. 18 on the theory of social balance.

17. G. Marwell, "Who is worried about the environment?", *Bulletin of peace proposals* 2, 1970, p. 187.

18. Three excerpts from a speech delivered on the Earth Day in Harvard University by George Wiley, director of the National Welfare Rights Organization are instructive *(cf. Earth day: The beginning. A guide for survival*, National Staff of Environmental Action (ed.), New York, 1970).

P. 214:

"Are you going to ask the poor people in this country to bear the cost of cleaning up air pollution and doing something about other environmental problems? In all likelihood a good many of the approaches that you are likely to take are going to be paid for directly at the expense of the poorest people in this country. This will happen in a number of ways. It will happen, for example, because most of the systems of controlling air and water pollution, if they are imposed, will simply be passed along to the consumer in higher costs. The poor people, the people at the bottom of the economic ladder, will essentially be given a regressive tax — they will be asked to pay the same price you pay in terms of higher costs for such basic things as electric power, heat for homes, and other commodities essential to life itself. Unless some serious planning is done, it is going to be the poor people who pay for those things you do."

P. 215:

"Is the ecology movement planning to place any serious priority on the problems of environment of the ghetto and the barrio, of our urban areas, where pollution is worse?
You must not embark on programs to curb economic growth without placing a priority in maintaining income, so that the poorest people won't simply be further depressed in their condition but will have a share, and be able to live decently."

as a pretext to distract them from development, that it will become one more obstacle to growth invented by outsiders unable (or unwilling) to understand the UDCs' specific problems and priorities. The neo-malthusian writings discussed above are not designed to dispel such misgivings [19].

6. The second radical trend (quite influential in Japan, but also present in other countries) takes a quite different and positive view. It insists, on the contrary, that environmental disruption is the poor man's concern as he is the one most severely hit. The issues so widely discussed to-day are not at all new and the working class has been exposed to all kinds of environmental hazards since the beginning of the industrial revolution. Moreover, if pertinent questions are asked about the way in which social costs arise and are treated in different socio-economic systems, environmental concern may act as a powerful eye-opener. As an anarchist theoretician put it, ecology is by its nature a science "critical on a scale that the most radical systems of political economy failed to attain" [20]. Finally, environmental concern, far from pushing people away from other burning issues, may act as a powerful lever for mass action, which will challenge at the same time all the evil aspects of the existing social organization.

In the second part of this paper we shall explore some of the questions and revisions suggested in the realm of political economy by the positive radical approach.

P. 216:

"*It is going to be necessary to have substantial government expenditures for the programs of environmental control or, indeed, of industrial control. That means that you will be directly competing with poor people for very scarce government dollars.* And if you are not in a position to mount a confrontation with the military-industrial complex, if you are not prepared to join with poor people in saying that this war in Vietnam has got to end, that we've got to stop US military imperialism around the world, we've got to cut out the vast and wasteful military expenditures; if you are not prepared to say that *we want to put a priority on dealing with urban environmental problems ; if you are not prepared to put yourselves and your movement and your organization on the line for those things, quite clearly poor people will pay the cost of your ecology program.*"

19. In a recent panel on development and environment, organized by the Secretariat of the UN Conference on the Human Environment (Geneva, June 1971) several speakers expressed the concern of UDCs of seeing environmental concern used as a pretext to slow down the pace of their development. Whatever the merits of this attitude, politically, it is one to be taken into account.

20. M. Bookchin, *Ecology and revolutionary thought*, New York, 1970, p. 6. Bookchin goes on saying that ecology is also an integrative and reconstructive science and that by insisting on the crucial role of diversity it lends itself to a libertarian interpretation, in which appear the concepts of a balanced community, face-to-face democracy, humanistic technology and de-centralized society.

Problem areas

1. *The definitional trap*

As usual, the definition of the scope of the subject we are dealing with in this paper presents conceptual difficulties. It is easy to define it narrowly as being merely the *economics of pollutions,* but this means abandoning the most precious part of the concept of environment, namely its all-inclusiveness. The alternative is, therefore, to include in the political economy of environment all the side-effects of economic activities which are disregarded by economic agents, as well as the economic feedback of the environmental changes thus provoked. In other words, the political economy of environment should explore the consequences of insulating, for the purpose of economic decisions, a given sub-system and referring exclusively to this as a framework for economic rationality. This is in line with the social and historical nature of political economy, since in different historical contexts and under different socio-economic regimes the isolation of sub-systems takes different forms. Wildavsky is, therefore, correct in saying that "the old economics was mostly economics. The new economics is mostly politics."[21] But two other difficulties are likely to arise. On the one hand the political economy of environment broadens its scope to the point of including both the economics of natural resources and social conditions of life — subjects which are not new at all. On the other, it may prove a dismal science if people are persuaded to use more comprehensive models for their decision-making. Its subject matter, like the *peau de chagrin,* will be shrinking ever more, to disappear altogether the day the decision making process is brought within the global system, considered in its entirety.

We need not bother too much, however, about either of these two points. Looking at old themes from a new and more global vantage point might prove quite useful, though the moment of really using the spaceship Earth as the framework for all decision-making has not arrived as yet. For the time being, environment appears, then, as the moving half-light between the isolated sub-system and that part of the rest, which has become too important to be disregarded altogether, but has not been included, for the time being, in the expanded sub-system.

2. *Some theoretical implications*

The tentative definition sketched above enhances the need to come to grips with two heroic and often unspoken assumptions of economists as a profession. The first postulates the possibility of a two-stage reductionism: all things can

21. A. Wildavsky, "Aesthetic power or the triumph of the sensitive minority over the vulgar mass: A political analysis of the new economics", in: R. Revelle and H. Landsberg (eds.), *America's changing environment*, Boston, Mass., 1970, p. 147.

be reduced to their economic dimension and the economic dimension yields itself to a quantitative treatment; a market or a quasi-market value can always be found or estimated. The second takes an associationist approach to build macroeconomics from microeconomic considerations. But we must now reintegrate a direct reflexion on use values [22] into economic or rather social science thinking [23] and seriously consider the possibility of finding in economics a "gestalt" approach. In other words, reflexion on environment might provide new arguments for those who inveigh against the tyranny of the "obsolete market mentality" [24] or, at least, emphasize the preoccupation of the economist with the supply of non-marketed goods and services [25]. How far should we go along these lines? Shall we be compelled to re-examine the very foundations of our discipline?

The profession is split on this issue. The majority tries to avoid taking such a radical position and, consequently, employs the best of its brains on patching up the existing models and paradigms of thought. Externalities are fitted into the traditional market model and any means will do to estimate prices or quasi-prices. A minority seems ready, however, to recognize the limitations of the economic approach, although it realizes that in doing so, it is undermining the vested interests of the profession.

There is still an intermediate position, held by those who recognize the importance of the "side effect" syndrome: "Gains are reaped and costs are incurred, but there is no market that relates the two. Most importantly, the costs that arise are borne not by those that cause them but by others who happen to be around but are outside the process — bystanders so to speak." [26] But quantification in market or quasi-market values seems preferable to them — even though obtained by simplifications and abiding by discredited models — than no quantification at all.

3. *Planning: problems of method or of institutions?*

The same debate continues with respect to environmental planning. On the one hand are those who consider the existing tools, such as cost-benefit analysis and input-output tables, as capable of taking care of the environmental

22. The remarks on the subject contained in Marx' *Grundrisse* seem to offer an excellent point of departure. See *Fondements de la critique de l'économie politique*, Paris, 1968, vol. 2, pp. 220-223.

23. Myrdal is right in emphasizing that the distinction between "economic" and "non-economic" factors should be transcended, the only scientific dichotomy being: relevant and less relevant factors. See G. Myrdal, "Cleansing the approach from biases in the study of underdeveloped countries", *Social science information* 8 (3), 1969, p. 16.

24. *Cf.* K. Polanyi, "Our obsolete market mentality", in: G. Dalton (ed.), *Primitive archaic and modern economics: Essays of Karl Polanyi*, New York, 1968, pp. 59-67.

25. See N. Wollman, "The new economics of resources", in: Revelle and Landsberg (eds.), *op. cit.*, pp. 131-145.

26. H.S. Landsberg, "The US resource outlook quantity and quality", in: *ibid.*, p. 123.

dimension, subject to some adjustments[27]. On the other, we find a growing number of authors warning against the illusion of finding suitable analytical methods for optimizing choices, once the environmental dimension is brought into the picture[28]. In between are the defenders of cost-benefit as a preferable alternative to no analytical method at all[29]. Their arguments are of a two-fold nature. They consider imperfect quantification, in spite of all, to be a useful obstacle to discretionary policy decisions. Moreover, they insist that qualitative assessment of alternatives anyhow involves implicit quantitative valuations and trade-offs which can be spelled out *ex post*.

Neither of the two arguments seems convincing to us.

It is an altogether different matter to spell out, formally, the results of a complex assessment and to use simplified quantitative criteria as a basis for the assessment. In the latter case, the analyst is likely to fall prisoner to his own conceptual framework; the quantifiable aspects are important because they yield themselves to analytical treatment, while all non quantifiable variables become unimportant because they prove intractable. Besides, experience shows how often and how easily analytical methods are manipulated to justify discretionary policy decisions. One might say, of course, that bad uses of a good method do not disqualify the method, but the economist should also be concerned with the uses of his science.

For these and other reasons, which need not be adduced here, many planners

27. An example of environmental cost-benefit taken to its extremes is offered in the procedures now under elaboration at the World Bank. Their complexity might have, as a first effect, a considerable slowing down of project elaboration, without necessarily taking into consideration the most sensitive aspects of the assessment, namely the interplay of natural and social environment. For the application of input-output, see W. Leontief, "Environmental repercussions and the economic structure: An input-output approach", in: Tsuru (ed.), *op. cit.*, pp. 114-134. For a more imaginative extension of the input-output paradigm so as to englobe the wastes, see A. Kneese, R.U. Ayres and R.C. d'Arge, *Economics and the environment: A materials balance approach*, Washington, DC, 1970.

28. A general warning against too many expectations attached to analytical methods is contained in two very important recent studies, the Report of the National Academy of Sciences on *Technology: Processes of assessment and choice*, Washington, DC, 1969, and OECD, *Analytical methods in government science policy: An evaluation* (authors: C. Maestre and K. Pavitt), Paris, 1970. See also OECD, *Science, growth and society: A new perspective*, Paris, 1971. The first and the third documents were prepared by panels presided by Harvey Brooks.

29. Two recent UN documents contain a very frank assessment of the heroic simplifications underlying cost-benefit analysis: arbitrariness involved in the consideration of remote effects, the need to assume that prices reflect values and market is perfect, resorting to the concept of the "willingness to pay", the impossibility to find a fully plausible, democratic social-welfare function (Arrow's theorem), the arbitrariness of the rate of discount of future with respect to present, etc. The authors consider, however, that in spite of being "philosophically" weak cost-benefit analysis can be reasonably well applied (ECE, Conference on Problems Relating to Environment, Prague, May 1971, *An introductory review of attempts to incorporate environmental issues into socio-economic thinking as presented in recent literature* and *The benefit-cost analysis of environmental pollution*).

have been arguing that cost-benefit analysis can be only applied to the assessment of technological alternatives to achieve a given output, but not for the choice of the output-mix [30]. The broadening of the social goals of development by emphasizing the environmental concern strengthens their argument.

We are, thus, apparently left with a vacuum. If cost-benefit is discredited, what should be proposed instead?

At the most general level, it seems reasonable to challenge the role of optimization as the central concept of planning and to reconsider the dialectics of goals and means in the context of heuristic rather than formal methods [31] of multi-purpose planning. In other words, it is necessary to look at the planning process as "an iterative exchange of information between agents and a central administrative body or as a bargaining discussion between representatives of various social groups, a discussion that follows some institutional rules" [32]. The way out of Arrow's dilemma must be sought on an institutional level. Participatory technology is being proposed as a countervailing force to technological alienation in contemporary society [33]. Participatory planning may prove to be the only workable method of integrating environmental concern into planning. The quality of life being after all, a fairly subjective concept, those who live it should be closely associated with all stages of environmental planning and its implementation.

At the level of operational concepts, environmental planning is likely to adopt a *normative* approach, laying down *social minima* as well as attainable goals expressed in a mixture of environmental and social indicators [34]. Normative planning has a bad reputation, on account of a not too commendable record in some countries. The more important it is, therefore, to begin imaginative work on this subject, linking it with the institutionalization of genuinely democratic planning procedures.

4. *The actors in the environmental game*

While the problems discussed above are of a general nature, the political economy of environment has also a more specific area of its own. It should try to identify the winners and the losers of the environmental game in different historical contexts and under different socio-political systems. The actors are

30. This had been, *i.a.*, Kalecki's approach who, on the other hand, used to insist on the need to apply "variant thinking" at all stages of planning procedures without necessarily resorting to formal methods.

31. See the stimulating article by G. Kade, "La théorie économique de la pollution et l'application de la méthode interdisciplinaire à l'aménagement de l'environnement", *Revue internationale des sciences sociales* 22 (4), 1970, pp. 613-626.

32. E. Malinvaud, "A planning approach to the public good problem", *The Swedish Journal of economics* 73 (1), 1971, p. 97.

33. J.D. Caroll, "Participatory technology", *Science* 171 (3972), February 19, 1971, p. 647.

34. This point has been emphasized in several papers by W. Kapp.

easy to identify: enterprises, governments and people. But the game is a very complex one (it is certainly not a zero-one game) and the interests involved are not always transparent [35]. We should thus aim at having a distinct political economy of environment both under capitalism and under socialism. In both cases the reasons for the externalization of costs by economic agents might be different. Internalization of profits and externalization of costs is inherent in the working of the capitalist enterprise under unhampered market conditions. The real problem is to know how effective the controls imposed by the State are likely to be and how far the latter is willing to go [36]. Now, in a collective socialist economy theoretically there should be no environmental disruption, except when it is deliberate or unexpected. Deliberate environmental disruption may occur when the short and medium-range rate of growth of the economy becomes the only criterion of development, whatever the immediate social costs incurred and the degree of mortgaging of resources for future. Single-purpose planning proves destructive in all circumstances.

The underdeveloped countries have some specific environmental problems. These are closely linked with the colonial and the postcolonial international division of labour [37], the massive destruction of environment brought about by monocultural exploitation of natural resources, as well as with the consequences of the transplantation of the industrialized world's consumption patterns. Moreover, considerable damage to environment accompanies several big development projects. The reasons may be threefold (besides the deliberate trade-off): inadvertance (lack of expertise), convenience (on finan-

35. To give just one example, J. Ridgeway in his book *The politics of ecology*, New York, 1970, tried to link environmental disruption with the policies pursued by international corporations in control of fuel resources.

36. The prospects for the USA are summarized in the following way by a radical author: "Recent financial reports indicate that the business of pollution control will in fact make a profit out of pollution while at the same time generating more pollution; more growth will be the remedy applied to the perils of growth. In short, that advertising will continue to cost more for business than research, that the consumers will be passed on any costs of 'pollution control', and that federal agencies, new or old, will continue to operate as captives of the industry they are to regulate." B. Weisberg, "The politics of ecology", in: R. Disch (ed.), *The ecological conscience-values for survival*, Englewood Cliffs, NJ, 1970, p. 157.

37. The historical perspective on a world-wide scale, is aptly described by G. Borgstrom: "In the last 300 years, the white man has mobilized the grasslands of the world to his benefit. He has gone all over and taken the prairies and the pampas, the grasslands of Australia, many of the grazing grounds of Africa, including the South African veld; all this chiefly for his own benefit. He has taken very little account of the people who were there originally; he has killed them off, chased them away, or provided them with calories devoid of adequate amounts of protein.

Seen in this perspective, the present large-scale exploitation of the oceans might be called our latest big swindle. As Western white men, this time we are going out to the grasslands of the oceans: the plankton pastures. We are mobilizing them, not to feed the hungry, not to feed the continents closest to these lush pastures, but to feed ourselves." G. Borgstrom, "The harvest of the seas", in : Helfrich (ed.), *op. cit.*, p. 76.

cial or administrative grounds so as to make it somebody else's headache) or lack of sociological imagination (inability to understand the interplay of natural and social factors) [38].

Suggestions for further research

In the light of the above considerations, and having immediate feasibility in view, the following four areas are proposed for the organization of research projects:

1. Adding to social indicators a set of environmental indicators. This implies, in the first stage, a joint effort on the part of scientists, physicians and social scientists and, then, an exercise in the methodology of planning, if the indicators are to play an operational role. Attention should be paid not only to social minima and to critical points, but also to the behaviour of the variables (morbidity is a poor criterion by which to describe a state of health; psychological stress is certainly no less important than nervous breakdowns; etc.).

2. Evaluation of recent trends in long-term planning, both with respect to methodologies and institutional arrangements aimed at integrating environmental concern into planning procedures. Once more, this subject should be approached in an interdisciplinary way. A very interesting by-product of research in this area could well be the assimilation, by economic planners, of new ideas in planning advanced by architects, urbanists, specialists in OR and social workers. The need clearly to differentiate the paradigms of medium-range and long-range planning could be taken as a working hypothesis.

3. To the extent that the institutional set-up for environmental planning should be participatory, its long-run success will be conditioned by the educational system's capacity to train and motivate people for genuine participation in public affairs. The implications of the environmental concern and of participatory planning for education should be spelled out. The project should try to convey to educational specialists the postulates of environmental planners.

4. Several big development projects in the UDCs, implemented with foreign assistance, proved quite destructive of natural environment and ill adapted to social environment. Environmental audits of such projects are, therefore,

38. For more details see the paper prepared by this author for Unesco on *Environmental quality management and development planning: Some suggestions for action*, submitted to the UN panel of experts on development and environment which met in Geneva in June 1971, published in *Economic and political weekly* 6 (30-31), 1971 (special issue).

urgently needed in order to identify the sources of bad planning and to propose remedial measures. Such measures should, whenever possible, be based on labour-intensive methods and could, at the same time, become pilot projects in participatory planning. The bulk of this research should be carried out by the countries directly concerned. But broad international co-operation is called for.

ERICH HÖDL • GERHARD KADE

On the political economy of environmental disruption

1.

Classical political economy is the political economy of private property[1]. It uncovered the laws of a society based on private property and took up arms for the developing system of manufacture — thus playing an emancipatory role in the dissolution of the feudal system[2].

Classical political economy declared itself for private property and for competition because, organised under these conditions, the removal of feudal structures and the development of productive forces could come about more quickly and thus social affluences (wealth) could be increased.

Within the transition period from feudalism to capitalism, classical political economy fulfilled its political function until about 1830[3]. After the development of the industrial system organised on these lines had led to a series of abuses (involving child labour, working hours, questions of housing, etc.), political economy renounced its critical function because now it could only refine the laws of private property and competition without calling their preconditions into question. As forms of organisation were never fundamentally discussed, political economy could not confront the historical task which is incumbent on a science: to probe the foremost problems of a particular epoch beyond their surface appearances and to give the results political relevance.

Classical political economy could no longer live up to its own claim to formulate laws of production and distribution (Ricardo)[4] and, because it did not revise its basic assumptions historically, had to become "vulgar"[5].

1. F. Engels, "Umrisse zu einer Kritik der Nationalökonomie", in: *Marx-Engels-Werke* (MEW), vol. 1, Berlin, p. 499 *sq.*
2. *Ibid.*, vol. 26 (1), p. 23.
3. *Ibid.*, vol. 23, p. 19.
4. D. Ricardo, *Principles of political economy and taxation*, London, 1908. MEW, *op. cit.*, vol. 26 (2), p. 100.
5. *Ibid.*, vol. 23, p. 95.

2.

Economic theory did not make the rapid development achieved by the industrial system and by capitalism, each of which laid down conditions for the other. It limited itself to the systemisation and refinement of the perceptions gained by classical political economy. It proclaimed its results as "eternal truths" [6].

Economic theory seized in particular upon those elements of the preceding classical economy which were no longer capable of development — either because they were historically out-of-date or because they were based on false assumptions [7]. This was due to the fact that it no longer understood itself as being socially critical. As the approach of classical political economy which had contributed to the growth of the manufacturing system was not changed to fit the new social situation, political economy became apologetic and could do no more than concentrate on the surface appearances of social processes.

This development was given decisive support by the formalisations prepared by the systematized theory and later by positivist theory [8]. The assumptions of classical political economy entered neo-classical theory in such a way [9] that formalisations could easily ensue. The debate on value criteria ("Werturteile") [10] draws the consequences from the programme of science already laid down by John Stuart Mill [11] and lays the foundation for econometrics, a theory of statistical economics. Mathematisation remains the most important feature of a science which gives no further explicit attention to its political function. The quantitative method constitutes a necessary but by no means a sufficient condition for economic research.

3.

A historical analysis of the problem of environment indicates its dependency on social forms. The nature relation defined as the relationship between society and nature is dependent on the organisation of society [12]. The pre-

6. *Ibid.*, vol. 26 (3), p. 255.

7. *Ibid.*, p. 476.

8. A. Comte, *Sur l'ensemble du positivisme*, Paris, 1848. A.A. Cournot, *Recherche sur les principes mathématiques de la théorie des richesses*, Paris, 1838.

9. G. Myrdal, *Das politische Element in der nationalökonomischen Doktrinenbildung*, Berlin, 1932. H. Albert, "Reine Theorie und politische Ökonomie: Die Problematik der ökonomischen Perspektive", *Zeitschrift für die gesamte Staatswissenschaft* 3 (117), 1961, p. 438 *sq*. G. Kade, *Die Grundannahmen der Preistheorie*, Berlin/Frankfort, 1962.

10. M. Weber, "Die 'Objektivität' sozialwissenschaftlicher Erkenntnis", *Gesammelte Aufsätze zur Wissenschaftslehre*, Tübingen, 1922, p. 146.

11. J.S. Mill, *Essays on some unsettled questions of political economy*, London, 1844.

12. A. Schmidt, "Geschichte der Natur im dialektischen Materialismus", *Existentialismus und Marxismus: Eine Kontroverse zwischen Sartre, Garaudy, Hyppolite, Vigier und Orcel*, Frankfort, 1965.

capitalist social forms are characterised by a communal regulation of the nature relation: the moulding of nature is performed by communal property according to social aims: social relationships (the most important being property) determine the nature relation[13]. As the productive forces progressively unfold to such a point that the changing of nature also determines the environment of the individual, the organisation of society must secure a nature relation which maintains the quality of life within the social framework.

The emergence of capitalism is connected with this form of property[14]. The use of a legal system which, when it first originated (Roman law), performed a function other than that within rising capitalism, led to private control over the communal structure of life[15]. The systematic extension of the rule of private property over nature and other means of production is accompanied by the separation of labour from capital which is itself the result of the accumulation of surplus value[16].

4.

The historical process of separation of labour from capital is the expression of an alienation process: as the worker is separated from the product of his labour into which he has put his life's activity[17], he becomes subject to alienation. If the worker relates to his product as to something alien, an appropriation by others must necessarily result — this is in capitalism the accumulation of private capital[18]. The alienation of man is thus engendered by private property and vice versa.

Nature as the "inorganic body" of man[19] now undergoes a kind of "alienation" from two sides: it follows the alienation of man himself and is reproduced by the existing and developing productive forces as a "second nature"[20].

With the total alienation by the separation of labour from capital and the far-reaching reproduction of nature, man and nature acquire the character of *commodities*. The capitalist mode of production necessarily and on a growing scale reproduces private property and nature as commodities which possess nothing more than *exchange* value. The fusion of man and nature

13. M. Weber, "Wirtschaft und Gesellschaft im allgemeinen", *Wirtschaft und Gesellschaft*, Cologne/Berlin, 1964, p. 257 *sq*.

14. MEW, *op. cit.*, vol. 3, p. 50 *sq.*; vol. 23, p. 741 *sq*.

15. *Ibid.*, vol. 3, p. 61 *sq*.

16. K. Marx, *Grundrisse der Kritik der politischen Ökonomie*, Berlin, 1953, p. 375 *sq*.

17. H. Marcuse, "Über die philosophischen Grundlagen des wirtschaftswissenschaftlichen Arbeitsbegriffes", *Archiv für Sozialwissenschaft und Sozialpolitik* 69, 1933.

18. K. Marx, "Ökonomisch-philosophische Manuskripte", *Marx-Engels-Gesamtausgabe*, vol. 3, Berlin, 1932, p. 39 *sq*.

19 *Ibid.*, p. 75 *sq*.

20. A. Schmidt, *Der Begriff der Natur in der Lehre von Marx*, Frankfort, 1962, p. 51 *sq*.

takes place and leads to an enormous heightening of productivity which under the prevailing conditions of organisation leads to the further alienation of nature. The mechanism of this process remains uncomprehended; its laws operate "behind the backs" of the participants[21]. Because the nature relation subject to historical change can explain the problem of environment, the "laws" of any particular form of society and their effects on nature have to be investigated.

5.

The interaction between society and nature which is dependent on the specific form of our society produces a second nature which corresponds to the level of development of the productive forces: its condition is historically determined. If the use-values produced for individual or productive consumption are not utilised, they are prone to the "natural organic change". The use-values produced by the interaction of human labour and nature therefore determine the state of the second nature which thus also determine the extent of environmental disruption[22].

The *commodity* character of nature must, with the growing development of exchange-value production, lead to a disruption of the environment. Corresponding to the separation between capital and labour there is a *commodity* production: it takes place only for the purpose of exchange[23]. The primacy of exchange-value is in capitalism only logical because exchange values permit the capital accumulation. Private property acquires its rationale through exchange-value and vice versa. If private property (as regards the means of production) can be said to be necessary for capitalism, the same is true of the competition for private property: it is true also of competition for the accumulation of capital and thus for natural resources[24].

6.

The emergence of private property succeeded the historically determined process whereby a high level of consumption became possible for individuals. Because the exchange-value remains the focal point, the interest in private ownership is limited to areas which allow surplus-value production. The creation of surplus starts from the area marked off by law; therefore pri-

21. MEW, *op. cit.*, vol. 37, p. 462 *sq.*
22. Schmidt, *Der Begriff der Natur...*, *op. cit.*, p. 60 *sq.*
23. MEW, *op. cit.*, vol. 23, p. 191. K. Marx, *Grundrisse...*, *op. cit.*, p. 116 *sq.*
24. MEW, *op. cit.*, vol. 23, p. 161 *sq.*; *Ergänzungsband* I, p. 490.

vate property is logical and the processes involved are controllable. By controllable is understood the technologically determined possibility for the production of surplus-value. The employment of non-private property, *i.e.*, property beyond the juridical control is thus possible.

7.

The theory of labour-value, which sees the process of production as of central importance, has two aspects: authority is exercised by the private appropriation of the surplus-value created in the process of production and the accumulation of surplus value furthers the division between labour and capital [25]. The ruling system develops according to both aspects: the first occasions the second and vice versa.

The progressive moulding of nature together with new discoveries leads to a further development of the productive forces. If the creation of surplus-value is a pre-condition and a consequence of the exercise of authority, then, through the construction of private property, a legal take-over of the social areas in which (high) surplus can be made becomes possible. Private property designates the area for the creation of surplus-value according to the law of exchange-value: $c + v + s$ [26].

Whereas with variable capital (wages) whose level is fixed by the standard of living and by the degree of emancipation, a maximisation of surplus-value is desirable in the case of a given exchange-value, the proportion of constant capital must be minimised. Constant capital contains private property regulated by law and can be reduced by the employment of external (social) property, it can be lowered. Thus out of the formation of exchange-value can be traced the characteristic seizure of common property ("freien Gütern") [27].

Because common property is subject to no law of value formation of its own, it is prone to the law of private property, for this operates consciously when actual surplus-value is created but unconsciously when concerned with the totality of society. Furthermore the inherent limit imposed on the private appropriation of property is indicated at the point where the rise of constant and variable capital leaves no further room for a production of surplus-value. Private property here lives off common property.

The production of exchange-value, if it is to be effective, depends on the level of mastery of the processes utilised. The limit to the formation of

25. Marx, *Grundrisse...*, *op. cit.*, p. 375 *sq.*
26. MEW, *op. cit.*, vol. 23, p. 226 *sq.*
27. K.W. Kapp, *Social costs of private enterprise*, Cambridge, Mass., 1950. T.R. Malthus, *Definitions in political economy*, London, 1827. MEW, *op. cit.*, 2 vol. 26 (2), p. 38, p. 135.

private property has extended on the basis of increasing technological mastery, *i.e.*, of scientific development, much further than that fixed by jurisdiction. The law of exchange-value operates beyond legal property relations.

8.

The fragmentation of property according to the individual mastery of technological processes has made competition [28] possible. By means of the increasing development of technologies and techniques of organisation, legal private ownership has expanded but has been far overtaken by the expansion as seen in real practical terms. Legalisation of the private ownership of resources is called for only when the private creation of surplus value is improved by the advantages outnumbering the obligations. Otherwise property remains in public hands.

The argument of mastery of technology is thus complemented by that of efficiency. Legal private ownership has its historical boundary and is forced no further since the actual practice of private ownership allows for the full enjoyment of profits as well as exemption from obligations. Co-operation between state and private enterprise becomes essential and a postulate established for the "incalculability" of public undertakings [29].

The development of the productive forces today necessitates the technological mastery of exchange-value production. Private property is defined only according to the efficiency of private enterprise and the consequences of real appropriation are compensated by the state. The economic theory of private property is thus invalidated.

9.

In the repeated attempts of economic theory to define social wealth, the up-and-coming marginal utility theory made use of the concept of scarcity [30]. Scarce goods, which must be useful in restricted supply, are suited to the satisfaction of needs and thus constitute wealth. By concentrating on this sharply delineated logic, the theory leads to an extension of the economic sphere within total society. The aims of economic activity are pronounced from outside according to the principle of ends and means [31].

The efficacy of such an economic science is restricted to the conveying

28. MEW, *ibid.*, vol. 20, p. 44 *sq.*

29. R.A. Musgrave, *The theory of public finance*, New York, 1959, p. 43.

30. L. Robbins, *Essay on the nature and significance of economic science*, London, 1932.

31. G. Myrdal, "Das Zweck-Mittel-Denken in der Nationalökonomie", *Zeitschrift für Nationalökonomie* 4, 1933, pp. 305-329.

of the scarcity-principle to new spheres which today are to be found in the field of the environment. The aims are viewed as if given from outside — currently by those debating environmental problems. Economics as a "thought technique" [32] creates the appearance of a politically neutral instrument engaged in solving problems of an ostensibly natural origin which cannot be explained by a depoliticised theory.

10.

The current definition of economic science became possible by the switching from the labour-value theory to the utility theory and signified the substitution of the market for production as the main subject of economic theory [33]. By this change theory has followed social practice [34]. The connection of market, production and consumption results by means of the dual projection of the theory of production factors. Using the optimal combination according to marginal productivity and marginal utility support is found for conceptions of an economics of equilibrium [35]. The concept of "pure" economics proves to be hostile to technology as it relates to the optimal *economic* combination. A disparity in the structure of technologies is accounted for in the data only when it expresses itself in different cost structures — that is, those aimed at the *market*. The environmental problems to which also technologies have given rise are omitted.

The limitation of economic theory to market phenomena [36] has excluded the differences between technologies in relation to their secondary effects just as completely as it has excluded the whole of nature and its change through human activity. All processes of consumption and production are investigated in each case under only one aspect: some have no historical past, the others no historical future.

11.

The lack of historicity and of a connection between social and economic processes in economic theory expresses itself in the *causation argument:* whoever causes environmental stress is to be held responsible for the damage [37].

32. J.A. Schumpeter, "Einführung", in: E. Barone (ed.), *Grundzüge zur theoretischen Nationalökonomie*, Berlin-Bonn, 1953, (2nd ed.).
33. Mill, *op. cit.*, H. Lehmann, *Grenznutzentheorie*, Berlin, 1968.
34. W. Stark, *History of economics in its relation to social development*, London, 1944.
35. Kade, *op. cit.*
36. Kapp, *op. cit.* "Environmental disruption: General issues and methodological problems", in: S. Tsuru (ed.), *Environmental disruption*, Tokyo, 1970.
37. Politicians in almost all countries base their proposals on this argument.

In as far as the act of causing stress serves as a criterion for indemnification political and theoretical discussion coincide: no interdependency exists between production and consumption and neither has a historical origin. The logical continuation of the causation principle leads to that problem familiar enough in political economy [38].

This situation necessitates a *historical* analysis which can shed light on how far producers and consumers influence each other in a manner determined by ruling authority.

12.

Present economic theory aids improvement of the conditions of operation and the performance of the economic dimension of society. At a particular level of development, plant economics broke away from its original source, political economy, and in part followed its own line of development. Although political economy also deals with areas lying beyond private property, it does not achieve more than a theory of commodity circulation and money economy. Because it turns its attention to the market — and must do so, for products are no longer anything other than commodities — it takes property relations for granted: its theory never penetrates their dynamics. The exchange of commodities leads via surplus-value to an extension of private property, the limits of which have already been indicated. Private property operates over the market and vice versa.

The environmental problems which emerge beyond the realm of the market also extend in significance further than the economic dimension of society, thus eluding economic theory. As we are dealing here with a social problem, its economic aspect can be grasped only by a political economy which confronts general power structures critically.

The environmental problems emergent in all forms of society must be comprehended as a function of ruling authority which in each case appears as a distinct type, discussable only in an analysis taking account of society. A society which in its essentials is determined economically cannot do without an analysis of the interdependency between economics and society and this must be performed by political economy. It is only the deficient awareness of this connection which prevents the growth of a political economy which sees itself as critical. The increasing fusion of nature and society and the heightening of productivity which follows from it leads under the existing form of organisation to the uncontrolled changing of nature and stress on mankind. The conscious piloting of future development is, with the perception of valid laws and of a re-orientation requiring widespread participation both possible and necessary.

38. F. Wieser, "Über das Verhältnis der Kosten zum Wert", in: F.A. Hayek (ed.), *Gesammelte Abhandlungen*, Tübingen, 1929.

GÉRARD MARTIN

Some possible approaches to environment

"Pollution, degradation of the ambient atmosphere, violation of the most elementary safety rules, shortage of public amenities [...] this contemporary conjuncture is no capricious whim of fortune. It is the logical outcome of a series of decisions founded on economic calculations dominated by a certain notion of what is profitable. When an economist perceives this reality, he must realise that he serves a truncated science whose shortcomings are, today, quite glaring; he is under pressure to deepen, or even to re-examine, the fundamental assumptions of this science."

This passage, from a recent article in *Le Monde* [1] by René Passet, demonstrates, if that were necessary, the magnitude of a problem of which the public at large is only beginning to become aware.

While by no means a specialist in environmental problems, since my Institute [2] specialises in scientific policy and futurology, and since we are, at present, working on the possibility of integrating social indicators into models of social change, it nonetheless seems to me that what is now grouped under the general heading of environment poses theoretical and methodological problems that are of importance to research in the social sciences. It is with some of these problems that I should like to deal here.

Firstly, we must define what we mean by environment. An initial approach might restrict the environmental field to questions relating to the protection of nature, to pollutants. This is a narrow conception, which does not allow us to comprehend the magnitude of the problems. As opposed to this, we may consider the environment as the ensemble of man-nature — objects-men relationships; this, of course, takes us a lot further than questions of marine-pollution rates or decibels of noise emitted by motorbikes. The whole question of the equilibrium of industrial society is thrown into relief, as much in its internal aspects as in those concerning its relations with less industrialised

1. *Le Monde*, January 12, 1971.

2. The Institut de Prospective et de Politique Scientifique (IPEPS), headed by Yves Barel, is part of the Institut de Recherche Économique et de Planification (IREP) of the Université des Sciences Sociales de Grenoble.

societies. From suffocation in the great increase in psychosomatic illness, contemporary society is confronted with environmental problems amounting to no more nor less than the happiness and the misery of mankind.

I have decided to broaden this approach in order to penetrate beyond the surface of a concrete situation and to attempt a more profound analysis. If one accepts this conception, one is directly led to question whether the classical tools of economic theory and analysis permit us correctly to grasp phenomena and to develop an appropriate policy for their modification; negatively, we are led to ask what alternative approaches could be used.

1. Theories and tools of economic analysis

An analysis of this topic is impossible without a prior reflection upon economic rationality; this will enable us to see which types of theory, plans and policies may be at issue.

1. *Economic rationality*

Economic rationality flows directly from eighteenth- and nineteenth-century rationalist ideology, from which economic doctrines have drawn their inspiration.

Thus, once one disposes of an input and an output, one will seek:
— To maximise out put for a given input,
— To minimise input for a given output,
— To maximise output and to minimise input at the same time, such a mechanism being applicable to all fields and to all levels of economic analysis.

All this is such that, for the individual, as for the social system as a whole, the golden rule for behaviour is the quest for the maximum advantage in return for the minimum cost.

Initially associated with the model of pure and perfect competition, this conception was, and still is, equally present in planning models, inasmuch as, and although, the essential elements of the free enterprise model have been transformed into a modern planning concept, the economic notion of reward-punishment being replaced by a variety of profit-cost concepts.

2. *Economic rationality and economy theory*

It is important to note from the outset that, confronted with new social problems and social change, economic theory and, consequently, the rationality underpinning it, operate a process of assimilation and recovery. Theory and rationalisation are, thus, in no way brought into question.

To my mind, this situation may be illustrated by the theory of externalities and the types of public intervention associated with it.

a) Deviations from the optimum

Starting from Pareto's general definition of the optimum, which consists in stating that a situation is optimal if any change in relation to it cannot lead to an increase in the welfare of some without diminishing that of at least one other, welfare depending on the sum of available quantities of goods, certain economic theorists have noted that certain situations could vitiate the achievement of such an optimum:

— The effects of economic activities that are not integrated into the market,

— The public character of a certain number of goods and services leading to indivisibilities.

These two types of situation must be corrected if the market is to continue to function, and this essential mission must be entrusted to the state.

b) Externalities and state intervention

"Externality characterises the phenomenon and its result by which an agent sees his utility vary under the impact of economic action (or inaction) by another agent, this action (or inaction) not being taken into account by market mechanisms."[3] Once this fundamental phenomenon, whose concrete aspects are, today, highly significant, is recognised, welfare theorists assign a corrective mission to the state where disequilibria thus engendered are concerned.

We thus hypothesise that the market mechanism is satisfactory, and that if there is a "market failure", we must envisage public corrective intervention; in this way, within such a system there are "as many market mechanisms as possible, and as many other mechanisms as are necessary"[4], the field of state intervention being very strictly limited by calculation of the cost of public intervention in relation to other forms of internalisation such as negotiation.

We are thus faced with a technical solution to a social problem which brings the entire problem back to a strictly economic rationality, as witnessed by the planning techniques used today.

3. *Economic rationality and planning*

As G. Kade remarks, "planning, as a method of approaching decision-making, is the ultimate consequence of the rationalist ideology from which eighteenth- and nineteenth-century economic doctrines flow."

3. B. Greffe, *La valeur en finances publiques*, Paris, 1970 (thesis).

4. G. Kade, "Théorie économique de la pollution", *Revue internationale des sciences sociales* 22 (4), 1970.

Starting from the economic rationality mentioned above, and extended to cost-benefit analysis, the development of planning occurred at the moment of meeting of three elements:

— The growing use of mathematics as a tool,

— The development of decision-making theory, or theories,

— Public interventionism, embracing the foregoing elements to the extent that "the combination of classical systems of rational decision-making and the idea of state intervention has given birth to a planning ideology that is at once rationalist and interventionist. Planning is conceived, moreover, as an action aimed at influencing the functionning of the social system as a result of an intervention policy founded on a rational decision-making model."[5]

This situation may be illustrated, on the one hand, by reference to cost-benefit analysis and, on the other, by reference to macro-economic models with fixed objectives.

a) Cost-benefit analysis

At first, cost-benefit analysis and its French application, RBC (Rationalisation of Budgetary Choice), appeared as an original attempt to get round traditional calculations and at least to introduce a little more clarity into public management. From certain aspects, then, it constitutes a form of response to the new problems of contemporary societies.

In fact, and despite the introduction of qualitative phenomena and what are, for the sake of convenience, called target groups, RBC remains a tool at the service of economic rationality:

— Because the quantification of the qualitative amounted to the monetarisation of benefits hitherto inexpressed, and to their integration into cost-benefit calculations;

— Because, if RBC remains conceivable at the level of a very limited project, it is powerless to embrace the totality of a system and its evolution, with the exception of the consideration of the automatic and consensual achievement of an optimum through the price-system.

Thus, the refinement and improvement of calculation can only restore the internal logic of the system.

b) Global functional models

Global functional models permit no more of a view of problems of social evolution than does RBC, nor do they orientate choices, or make them explicit.

In effect, the action of most planning models [6] is defined by the transformation M of an initial situation S into a final situation S':

5. *Ibid.*
6. *Ibid.*

(S)————————————————M————————————————→(S′)

The transformation of S into S′ assumes that the process is broken down into specific phases representing the ends-means dichotomy.

Phases 1 & 2	determination of objectives		initial situation
Phase 3	└——→	choice of instruments	←——┘
Phase 4		↓ putting into operation	
Phase 5		↓ control	

Hence an initial situation:

$z_1, z_2, \ldots z_n$

$x_1, x_2, \ldots x_m$

with $z^+_1, z^+_2, \ldots z^+_n$ set of objectives z_j

and $x_1, x_2, \ldots x_m$ set of instruments x_i

the programme is then expressed by $x^+_1, x^+_2, \ldots x^+_m$ set of instrumental variables.

In this context, planning consists in determining the set $x^+_1, x^+_2, \ldots x^+_m$ compatible with a determinate set of objectives z_j.

Planning is reduced to a functional transformation process in which the planner is assumed to be in possession of all information concerning possible solutions, their consequences as well as a logical order of collective preferences. This, then, amounts to saying that the ensemble of instruments x_i is optimal in relation to the ensemble of objectives z_j.

We have, then, a relatively closed model involving deduction of the rational decision with the centralisation of diagnosis and evaluation of choices. The implicit hypotheses being that all information is available to the decider and that mathematical methods provide a satisfactory means of resolution.

In sum, we can see that economic rationality governs the ensemble of theories and practices in economic analysis. In this context, the treatment of environmental problems, as defined at the beginning, will merely be the equivalent of social policies practised hitherto, that is, an *a posteriori* public intervention which, even if it makes the polluter pay the cost of the disutility introduced by his role in the pollution, for example, will only be situated at the apparent level of these problems, and in a short-term perspective. This restrictive appreciation does not mean that we ought not equip ourselves with the analytical tools available as soon as possible; on the contrary, no delay can be tolerated in this matter. It signifies simply that, if we are to get to the heart of things, we must both enlarge our temporal perspectives and envisage the use of new instruments. In short, we must view the situation from a wider angle.

2. Alternative approaches

Very generally, we can distinguish two alternative types of approach. Firstly, those involving a renewal of the classical instruments; secondly, those, still hesitant, which tend radically to modify our perceptions of social phenomena.

1. *Renewal of the economic approach*

There seem to be two important elements here. They concern, on the one hand, the integration of social indicators into cost-benefit analysis and, notably, into RBC or PPBS (Planning-Programming-Budgeting Systems) and, on the other, the attempt to develop a system of social accounting.

a) Cost-benefit analysis and social indicators

The integration of social indicators into PPBS and RBC type techniques satisfies a concern that is highly significant due to the fact that the State is now concerned with the improvement of techniques of public action, when that becomes socially necessary.

In effect, at each historical moment, models and techniques of formalisation correspond to the needs of the economic system: a society will secrete the instruments it needs and no more. In this way, from a certain state of economic theory, the state will demand a system of representation adapted to its action and to the new social problems which may emerge, such as the environment today, for example. It will be seen that, as the state plans and refines its productive, transfer or reparatory activities, the system of representation becomes more exhaustive, its statistical base covers a broader and more detailed spectrum of relations. This is why we have a set of technical means designed to facilitate information and knowledge at a given moment, and whose social role is, simultaneously, to facilitate decision-making, to broaden dialogue and, finally, to contribute, as much as possible to the presentation of societal equilibrium in its entirety.

Cost-benefit analysis as refined by social indicators constitutes an example of this process. The methodological research involved here is interesting. Nonetheless, it poses a certain number of questions concerning problems of measurement, techniques of quantification, choice and typology of indicators and, finally, their prospection and the linking of means to objectives.

1) Techniques of quantification

The first problem concerns the measurement of social variables. In effect, the exclusive use of monetary language runs the risk of impoverishing the field opened up by the "social indicator". If, on the other hand, one uses physical language, one is liable to come up against difficulties in aggregation that will be insoluble without the use of a scale of values expressive of the level of indicators.

"If advanced, or exploratory research were possible, it seems to me that it would be necessary to study the possibilities of *time* as an instrument of measurement. This assumes: 1) The establishment of a typology of time that would go well beyond the traditional distinction between labour and free-time. We would need to attempt to symbolise daily life: 'cultural' time, 'civic and social' time, constraint-time (transport, administrative formalities, innovative time, educational time...) As will be seen, it is a question of trying to utilise time as an instrument for the measurement of style or quality of life. 2) Taking into account the differences in 'quality' or intensity of time. 3) The essential — to my mind — distinction between the measurement of time on an individual scale and on the scale of society." [7]

In second place, we must weight the different indices which intervene in the construction of a social indicator. For the time being, the weighting of indices can only involve qualitative judgements.

2) Choice and typology of indicators

The foregoing difficulties are aggravated when one wishes to select and classify indicators.

— It is extremely difficult to assess the validity of an indicator for purposes of economic policy. On top of that, the choice of an assortment of indicators which would enable us to form a judgement on a given social theme has not yet been mastered, and one might even go so far as to say that the formulation of political options might be necessary here.

— The typology of indicators is another problem that has yet to be resolved.

As J. Baudot has noted, the integration of social indicators into a system may be rendered necessary if they are used not merely for the measurement of current situations and objectives pursued but equally for the means being utilised. In American work, the notion of indicator of means seems to have been rejected, for an exclusive link is established between variations in the indicator and variations in the size of the credits allocated to a public programme. As American researchers are not unaware that an indicator can and must be sensitive to a legislative or regulatory measure, or to a simple modification in behaviour, this exclusive link is evidently deliberate and amounts to making social indicators into factors enabling them to assess the effectiveness of budgetary choices within the framework of PPBS. Henceforth, indicators of means are useless, because these means are directly measurable. One may note, however, that the Americans are not, for the time being, abandoning pyramidal constructions: goals and intermediate objectives.

Conversely, where France is concerned, the utilisation of the dissociation between indicators of means and indicators of objectives has been retained in preliminary works on indicators.

This dissociation is useful in part, to the extent that it could be interesting to have a synthetic, coherent idea of the various means utilised by different decision centres for a single phenomenon. Conversely, it fails to resolve a certain number of problems:

7. Y. Barel, *La modélisation socia'e : Pourquoi et comment*, Grenoble, IREP, March 1970 pp. 10-11.

"Means formally orientated towards a precise end have, in fact, direct and indirect incidences upon one or several other ends: the means for a health policy affect morbidity and mortality, but also the rate of activity and the social situation of the aged. The means themselves, moreover, react on each other, are constantly interacting and even cancel each other out [...] Consequently, how will it be possible to allocate means to ends, to measure the effectiveness of means, to impute variations in objectives to variations in efforts being undertaken, without possessing an explanatory system, a social theory enabling us to control indicators of means and indicators of objectives." [8]

It would thus be illusory to think that any social phenomenon whatever, could, by nature, be either a means or an objective. Any phenomenon, in fact, is a means at certain moments, and an objective at others; often enough it is both at the same time. Consequently, the distinction between means and objective is fluctuating, conventional and is utilised for the convenience of a specific research project. Conversely, if it is too early to speak of indicators of means and indicators of objectives to the extent even that social indicators are often goal-indicators passed off as objective-indicators, one cannot, nonetheless, reject the concepts of means and goals.

3) Projection of indicators

This question is directly linked to the foregoing problem. It is not only necessary to determine a realistic level of indicator for the objective to be attained, but also to achieve liaison and coherence between policies and means in one field and objectives being pursued in other fields.

Horizontal coherence must, therefore, simultaneously resolve the problem of liaison between objectives, liaison between means as well as liaison and relations between means and objectives.

We have here an important problem concerning relationships between variables. In this analysis, the correlation method is not necessarily the best, as it does not always express relations of causality.

On another scale, the temporal permanence of the indicator, and the eventual abandoning of a redundant indicator are problems yet to be resolved.

These, to my mind, are the difficulties presented by the integration of social indicators into the processes of collective decision-making.

b) Social accounts and social accounting

If economic accounting and, notably, national accounting present a certain number of advantages, its use in the study of welfare, social development and environmental problems remains limited.

As distinct from social theory and social planning, there is what might be termed a certain isomorphism between national accounting and economic theory. In effect, when national accounting emerged, it was able to base itself on a relatively elaborate economic analysis, one that was partially utilisable for planning purposes. It is for this reason that, when an analyst notes

8. Baudot, *Méthodologie des études à long terme dans le domaine social*, Grenoble, IREP, 1969, p. 55 (mimeo).

any movement whatsoever in a national accounting item, he can, not precisely, but with a fair approximation, calculate the repercussions of this observed movement upon other items and explain its significance in terms of economic policy and theory. Inversely, progress in economic theory and changes in economic policy may be reflected in national accounting.

As opposed to this, national accounting is insufficient as an instrument for the measurement of welfare and the state of social development. This is why a certain number of writers have considered it necessary to attempt to develop a system of social accounting or of social concepts based on economic accounting.

This is notably so in the case of Mancur Olson when he declares that "currently existing economic indicators and national economic accounting furnish an exemplary model which may be used to orientate the development of improved social statistics". Similarly, Daniel Bell declares that "we need a system of social accounting that will enlarge our concept of costs and benefits, and which will situate economic accounting within a wider framework".

1) Two types of social accounting

Social accounting may be developed in two ways:

— Either by creating a wider framework encompassing national accounting, on condition that a single instrument of measurement is used; the framework will give an estimate of social progress;

— Or by developing social concepts which can be added to, or articulated with national accounting ; the British Central Statistical Office is moving in this direction.

2) Limits of social accounting

If, as with the development of a system of social indicators, the goal of social accounting is indeed the development of an instrument of coherence, one may question whether social coherence may be ensured, or assessed, as precisely as economic coherence.

In effect, certain questions raised above, it seems, ought to be noted on this point. The difference in nature which exists between the system of social indicators and economic accounting essentially rests on the fact that economic accounting supposes a homogeneous measurement unit, with additive properties, and the existence of one or several global aggregates, while a system cannot be said to be an accounting. A second reason, moreover, is that the mode of symbolisation of social phenomena cannot be the same as that for economic phenomena. In economics there exists, in effect, a social phenomenon, the object of a generalised consensus: value, which entails prices. The proof is that conflicts over distribution admit this by definition. Economic accounting thus possesses a homogeneity that is directly inscribed within the most concrete social reality. Conversely, social symbolisation is not based on such a social phenomenon, but still rests on a conceptual symbolisation in such a way that, in this field, not every homogenising operation has an immediate social correlative, remaining, rather, a partial and limited conceptual operation. It is important, therefore, in social planning, to respect the fundamental heterogeneity of social phenomena, and this implies that the broadest possible approach cannot, to my mind, rest on the concepts and techniques of economic accounting.

2. *Attempts at new approaches*

It was Bertram Gross, I think, who was the first to attempt to renew the approach to phenomena linked to interdependencies[9].

a) The Gross system

Noting the growing inflation of disordered statistical data, Bertram Gross attempts to take "overviews" of society and social change. It should be noted, however, that Gross does not claim to have developed a new theory of social change: he desires simply, but ambitiously, to take account of the ensemble of societal phenomena within the most exhaustive model possible.

The core of his analysis rests on the development of a generalised accounting system whose fundamental variables are structural and performance variables.

The structural variables group those measurements facilitating a judgement on society's "future capacity to perform"; performance variables are aimed at an assessment of the manner in which society satisfies individual needs at a given moment.

More precisely, "the state of a nation, at any moment in the past, present or future can be analysed in terms of two closely linked, multidimensional factors: the *structure* of the system and its performance. The elements of the structure of a system concern internal relations, while the elements of performance concern the acquisition of factors and their transformation into products (input, output). These dimensions of structure and performance furnish a conceptual framework for the organisation of all information, both quantitative and qualitative, concerning national projects, and the extent to which they are fulfilled or not. The distinction (between structure and performance) is analogous to that which exists, on a purely physical level, between matter which has a mass, and which occupies space, and kinetic energy, which consists in activity. On every level, structure and performance are aspects of the same approach. The first may be considered as consisting in slow, long-term processes, and the second, in rapid, short-term processes." [10]

There is no question, within the framework of this note, of developing in detail the elements of the Gross system. Suffice it to indicate the interest of this approach. As Y. Barel has remarked:

9. R.A. Bauer (ed.), "The state of the nation: Social systems accounting (Gross)", *Social indicators*, Cambridge, MIT Press, 1966, pp. 36-48.

10. Y. Barel, *Analyse de systèmes et méthodologie des études à long terme dans le domaine social*, Grenoble, IREP, June 1970 (note mimeo).

"B. Gross emphasises that we expose ourselves to numerous disappointments if we seek *directly* to measure the performance of a system independently of its structures and their evolution: performance is, in effect, linked to structures and their evolution. One might say that one of the major reasons for the relative failure in the quantification of social facts comes from the hypothesis — often implicit — and the illusion that structural factors do not intervene in performance or, if indeed there were intervention, that it could be considered as an invariant. The result of this was that the study of the structure-performance relationship was not placed at the heart of the analysis of social forms and causality."[11]

Gross' contribution is, thus, very useful to our knowledge of social phenomena and their relationships. It should be noted, nonetheless — without entering into a detailed critique — that Gross' work is highly ambitious. In fact, the social sciences are not yet capable of taking the ensemble of variables in a given system into account. The will to exhaustiveness, moreover, expressed in a global model, even if, as Gross attempts, the model is adjusted to the aims and desires of the population, runs the risk of presenting a static physiognomy of society by eluding the serious problems of weighting.

b) Some pointers for a new approach

The new approach we propose focuses around two elements:

1) The sectorial approach and integrative approach

The debate between the sectorial approach and the integrative approach is not merely methodological; it also covers a social problem. Because, above all, it is within observable social reality that the problem of relations between global society and the specific structures or processes constituting it is posed: the problem of the relation of the parts to the whole... Social reality and its dynamics condition the methodological debate and illuminate it by specifying the links which exist between the approach to a problem and the problem itself[12].

But,

"Contemporary social reality permits us to advance the thesis that the most developed societies in today's world are the seat of a contradiction which gives many to question whether it may not be capable of provoking the shattering or the blockage of these societies. The contradiction, expressed very compactly and schematically, consists in the fact that these societies are undergoing a dual process of integration and disintegration or, indeed, are only accomplishing a partial, malformed and anarchic integration, under the form of discrimination rather than cooperation. The integration appears only via the confrontation of sections of the social body. It is imposed and undergone and, hence, not controlled by society as a whole. It pays for momentary stability with longer - term instabilities.

What characterises contemporary societies is less the existence of this integration-disintegration contradiction than the degree of its intensity and the new forms which it assumes. The fact that the same forces partially account for both integration and disintegration renders the contradiction particularly powerful and difficult to surmount."[13]

---

11. *Ibid.*

12. Y. Barel, *Prospective et analyse de systèmes*, Paris, Documentation Française, April 1971, p. 17 (Coll. Travaux et recherches de prospective).

13. *Ibid.*, p. 17.

It is at this level, I think, that the environmental problems as raised initially can be situated in a new manner.

Henceforth, the integrative approach constitutes a form of response to the fact that, at present, as much on the level of action as on that of comprehension, liaison between each sector of social life and its "environments" is not yet effective. The sectoral approach consists in considering, for the solution of certain problems, a social system or sub-system as relatively closed or autonomous. The integrative approach consists in rejecting this hypothesis of "closure" for the solution of other problems, in favour of considering each sectoral ensemble as an element in a vaster ensemble. The integrative approach is not, thus, a global approach, albeit it may well be capable of developing into this. From a methodological point of view, it is the fact of considering every ensemble under examination, including, for example, that of the society of a specific country, as an element of a vaster system.

2) Systemic approach and systems analysis

There is no question of dwelling upon systems analysis here, unless to say that, although posing difficult problems concerning definition [14], one turns to it on account of its interdisciplinary fertility and its common preoccupation with the interpretative approach, as much on the cognitive as on the decision-making level.

On the cognitive level, the systemic approach can furnish new conceptual tools. This is so in the case of system and environment concepts, of closed or open systems, of the analysis of relations between the part and the whole. But, over and above these "spatial" concepts, the systemic approach enables us to envisage a temporal type integration of the past, present and future behaviour of a given system.

At the decision-making level, systems analysis introduces a greater degree of clarity into the processes and modalities of decision- and choice-making. Some current research is even concerned with problems of the ordering objectives among themselves.

Certainly, and this point must be emphasised, the systemic approach and systems analysis are still at a very hesitant stage, especially insofar as relations between cognitive and decision-making levels are concerned, but their fertility is promising for the future. The Institut de Prospective et de Politique Scientifique has, moreover, already carried out an initial application in the field of scientific policy [15], and is currently studying the possibilities of integrating social indicators into models of social change; the aim of this research is to attempt to establish the link between social theories and indicators in such a

14. *Ibid.*, second part.

15. Y. Barel and C. Roig, *Analyse de systèmes de la politique scientifique*, Grenoble, IREP, June 1971 (mimeo).

way as to identify the conditions for the development of a system of social indicators[16].

Naturally, the elements I have presented above are of a very general nature. All I was concerned with, here, was to raise certain methodological problems posed by the current environmental question.

Of course, the approach I have chosen is not entirely exclusive of others — the economic approach or the renewed economic approach. It should be seen in a long-term perspective aimed at perfecting the instruments of social knowledge without, at the same time, ignoring the demands of decision-making. In effect, it seems to me — though this is as yet only an intuition — that if research into social indicators should one day be successful, its use in planning and collective choice-making will not be able to ignore economic analysis.

16. G. Martin and B. Jobert, *Étude préliminaire d'une intégration des indicateurs sociaux dans les modèles de changement social: Essai de méthode générale*, Grenoble, IREP, January 1971 (mimeo).

ROBERT SPIZZICHINO

Quelques réflexions

A propos des problèmes économiques posés par l'aménagement et le contrôle de l'environnement, je voudrais m'inscrire dans la perspective des idées explicitées par les professeurs Streeten, Kapp et Sachs, et préciser des voies de recherche possibles à la lumière de certaines expériences déjà réalisées.

Si effectivement on ne peut que constater actuellement les insuffisances théoriques et pratiques des outils économiques mis à la disposition des fameux "décideurs" — dont il sera bon un jour de se demander qui ils sont — il faut bien avouer qu'on est dans l'embarras face à un certain nombre de problèmes immédiats, et que l'appel à la recherche constitue certes une nécessité, mais aussi un refuge commode.

Pour notre part, il est évident que la réflexion sur l'insertion d'une dimension "environnement " dans les indicateurs sociaux prend une acuité bien particulière du fait des propositions qui vont être faites à Stockholm sur l'échange d'informations, non pas seulement en provenance des pays développés et à *l'intention* des pays en voies de développement mais surtout *entre* ces derniers. Il est prévu en effet de mettre l'accent sur les informations économiques et sociales et les informations opérationnelles.

Cela n'est naturellement pas suffisant, et ce travail est inséparable d'une réflexion sur l'utilisation de ces indicateurs dans des processus de planification. C'est surtout dans ce domaine que certaines expériences méritent une attention particulière.

Émanant des recherches d'un groupe pluridisciplinaire anglais (ingénieurs, chercheurs opérationnels, urbanistes, architectes, sociologues) en charge de la planification urbaine à Coventry, et reprise en France sur des problèmes d'aménagement et de développement régional à divers niveaux, *la théorie de la planification stratégique* commence à se faire jour à travers des exemples concrets d'application.

Cette théorie — peut-être assez proche, quant aux attendus, de ce que Sachs appelle la planification participative — mêle étroitement les méthodes de rationalisation des choix (coût, bénéfice, évaluation et sélection des alternatives, arbres de pertinence, programmation en avenir incertain, analyse de sensibilité) avec une analyse sociologique tirée de travaux sur la sociologie des organisations, et la théorie des conflits.

Elle s'attache en conséquence à d'abord analyser la planification comme un processus de choix stratégiques exprimés en termes de jeux de pouvoir, et seulement dans un second temps, à ne rationaliser que les chaînes de décision pour lesquelles la rationalisation est pertinente avec la nature du problème posé, ce qui permet de suivre des plans et des programmes en termes combinés de données quantitatives et qualitatives (méthode des chaînes de cohérence).

D'après l'état des travaux en cours, il semble que ceci soit riche de possibilités. Il serait peut-être utile de l'expérimenter plus avant et de parfaire cette voie à travers :

— Un certain nombre de projets productifs dans les pays en voie de développement dans lesquels l'aspect développement apparaît *a priori* comme antinomique de la protection de l'environnement,

— Le suivi de la mise en œuvre de plans quinquennaux de développement.

J'insiste pour terminer, sur un point : quelle que soit la valeur des hypothèses de travail et des théories sous-jacentes, ce n'est qu'à travers un contact concret avec la réalité, pour multiforme qu'elle soit, que s'élaborent les instruments dont nous ressentons tous le besoin.

RÉFÉRENCES

Friend, J.K.; Jessop, W.N. *Local government and strategic choice*. Londres, Tavistock, 1969.

Bureau d'Études et de Réalisations Urbaines (BERU); Mission d'Étude de la Basse-Seine (MEBS). *Mise en œuvre du schéma directeur de la Basse-Seine : Vers une approche praxéologique des problèmes d'aménagement*. Rouen, BERU-MEBS, 1970.

Bulldoc 31-32, 1971. (Numéro spécial : *Sociologie de la décision*.)

MARION CLAWSON

Economic development and environmental impact : International aspects *

An output of economic goods and services inevitably results in environmental impact of some degree. One cannot obtain iron or other metal without mines, nor petroleum without wells, nor crops without farms, nor timber products without forest harvest. Each of these actions or situations leaves some scar upon the environment. It has ever been thus.

The extent of the physical impact of resource development for economic output depends upon the technique of such development and use, upon the ecology of the area concerned, particularly upon its ability to absorb wastes and to heal itself after disturbance, and other factors.

The psychological impact of the resource development depends upon many factors, which may be summed up in one catchall word : culture. How people perceive the environmental disturbance arising out of resource use, what their personal value standards are, what their concepts of the good life may be, and similar factors affect, if not determine, their psychological reaction. The same physical effect upon environment may thus produce different psychological effect, depending upon the persons involved.

We assume that people act rationally in economic development and in resource use, given the frame of reference within which they operate. All are limited, influenced, and guided by personal and cultural history, by

* In the preparation of this paper I have drawn heavily on the research studies of several colleagues at Resources for the Future, especially on the work of Allen V. Kneese and his associates. A recent publication which presents their thinking, and which draws upon and to a degree summarizes previous work by the same group and theoretical and empirical studies by others, is *Economics and the environment : A materials balance approach*, Resources for the Future, Washington, 1970. I assume the readers of this paper are, or can become if they so choose, familiar with the studies of Kneese and associates; hence I shall not cite them specifically, or review their findings. I seek instead to extend their basic analyses to the international sphere, and more particularly to the inevitable conflicts between economic development and the natural environment, especially as these conflicts contrast high and low income countries.

information or its lack, by economic resources available for economic processes, and other factors and forces. Put differently, one may influence or persuade people, but can compel them only with difficulty and within limits.

Some aspects of environmental impact

The production of consumer commodities or of intermediate production materials leads to their use or " consumption ", and this in turn leads to residuals which must be disposed of in some way. The total tonnage of fossil fuels, minerals, plant products (including forest products), water, and other inputs into the production process is used to produce some good or service which consumers use, directly or indirectly. These input materials are not really consumed, in a physical sense; the services they provide are consumed but the materials themselves persist, often in changed form. This is simply the law of the conservation of matter, applied to the usual economic processes of production and consumption. The residuals must be discharged to the air, or to water bodies, or added to the land. The tonnage of residuals equals the tonnage of inputs, except as oxygen from the air adds to the tonnage of residuals, and except as additions or subtractions to inventory temporarily modify the flow of residuals; and, for any given geographical area, trade with other areas may modify the local balance. It is impossible to attempst an increase in production or in consumption without at the same time experiencing an increase in residuals.

The environmental aspects of residuals have several characteristics. There is the matter of certainty or uncertainty of environment effect; for instance, there has been a major controversy in recent years as to whether the globe is warming up or cooling off, as a result of man's discharges to the atmosphere. Impressive evidence and theory can be adduced on each side of this argument; some forces operate to warm up the globe, others to cool it off, and the long-run balance is by no means clear at this juncture. Even when a clear trend is evident, a further question arises : will some form of offsetting or control measures arise more or less "naturally" or by likely human action, or will the evident trend continue to crisis or to catastrophe? Then there is the matter of persistence or decay of residuals, which frequently gets down to the contrast between inorganic compounds made by Man and organics which occur in Nature. The forces of decay, the volumes with which they must cope, and the time span in which they may operate may all be decisive in this connection.

Then there is the matter of the possible extent of damage, from some form of residual or environmental impact. Some impacts are merely annoying, as perhaps unpleasant odors ; others may lead to physical damage to present individuals, immediately or over their lifetime ; still others may cause, or are suspected of causing, genetic damage to present individuals which will show up only in later generations ; and still others may lead to destruction of the total environment. It is possible, for example, to postulate a continuation of trends in discharge of materials to the upper atmosphere which would lead to a warming up of the whole globe to a level where human existence would be impossible. Closely related to this matter of extent of damage is that of urgency, or time horizon. Some residual discharges or environmental impacts are immediate in their effect, while others are likely to create ill effects noticeable to the ordinary person only after some decades or longer. Yet some of the latter may be urgent, in the sense that the lead time, between decision to act and noticeable results, is so long that early action is called for.

Some environmental impacts are irreversible, as when a species becomes extinct. Others may be quickly reversed ; if new air pollution in a city were to cease, rain and snow would shortly clean up the local atmosphere. Innumerable intermediate situations exist. Even when reversibility technically exists, costs and time may be involved to restore an earlier condition.

Environmental impacts differ greatly in their incidence, both among individuals in any given area, and between geographically separate areas. Frequently environmental degradation takes the form of one person or group gaining the benefits, while others suffer the loss ; the belching smokestack is the old example of some experiencing damage while others gain. The incidence problem is often complicated ; in the foregoing example, how much do local residents benefit from higher employment and larger local volume of business ? Residuals often exert their most marked effects down wind or down stream ; discharges are made at one point, while ill effects are felt primarily elsewhere. The ill effects may be local, regional, or global, movements of water- and air-borne wastes are notorious in their disregard of political boundaries.

The environmental impact of residuals is also highly dependent upon the volume or scale of the latter. Actions which may be comparatively harmless at one scale of activity may become intolerable at another. The more or less natural environment has considerable capacity to absorb residuals, the exact capacity depending in part upon the kinds of residuals and upon the forces and processes of decay. Up to some threshold level, additions to residuals may exercise limited effect, while over that threshold the same quantity of added residual may have a marked, or even devastating, effect.

Finally, the environment within which Man lives is increasingly what he makes it. Man has been one force in the natural environment for many thousands of years, but his role has increased in modern times, and dramatically so in the most recent two or three generations. There is, for instance, no longer any wholly unmanaged or untouched wilderness area in the world where Man exerts no effect. To say that Man's influence is all-pervasive does not in the least mean that it is uncontrollable and that ill effects are inevitable ; on the contrary, the same use of knowledge, the same science, the same technology, and the same economic machine which produces environmental ill effects can be directed, if Man has the will to do so, to environmental protection, preservation, and even enrichment.

Dynamic forces

Over time, total population, economic output per capita, techniques of resource conversion and utilization, and other factors may change. Other factors remaining the same, more people in an area (nation, region) mean more environmental impact. Likewise, more economic output per capita results in more environmental impact, other factors remaining constant. These relationships may be neither linear nor proportionate. The effect of changing techniques of resource conversion may be either to increase or to decrease environmental impact; some new techniques may be environment-conserving, while others may be relatively environmentally destructive.

The possible interactions of changing population, changing economic output per capita, and new techniques of conversion are numerous and complex. Much depends on relative rates of change. Thus a country or region growing slowly in population but rapidly in economic output would have one set of environmental impacts, whereas a country with a high rate of population growth and a low rate of growth in economic output per head would have a different set of impacts. If conversion techniques be accepted as given, which they may be in the short run, then environmental impact would be reduced by reduction in either rate of population growth or in rate of growth in economic output per head, or both. We see no *a priori* reason to expect that high rates of either are more easily reduced than are low rates of each.

Trade-off between output and impact

At any time, with given resource conversion techniques, a trade-off between economic output and environmental impact is possible in any area. The nature of this trade-off may change over time, as conversion techniques change. The ratio between units of output (however measured) and units of environmental impact (however measured) is not necessarily constant throughout the range of the trade-off. It seems highly probable, however, that at any level of output, more environmental conservation is possible at some sacrifice in output.

Within the relevant frame of reference, the individual or the group chooses that combination of economic output and of environmental impact which best satisfies his or its scale of values. Many factors affect this choice, but surely the relative level of income is one. When income is low, most individuals, groups, regions, and countries will place a relatively high value upon more economic output, even at some sacrifice in the form of increased environmental impact. When income is relatively high, the person or the group can sacrifice some economic output or modify resource conversion techniques in order to reduce environmental impact, with less loss of basic human necessities (food, shelter, clothing, etc.). However, "luxuries" may be so firmly embedded in the person's or group's value standards that they will be preferred over some particular reduction in environmental impact.

Nations and regions

The trade-offs between economic output and environmental impact are greatly exacerbated by national boundaries. Different countries share economic output and environmental impact in different proportions, when raw material, capital, finished products, or services flow across national borders. One country has the deposits of iron ore, the mining of which necessarily involves some degree of environmental impact ; but the sale of its ore provides it with foreign exchange needed to buy desired industrial products. The importing nation gains the iron, to make steel for automobiles ; but it also has the auto hulk to dispose of or recycle, to say nothing of the air pollution associated with the automobile's use. Numerous other examples could be cited, of differences in benefits or in impacts for the countries involved.

The problem is complicated further by the difference in interest among groups within each country. One group in the exporting country may gain the income from mining royalties while others suffer the environmental impact. While there may be real differences between the total situation of the exporting and that of the importing countries, it is a serious mistake to assume that either is a single entity.

Differential economic gains and environmental impact in two or more countries are significant, in part because each country is a sovereign nation. All manner of national pride, prestige, and interest may be involved. But there are many similarities between international problems and interregional ones within the same country. Resource exploitation in an economically less developed region, with its attendant local impacts, may provide more income to the importing region, while its contribution to the economy of the exporting region may be basic. Many regions of the United States have sought economic development in their frontier past, almost without heed to the environmental impact, for instance. Most of the discussion which follows is equally applicable interregionally within countries as it is internationally.

Problems and opportunities of high income countries

Average per capita income varies from very low to very high, when nations are compared ; there exists a continuum between extremes, with some nations at all intermediate levels. Nevertheless, it is useful to distinguish between "high" and "low" income countries, without defining either precisely. We prefer this income characterization to the common euphemisms of "developed" and "developing". A high income country, such as the United States, may be developing in the sense that average per capita income (as conventionally measured) and average well-being (however measured) are rising. A low income country may be developed, in the sense that it has reached some sort of lesser summit or plateau in its economic and social development above which it cannot rise without major outside help.

On a global scale, most high income countries have modest rates of population growth. Canada, the United States, Japan and Western Europe are countries or larger regions where population growth rates range from average to low, on the world-wide scale. Consequently, the impact of population growth upon environment ranges from average to modest in these countries ; other factors in these countries do, however, lead to greater environmental impact. There are cogent reasons for further reducing the rate of population growth in the high income countries, although the population problem is not acute in most of them nor does it promise to become so in the next generation. But no reduction in rate of population growth will *alone* have much impact on the environmental problems of those countries.

The relatively high average income of high income countries does result in relatively severe environmental impact either within such countries or in the areas from which they draw materials or both. High income areas require large amounts of raw materials, at any given technology of converting such materials to finished products. Likewise, they create large volumes of residuals which must either be recycled or otherwise disposed of. A country which produces no paper has no problem of papermill wastes ; and if its consumption of paper is very low, its waste paper problem is minimal. High income countries invariably consume a lot of paper; paper-mill wastes arise somewhere, unless controlled in the mill; and waste paper is a major residual.

At the same time, high income countries possess great scientific, engineering, and economic capacity to cope with environmental problems if they have the will to so use it. New technologies of production, consumption, and recycling can be invented, developed, and applied. If the objective is to reduce or to minimize environmental impact, the high income areas can devote substantial economic resources to this end, with only modest declines in average consumption. In a period of prosperity in the United States, the *gain* in average per capita income between one year and the next will be greater than the *attained level* of average per capita income in many low income countries. Accumulated capital in high income countries permits substantial new investment in environmental impact-reducing measures, if this is the best way to achieve a desired reduction in environmental impact.

High income countries can, if they will, do much to reduce environmental impact. Doubts arise as to the individual and collective will to make even modest sacrifices to this end — sacrifices which match the oratory. There exists an economic momentum at both the total and the individual scale which is hard to modify. Neither producers nor consumers, pursuing individual interests within a total framework, are likely to do much, if anything significant, to reduce environmental impact. A few housewives may buy beverages in returnable containers and conscientiously return the containers, and a few businesses may adopt genuinely environmentally impact-reducing measures without compulsion of law or regulation. But such measures are likely to be few, limited in scope, and transitory.

If high income countries are significantly to reduce environmental impact, consistently over a long period, then group-imposed inducements and compulsions on both consumers and producers are almost certainly necessary. Laws, administrative regulations, taxes, subsidies, group-determined pricing arrangements, and other measures will be needed in varying combinations. With few exceptions, this means governmental action; popular support will be essential, but insufficient by itself. Legislation to compel or induce action will inevitably encounter resistances; there is nothing inconsistent in either a producer or a consumer supporting measures to reduce environmental impact when the major adjustment falls on someone else, and in opposing them when he must make the major adjustment. Legislation imposing constraints (and including inducements) on producers will involve a majority imposing its will on a minority; the latter can make up in intensity and in tenacity of effort what they lack in sheer numbers. Legislation imposing constraints (including inducements) upon consumers will usually involve a majority disciplining itself — possible, but not easy.

Problems and opportunities of low income countries

In low income countries, a substantial portion, if not the vast majority, of the people are poorly fed, badly housed, lack adequate medical care, have poor educational opportunity, or are poorly clothed — or commonly suffer all these deficiencies, often to a more or less comparable degree. The marginal utility of real income is very high, in a basic human sense. If incomes rise, some of the increase will be spent to remedy each of these deficiencies, and perhaps others. Neither individuals nor countries will use all of the increased income for better diets, nor all for better health, nor all for any other single purpose. Improvement in diet will stop far short of what the expert thinks desirable, as long as deficiencies exist in housing, health, education, etc. Moreover, some part of increased income will be used for entertainment or pleasure, even while some of the "basic necessities" remain deficient.

In the scale of values for expenditure of available income, the low income individual or country puts environmental quality in a distinctly subsidiary role. They may not be insensitive to environmental quality, but hunger is urgent. In the past generation, low income countries have used only minuscule portions of domestic economic resources or of economic assistance from abroad for environmental preservation, enhancement, or rehabilitation. Many political leaders of low income countries have expressed their preference for economic development rather than for environmental protection. But the actions of these countries have been far more eloquent than their words, though to the same ends.

In addition to differences in the income-environmental-impact ratios in the low as compared with the high income countries, some rationale to the relative neglect of the environment lies in the fact that the capacity of their environments to absorb wastes may equal or exceed the volume of wastes produced. Waste disposal practices wich are tolerable (and efficient) at low levels of economic output and hence of waste generation, may be intolerable when volume of waste rises to a much higher level. The ecologic structure of an area has a capacity to absorb and to recycle many waste products, especially those of natural origins, and this capacity may be adequate to the task in some lower income nations.

By and large, low income countries of the world have high rates of population growth. Application of modern medical knowledge has drastically and recently lowered death rates, though generally not to the levels of the richer countries. Birth rates remain high, often unchanged, and the classic population explosion experienced by any species when one major limitation is removed and others have not yet become operative ensues. Many African, Asian, and Latin American countries currently have rates of natural increase of 2.5, 3.0, and even 3.5 percent annually, compared with 1.0 percent or less in many richer countries. With extremely few exceptions, these countries have not lowered their rates of natural increase significantly. Most, indeed, have not really tried. Many, if not most, see no real need to reduce rate of population growth ; others, as India, concede the need but have not, as yet, made significant progress. Some such nations, or at least some people in them, have resented suggestions that they should try to limit population growth ; they interpret such suggestions as a form of racial warfare, to maintain them in economically subordinate positions.

The population problem is, however, acute in most lower income countries. Given the present major discrepancy between birth and death rates, given the "demographic momentum" which exists in most of them, and given their typical unbalanced age structure (vastly more young people, due to recent high growth rates, than in developed countries), any ultimate stabilization of population seems two or three generations away. An ultimate stability level five or more times their present population seems the best that can be hoped for. And attainment of even this result requires major effort in the near future, continuing over the next several decades. This is an extreme example of the fact that a problem may urgently require action simply because of the long lead time between initiation of the action and probable results.

Equally important with implications of total population growth are those for growth of urban populations in low income countries. Urbanization is proceeding as rapidly in low as in high income countries, and without either the economic or the technical base to make urban living economically and socially acceptable. Low income countries are just now beginning to experience some of the urban environmental degradation which has become so serious in higher income countries in recent decades — air pollution, smog, traffic congestion, water pollution, crowding and attendant ills, and others. Those low income countries which believe their environmental problems are not yet serious should take a new look at their emerging urban problems.

Low income countries have less indigenous research to apply to their environmental problems. Low incomes are generally reflected in low educational opportunity and in low support for research — indeed, it could scarcely be otherwise. While low income countries can import research results from higher income countries, in many cases the imported research is not applicable or requires a degree of adaptation which in turn requires research not readily financed in the low income areas. The immense accomplishments of soils and other agricultural research were developed for temperate zone agriculture, for instance ; while much agricultural research is underway in tropical zones, much is financed by, and led by personnel from, higher income countries, yet the research accomplishments in tropical agriculture lag enormously behind those of temperate zone agriculture. Generally, similar relationships exist for research in many other fields. Some critics have gone so far as to assert that science and technology have worsened the economic position of the lower income countries, because they have made the richer countries less dependent upon the natural resources from the lower income areas.

But lower income countries are handicapped in their application of such science and technology as do exist, if they desire to reduce environmental impact. They lack capital ; often they lack enough entrepreneurial talent. When they hire engineering and other talent from richer areas, the latter often have little or no interest in keeping environmental impact down ; their function, as they see it, is to "develop" the resources as efficiently as possible.

In sum, low income countries often lack the ability to cope with environmental impact, and give a higher priority to other uses of their available resources. Their environmental problems are likely to arise more from their rate of population growth and from the inducements to export raw materials to high income countries and regions, than from their economic consumption.

Interest of high income countries in environmental problems of low income countries

High income countries may properly have an interest in the environmental problems of low income countries, but the degree of this interest may vary over a wide spectrum, ranging from largely or wholly altruistic to self-interest of the higher income area. Although a continuum of relationships undoubtedly exists, it may be helpful to describe a few more or less discrete situations or relationships.

1.

A situation or relationship may exist in the low income country, which is now or will be in the future damaging to the residents of that area, but which has no discernible effect, direct or indirect, upon the high income country. For instance, self-sufficient farmers in a low income country may be farming in such a way as to create a severe erosion problem ; in time, if not now, crop yields will fall, and severe food shortage will develop ; but this area does not trade significantly with any high income country, so that no indirect or direct effect of the imminent worsening of the environmental situation in the low income area will be felt in the high income area. The citizens and the government of the latter may have an interest in the problem of the lower income area, in the sense that every man should be concerned about his fellow man — but not more.

2.

A somewhat similar situation or relationship might exist, except that the agriculture in the low income area did produce some exportable surplus, which was traded directly to the high income country, or indirectly in the sense that it entered a market in which the latter either bought or sold, even though no goods flowed directly from the low income area to the high one. In this case, in addition to the general concern for the welfare of others, the high income area would feel some concern — slight, but still some — for its own welfare, since the terms of trade for its raw materials or finished products might be affected, though probably only to a minor degree.

3.

The next logical step is somewhat similar to the foregoing, except that now the degree of interrelation between high and low income areas is relatively great. Thus, in the foregoing example of soil erosion, one of the main crops would be imported by the high income country, forming a major source of its supply. Or there might be a vital trade in any product of mine, farm, or forest. If the deteriorating environmental situation continued, then in time, the supply of products to the high income country would be reduced or raised in price or both. Or the low income country might impose environmental controls of some kind, the effect of which would be to raise the costs of production, reduce the supply, and hence increase the price of some commodity imported by the high income country. Under these circumstances, the high income country would have a direct interest in the environmental situation of the low income country as part of its own self-interest.

4.

The low income country might be intent upon a program of resource exploitation which would lead to the virtual destruction of some resource, which is valued highly by the citizens of a high income country. An African country might embark upon a program which threatens some species of wild-life, or would damage some outstanding waterfall. In this type of case, the low income country would seek a use of its natural resources which it thought would bring the highest income to it, or at least to the owners of the land; residents of high income areas would experience some loss, perhaps a great one, as this resource was destroyed or so changed as to have lost its value for them.

5.

A still greater degree of interest, from the high income country toward the low income one, would arise in those cases in which the low income area was pursuing some line of action directly harmful to the high income area, producing an effect which was unavoidable by the population of the high income area. For instance, if the use of DDT or some other chemical in the low income area had serious world-wide effects, or if some program of land use led to atmospheric pollution which in turn caused serious changes in world temperature, then the residents of the high income areas would have a direct personal interest in the environmental situation of the low income area, in addition to any concern they might have for the residents of the latter. Direct intervention, if it could be successful, would thus be in their own self-interest.

Each of these situations could be elaborated, and other examples given; intermediate situations obviously exist. But these may help to illustrate the range of situations or relationships which do or might exist, and the extent to which the self-interest of the citizens of the high income areas would be involved.

Interest of low income countries in environmental problems of high income countries

If the high income countries have a number of legitimate interests in the environmental problems of the low income countries, the latter equally have a legitimate interest in the environmental problems of the high income areas. To some extent, the interests are reciprocal and parallel; to some extent they differ. The following type situations may be recognized:

1.

The high income country pursues a program of resource use and development with environmental impact which the people, or at least the leaders, of the low income areas deplore, but which has no measurable effect upon human welfare in the low income area. The high income area may permit unlimited proliferation of billboards along its highways, or may permit suburban sprawl that wastes land and is unattractive, or may permit the invasion of its parks by highways, or engage in other activities which lower the quality of life for its residents, but from which it would be hard to identify any effect upon the lives of people in the low income areas.

As in the parallel reverse case, the citizens of the low income country may express a concern, of one man to his fellow man, over this situation, without feeling any self-interest in its modification.

2.

The high income country might consume resources profligately or wastefully, but with only a limited impact upon the low income country, because trade between them or to a common market is limited for the commodity or service concerned, and because there is no direct physical impact or fallout. There may be a future impact of greater proportions, but the present and immediate future impact is small. An example would be large scale water pollution, which greatly lowered the quality of rivers and lakes in the high income area, but with little impact, direct or indirect, upon the low income area.

3.

A somewhat similar but more severe situation would exist when a high income country consumed some kind of natural resource profligately, and at the same time bought foreign natural resource products at prices which induced a large production of the same or closely similar resource in the low income country. The situation would be further exacerbated if the importers in the high income country felt no more concern about environmental impact in the low income country than they were forced to acknowledge by legislation or by an aroused public opinion. Many examples could be cited : exploitation of oil resources in low income countries and regions, exploitation of mineral resources in the same areas, importation of crop products without concern for the circumstances of production, etc. The low income country would be torn internally by conflicting desires — the desire to take advantage of a good market, to earn needed foreign exchange, the concern over environmental impact, often the concern over excessive dependence upon a foreign country, and over its long-run future when the richer deposits of the natural resources had been exhausted. This is clearly a very common situation in the world today.

4.

A variant of the foregoing would be the situation in which consumers in the high income country offered such attractive prices for some resource of the low income country that citizens of the latter, or at least some of them, could not resist actions which they realized full well would lead, in the long-run, to severe environmental effect, including destruction of the resource. An example would be the willingness of consumers in high income areas to pay such prices for alligator skins (or for any other biological materials) as to lead to such extensive poaching in the low income country as to destroy alligators entirely.

5.

Producers or consumers or both in the high income country might take actions, in their own self-interest as they interpreted it, which would directly harm the population of the low income countries but which the latter could not avoid by any action they might take. The same examples used in the parallel but reverse case apply here : use of DDT or other chemicals which become dispersed world-wide and which do harm to people, high level air pollution which affects world climate, etc. In each case, of course, the actual damage to the low income areas would have to be proven, not merely asserted, for this example to apply. These are typically physical, not trade effects.

6.

The high income country might adopt and make effective environmental controls of some kind which would markedly affect the export demand for the resources of the low income country ; this effect might lead to either greater or to less environmental impact in the low income country. A similar situation would arise if the high income country developed a new production technology which had the same effect of greatly affecting the demand for commodities from the low income country. The essence of this type of case is that the high income country enacts legislation or develops new technology or otherwise takes some action, on its own initiative and for its own reasons, but which has a marked effect upon the low income country, either positively or negatively. A high income country might enact legislation to prohibit trade in endangered species of wildlife or in their products, as in fact the United States has recently done ; with a reduced market, exploitation of the resource in the country of origin becomes less profitable. Or an industrial country may develop a new product which replaces a former raw material, as has happened with artificial and natural rubber over the past generation, or as conceivably could happen with artificial and natural coffee in the future.

7.

The high income country might develop new techniques or new materials, for reasons of its own presumed self-interest ; but techniques of direct applicability in low income countries, which the latter could not develop on their own, and which have marked environmental impact when used in the low income countries. Many examples could be cited here — all chemicals, many kinds of machinery, many resource extraction or processing techniques, and others. The environmental impact in the low income country might be either adverse or positive, leading to either accelerated erosion or other environmental impact or permitting some reduction in an existing situation of environmental deterioration.

Ways in which high income countries affect environmental impact in low income countries

If a high income country wishes to affect environmental impact in a low income country, for whatever motives, what tools or means are open to it ? National sovereignties are involved ; while a rich and powerful country may exert many pressures on a poor one, yet the latter is independent and sovereign. Both legal and political considerations may limit action or affect the form of action. A number of mechanisms might be employed, singly or in various combinations, by means of which a high income country could affect environmental impacts in a low income country.

a) By means of education in all aspects of natural resource use, and by means of social science research, the high income country might help the low income country to analyze its economic and natural resource problems and to work out a more rational solution, within the frame of reference of the low income country and with its present technologies. Implicit in this method is an assumption that many low income countries do not now pursue their own self-interest rationally. Many conservationists have pointed to situations in which low income countries have embarked upon major river development projects, with inadequate consideration of their adverse effects upon the environment. A more careful analysis, with more careful calculation of costs and benefits, in environmental as well as in monetary terms, might well lead the low income countries to reject the development proposal in its entirety, or to take steps to reduce the adverse environmental effects, or to take measures to increase the positive results. The low income country could often point out that its mistakes, if any, had been in large part foisted upon it by foreign engineering firms, economic advisors, or others from outside, and that any help from richer countries in reducing environmental impact was mere restitution for an injury already inflicted. While this type of measure would be helpful in all of the situations of environmental influence of a high income country upon a low income country, previously discussed, it would be helpful in all of the situations of environmental influence of a high effect upon the high income country, of some resource exploitation program of the low income country, was low.

b) The foregoing shades into another type of situation, in which the high income country might help the low income country to develop some new technique of resource use, or to adapt to its conditions a technique developed elsewhere with the objective of minimizing environmental impact. Tropical African countries developed a system of land and soil management, based upon clearing the forest, farming for a few years, and allowing the area to grow back into forest; perhaps the best system that could have been devised to meet the conditions under which it actually developed, this system is under increasing pressure as increased population leads to shorter and shorter rotations. A wholly different approach to tropical soil management may be necessary, and some research done to date suggests that a much more intensive form of land use without serious erosion is possible. This is but one type of situation in which research financed and aided to a major degree from high income countries might be highly influential in reducing environmental impact in the low income countries. Similar illustrations could be found in the exploitation of tropical forests, or in mineral exploitation. In each case the essence of this type of example is that new research opens up new horizons.

c) The high income country might offer a subsidy to the low income country to enable or to induce it to employ some new measure or new materials, less harmful in its environmental impact than the present measure or measures. To use the DDT case again, a new insecticide specific to malarial mosquitoes might be developed but be much more costly than the DDT. High income countries, in their own self-interest, might subsidize the use of the substitute, if they are in fact convinced that widespread use of the DDT in low income countries is harmful to the citizens of the high income countries. Such subsidies could be applied rather easily, simply by making the new material available at a reduced price. The subsidy might take the form of a capital grant to enable the low income country to develop a production capacity; or it might take the form of a current input as in the case of the reduced price; it might be for a short period of time until the low income country was able to carry out its own program, or it might be more or less indefinitely. This type of action by a high income country would apply particularly to the kind of situation described in item 5 above, wherein the low income country was pursuing a course of action likely to be directly harmful to the residents of the high income country.

d) The high income country might extend a subsidy to the low income country, as a sovereignty, or to some of its citizens, to persuade it or them to modify some production process which has unfavorable environmental impact. The type of action suggested here is concerned with some method of operation in contrast to some use of material, as suggested in the foregoing illustration. It is also limited to some known methodology, as contrasted to the research possibility outlined previously. But it bears some resemblance to each of these earlier examples. The methodology of resource use which it was desired to modify might be one which had adverse effects on the high income country, or it might also include those which the high income country deplored but did not suffer from directly. In general, one may expect that continuing subsidies to modify production methodology would be hard to enforce, to supervise, and even to monitor ; the high income country might easily find itself paying for practices that were not performed, or practices that would be carried out without a subsidy. One can imagine that measures of this type would find far less acceptance in low income countries than would, for example, subsidies to the price of some substitute production materials, as discussed above. The United States did extend large subsidies to Mexico to enable it to eradicate foot-and-mouth disease in cattle ; but the Mexican cattle producers were eager to get back into the American market and accepted help — and the attendant actions and controls — as a means to that end.

e) The high income country might exercise some control over capital flow to the low income country for some end of reduced environmental impact. This control over capital flow could be either to restrict capital movements where undesirable environmental impact seems imminent, or to stimulate them to produce some action designed to reduce environmental impact. A single rich country could exercise some control over capital flow ; a consortium of rich countries could exercise more control ; and they, in conjunction with international or interregional lending institutions, could exercise still more control over capital flows. The controls might extend to terms of projects, as well as to volumes of capital. It is noteworthy that the World Bank has added an ecology department to appraise the ecological consequences of proposed loans. Even a single country could be influential, even if the low income country obtained capital elsewhere. Loans to permit economic use of previously flared natural gas would be one illustration of stimulation of capital flows to reduce environmental impact of wastage ; refusal to make loans for river development projects which seemed likely to create serious adverse environmental impacts would be an example of the use of credit restriction.

f) The high income country or countries might exercise control over trade from the low income country or countries, as a means of reducing unfavorable environmental impact in the latter. For instance, the high income countries could refuse to admit importation of live animals or of products from animals of endangered species ; as noted, the United States has recently taken some steps in this direction. Or the United States might refuse permission to land to any SST, thus removing much of the economic support for such aircraft in any country. Or a consortium of high income countries might make a concerted drive against the importation of opium. As the latter example suggests, trade restrictions are not always fully effective but in some cases they might be decisive. The legality of imposing trade restrictions is high but the politics are less firm.

g) High income countries might exercise some controls over their domestic firms, in ways that would reduce environmental impact in low income countries or elswhere. For instance, the United States might put stiff requirements on control over oil spills or discharges at sea, as a condition of operation of any petroleum company in the United States. Or domestic firms could be required to stay out of some lines of resource exploitation, or to engage in some line of environmental protection in low income countries as a condition to operations on the domestic scene. There may well be legal problems here as to how far courts would uphold such measures ; political problems, or how far legislatures would go in imposing such controls, may be far more important ; and enforcement problems would surely be difficult. Nevertheless, high income countries cannot evade some responsibility for how their companies act abroad any more than a mother can avoid some responsibility for how her children act at the neighbor's house.

h) Lastly, high income countries may enter into, and stimulate, treaties, agreements, and conventions about resource use designed to reduce environmental impacts. The history of such efforts to date does not lead to much optimism. It is hard to get all the countries most directly involved, both rich and poor, to join ; it is still harder to get them to fulfill their obligations or to take effective action. If one or more countries does not fulfill its obligations, the others are unwilling or unable to force it to do so, in many cases, and the whole enterprise shortly breaks down. Conventions about fisheries and the hunting of whales have had a notable record of nonperformance ; is there reason to believe that treaties or conventions about use of DDT or other chemicals or about atmospheric pollution on a world-wide scale would fare any better? Nevertheless, treaties and conventions may be useful especially if backed up by some of the measures previously discussed.

Ways in which poor countries might affect the environmental impact of actions taken by rich countries

What can the poor countries do to reduce the environmental impact upon themselves of actions taken by the rich countries? We shall not consider the actions poor countries might take to reduce environmental impacts within the rich countries; while this range of actions has logical similarities to the foregoing measures that rich countries might take to influence impacts within the low income countries, in practice the interest and influence of the low income countries upon situations in the high income countries is low. A number of measures are, at least in theory, open to the low income countries to protect themselves.

They can establish, by law and administration, the conditions on which their natural resources can be exploited to provide commodities to sell to the high income countries. This could apply to the exploitation of oil and gas resources, to harvest of products, to the mining of metals, to the production and trade in agricultural commodities, and to others. The low income country could establish what is permissible, and what is not, in methods of resource development and utilization. They could explicitly deal with air and water pollution, with erosion and forest degradation, and similar matters.

The low income countries can forbid or regulate the import of materials, especially chemicals, that might have a deleterious effect upon their natural environment. This could be an absolute prohibition, or the establishment of conditions unnder which imports could be made and materials used.

The low income countries could prohibit the export of specified raw materials, if these were deemed essential to national well-being. While such actions have been uncommon for natural resources, they have been applied (often with inadequate effect) upon export of cultural objects.

The problems of the low income countries, in trying to protect themselves against environmental impacts arising out of the actions of rich countries (or their citizens and firms) are only partly legal. Political pressures from the rich countries may make it impossible for the poor countries to use the legal powers they have. The low income countries have little economic power to affect the actions of the richer countries — indeed, "rich" and "poor" largely mean this. The low income countries surely cannot threaten to withhold their capital from use in high income countries, in the way that the latter can do. Only by concerted action among low income countries would it be possible to withhold natural resources from the higher income countries, in any bargaining struggle. While some modest successes have been attained by the oil-producing countries in the past year, one may doubt if such concerted action is likely to be adhered to over a long run. For one thing, the poor countries are ambivalent; they want better bargains from the richer countries, but they also want trade and the monetary gains arising therefrom. There are diverse interests within each low income country, that reduce its capacity to use what limited bargaining power it may have, vis-à-vis the richer countries.

The best mechanism the poor countries possess, in their dealings with the richer countries, may well be the international organizations — the UN and its various branches. Such international organizations give the low income countries a platform from which they can criticize, cajole, and implore the richer countries to take lines of action more favorable to the low income countries. Sometimes they can get some action in this forum — not often perhaps, and less than they would like, and yet perhaps more than they could get in any other way. After all, even the most powerful nations are sensitive to world public opinion.

But it may greatly be doubted if the poorer countries will choose more environmental protection, if they succeed in winning any concessions from the richer countries; they may well prefer better terms of trade in the markets, or greater economic investments, or some other relationship which will favor economic development more than it would favor environmental protection. The poor countries are, largely by definition, weak economically; and their choices are more likely to be for economic development than for environmental preservation.

International competition and environmental prospects

But the choice for economic development, instead of for environmental protection, may not be limited to the poorer countries. Any nation whether rich or poor, which embarks upon a program of environmental protection, raises the apparent cost of materials for domestic use and for export. We say "apparent costs", because it may simply be making the market price reflect more or all of the real costs of production, some of which had previously been evaded by the producers. Nevertheless, the market prices of raw materials will increase if effective environmental controls are established. The extent of the increase may be less than often assumed — more likely in the range of 1 to 10 percent, than higher. Market price increases will surely affect the money costs of production within the country, and the money price of export commodities.

Will either rich or poor countries willingly undertake environmental programs which will raise the money prices of their raw materials? The rich nations may fear that their rich rivals will pass them up, if they do so ; Japan, the United States, the USSR, and other countries are clearly in this general situation. But the poor nations may fear loss of their export markets ; if the cost of their iron ore, or their copper, or their oil, or their forest products rise, will they be able to retain their export markets ?

A similar problem is faced within every country, as regions or localities or firms seek to compete for the national market for raw materials. In the United States, there are severe limitations on the laws and programs that a single state may adopt ; if too stringent, these may well drive business elsewhere, with consequent economic loss. Within a single nation, this situation may be met by having the national government pass laws and establish standards, thus raising the whole plane of competition within the country. With effective national standards, no firm can play one state or one locality against another, seeking more lenient environmental protection. But there is nothing comparable at the international level ; the UN is not a world government in this sense, nor is it likely ever to be. One cannot but be pessimistic about the prospects for world-wide action on environmental problems, even those with global ill effects.

ELIZABETH WHITCOMBE

Development projets and environmental disruption: The case of Uttar Pradesh, India

The current concern, in the western world, with environmental disruption in the context of economic planning, focusses largely on the impact of industrial development — the expansion of a vast and long-established industrial base — on the resources of the biosphere and the mechanisms which create and preserve them. Attempts to promote world-wide discussion preparatory to action on these issues have, predictably, met with less enthusiasm in those countries whose economic structure is primarily characterized by a crippling dependence on agriculture as prime source of wealth and employment. Recommendations to restrict industrial expansion on the grounds of a necessity to conserve dwindling natural resources and as a defense against increased pollution can be interpreted by the poorer countries of the world as a device to slow down their national and potentially competitive industrial programmes. Such programmes are legitimately seen as the remedy for the present over-reliance on an impoverished agricultural base underlying the economic predicaments of these countries. In this respect, the by-products of industrial growth, *viz.* environmental pollution, ecological disorders and a gradual depletion of certain natural resources would seem a small, and acceptable, price to pay for the relief of current levels of poverty. Further, the hue and cry raised recently in the west over environmental issues has done little to encourage a balanced assessment of the relative capacity of the physical mechanisms of the biosphere to adjust to new demands: in short, to construct a scale by which degrees of environmental disruption may clearly be categorized according to capacity and rate of reversibility and reparability, in the interests of economic planning.

The world's poor countries are nonetheless faced with a major environmental problem in the consequences of inevitable technological innovation in agriculture. This has its counterparts in the west also, but owing to the relatively minor dependence in modern times on agriculture, such consequences have till recently been considered economically insignificant. But the ecosystems predominating in the world's poorer regions are primarily characterized by precariousness. Disturbance of them frequently involves rapid decline in productivity. All agricultural development even if ancillary to industrial expansion, demands technological innovation just as industry does, and must disturb ecological balances which ruled prior to innovation. The problem of economic planning for a continuing optimal use of agricultural resources to relieve, in the first instance, the disparity between population growth and the increase in food production, is to design techniques which can raise levels of production and, at the same time, compensate for their impact on those areas of the agricultural environment where neglect of the consequences of innovation would seriously limit the realization of planners' aims. The environmental problem is therefore as central in these areas to economic planning as it has been to their agrarian history to date. Fundamental physical constraints must be accounted for and scales constructed of their relative significance in relation to the range of risks to which farmers of various economic categories may be exposed in their adoption of new techniques.

Northern India offers a "natural laboratory" for the detailed examination, over a precise time-scale from the mid-19th century to date, of successive innovations introduced piecemeal, in accordance with a policy of maximization, into the world of monsoon agriculture. The history of these innovations and their more pronounced physical and economic consequences is well documented in the records kept by the British Indian government in its several departments. An analysis first of the 19th and early 20th century background and second, of the post-Independence innovations may prove helpful in providing a framework for the estimation of a scale of relative costs involved in the application of certain techniques aimed at intensification in such a set of agrarian conditions, and for marking out areas where compensatory measures are demanded to prevent the persistent limiting of levels of production below optimal standards. The present paper offers a preliminary outline for such an analysis.

"Most certainly the question, are we making the most out of the land, must be answered in the negative; [...] because the land itself yields nothing like what it should."[1] Forming his conclusions thus in 1879 on the state of Indian agriculture, Allan Octavian Hume — the founder of the Indian National Congress — drew not merely on his nine years' experience as secretary to British India's newly-formed Department of Agriculture. Hume had earlier accumulated, in the course of his career in the revenue administration — as magistrate and collector of several districts, most notably Etawah, of the North-Western Provinces (which, with Oudh formed the United Provinces, now Uttar Pradesh) — a store of observations on agrarian principles and practices of the Doab. It was clear to Hume that the primary fault of persistently, and increasingly, poor agricultural performance was not to be laid at the farmer's door. On the contrary, " it is due to the patient, frugal

1. A.O. Hume, *Agricultural reform in India*, London-Madras, 1899, p. 4.

and not unintelligent husbandmen of India to admit freely that, looking to the conditions under which they labour, their ignorance of scientific method, their want of capital (and all that capital enables a farmer to command), the crops they do produce are, on the whole, surprising..."[2] The root cause lay rather in the state to which the soil had been reduced, in the fact that "agriculture in India has become, and becomes daily, more and more, what Liebig happily designated a system of spoliation"[3]. Low yields were the index of a declining productivity — for which not only the cause, but also the remedy, was immediately clear: "With proper manuring and proper tillage, every acre, broadly speaking, of land in the country can be made to yield 30, 50, 70 percent (according to circumstances) more of every kind of crop than it at present produces, and this with a fully corresponding increase in the profits of cultivation."[4] This was the essential beginning. Other improvements must necessarily follow in co-ordination: the arrest of the processes of salination and the reclamation of the already vast tracts of salt land; judicious, small-scale mechanization; the relief of peasant indebtedness and the provision of comprehensive public credit for agricultural purposes.

Hume's recommendations as to the urgent improvement of agrarian conditions had been rapeatedly shelved through the opposition and in favour of the prior concerns of the Department of Agriculture's two senior partners, Revenue and Commerce. In the North-Western Provinces, large-scale irrigation schemes progressed throughout the second half of the 19th century to cover all but the eastern Doab with a network of canals, stimulating the cultivation of soil-exhausting commercial crops — indigo, cotton, sugar-cane, wheat — but the provision of nutriment for the soil, in the form of organic or inorganic fertilizer, was nowhere organized in co-ordination. Irrigation was the preserve of the canal department, the senior technical service of Government; agriculture, a newcomer to the bureaucratic scene, had never the means to carry out schemes for comprehensive improvement which fell within its purview. Proposals for the relief of scarcity in organic manures by the selection of areas for fuel and fodder reserves were rejected by the revenue administration as impractical. The manufacture of chemical fertilizers from the saline-alkali deposits in central and east districts of both the North-Western Provinces and Oudh (a symptom of severe ecological malaise) was effectively prevented by the Salt Tax levied by the excise. For the first decades of the 20th century, agricultural developments tended to follow rigidly the lines laid down by their 19th century antecedents: the building of the Sarda Canal, the formation of the sugar-cane agro-industry around the staple commercial crop of the Provinces, small-scale improvements in agricultural machinery and varietal experiments (chiefly on export staples). By the early 30's a significant

2. *Ibid.*
3. *Ibid.*, p. 24.
4. *Ibid.*, p. 20.

advance had been achieved in what is now known as minor irrigation: Sir William Stamp's pioneering tube-wells first developed in the field in parts of the (highly productive) Meerut division. The application of chemical fertilizer, in the form of (imported) ammonium sulphate, barely passed the experimental stage. It was not until 1946-1947 when A.B. Stewart conducted his balanced-dressing experiments with phosphatic and potassic as well as nitrogenous fertilizer on selected cultivators' fields in Kanpur district that the essential chemical components for the improvement of the fertility status of the soil were established. It remained to co-ordinate these with irrigation and to develop at the same time crop strains which would ensure higher and better quality yields. The 50's saw considerable activity along these lines in the established agricultural institutions — most notably the Kanpur College, now the Institute of Agricultural Sciences. But, as in Hume's day so in the days of his successors in the Congress, the selection of priorities reinforced by budgetary restrictions prevented both large-scale experimentation and adequate diffusion of improved techniques. This position was dramatically changed by the end of the decade. Programmes for the 60's, for intensive agricultural district and area development (IADP and IAAP) heralded by the establishment of agricultural universities on the model of US land-grant colleges with sister relationships to their US counterparts, marked the reversal of priorities for planning for industry in favour of agriculture. These schemes, based on an all-round, "package" of practices — fertilizer, irrigation, plant protection — have culminated in the High-Yielding Varieties Programme, in operation in UP since 1966-1967, based on the dissemination of exotic dwarf wheats and rices. Here at last were the co-ordinated improvements for soil and for seed required for planned agricultural development [5].

The selection of the Tarai and, more precisely, of the 3 000 acre Government farm near Rudrapur as the site for the UP Agricultural University and the focal point for the dissemination of the new intensive agriculture programmes in co-ordination with the Indian Council for Agricultural Research and the State Department of Agriculture, was apposite. The fertility status of Tarai soil, newly reclaimed (between 1946 and 1952) from jungle and malarial swamp, is the highest in the state. The groundwater reservoir of the region, fed directly through the gravel beds of the Bhabar tract to the north from runoff from the Siwaliks and ultimately the Himalayas, has been assumed to be virtually inexhaustible. The high water-retention capacity of the soil is a function of its rich clay-mineral component. These conditions have been fully exploited by the new agricultural strategy in a consistent drive to maximize high-yielding acreage and high per acre yields in the region. Investment in agriculture has tended, predictably enough, to flow most freely where risks are least: the typical Tarai farm, of a minimum of several hundred acres

5. See in appendix the table of sample expenditure on agriculture in the 19th and 20th centuries.

under co-operative registration, represents in its combination of abundant natural resources and private capital the ideal in creditworthiness, a fact appreciated not merely by the Reserve Bank's Agricultural Refinance Corporation, the State Bank of India, and numerous commercial banks but by the World Bank also, as exemplified by its assistance to the newly-formed Tarai Development Corporation. Agricultural performance in the Tarai to date has justified expectations: by following recommended mono-cultural practices to maximize potential productivity for wheat, regular applications of 140-160 lb. nitrogenous fertilizer per acre, plus 80-100 lb./acre each of superphosphate and muriate of potash; five, six or even seven regular irrigations at precise, optimum timings in the life-cycle, objectives of aggregate rice and wheat yields of 100 quintals/hectare over a single, two-harvest agricultural year are not unreasonable.

How far can this pattern be followed in the greater part of the 48 000 000 acres which make up the cultivated area of UP? How adaptable is the new pattern of monoculture proving to the complex disparities which form the present-day geomorphology of the alluvial plains? A more modest version of wholehearted response to the stimulus of the new agricultural strategy is to be found in the north-western uplands of the Meerut and upper Rohilkhand divisions: the home of UP's agricultural aristocracy, as distinct from the pioneering *nouveaux riches* of the Tarai. Uplands-Meerut cultivation and Jat cultivators were a by-word for agricultural prosperity in Moghul times; their sugar-cane and wheat production aroused the admiration of the first British administrators. Large-scale canal-irrigation, an innovation which became the basis of modern Indian agriculture, was first introduced into the Meerut districts in the early 1830's (the East Jumna canal system). The object of irrigation, then as now, was to maximize production and its profits; the stimulus it provided to the cultivation of sugar-cane and wheat in the region satisfied that objective. The tradition of such cultivation — the proportions under each crop varying in accordance with market conditions — has persisted to the present day, with concomitant facilities: abundant irrigation from both canals and tube-wells; public credit distributed through cane as well as regular co-operative societies; a competitive market for sugar-cane ranging upwards from village-level refineries to sugar-factories; a proportionately greater mileage of tarred and concrete-track roads than in other UP districts; rubber-tyred "Dunlop" carts. Fundamentally, these uplands regions have a distinct geomorphological advantage: natural drainage is for the most part adequate, and the permeability coefficient of the soil such as to ensure downward percolation of moisture at a fairly uniform rate. But to the south of the Meerut division, where the uplands proper merge with the central and lower Doab drainage basin, the dominant problems of the UP plains become increasingly evident. In south Meerut and south-west Bulandshahr the general gradient of the land slopes off, in the central Doab, to less than a foot per mile, with long shallow depressions, at irregular intervals. During the rabi (winter-spring) season, dark-green Mexican wheat fields stand out against ragged patches of grey-white, waterlogged and saline soil — varying in size from a few square feet to vast tracts of 1 000 or more acres barely covered at intervals with stunted, vestigial monsoon grasses: the product of defective and impeded drainage. From the north-west through to the south-east, the proportions of green to grey-white — a contrast seen at its most stark in February-March, when there is least residual moisture in the soil — indicate the extremes in fertility: the ratio of highy productive to severely deteriorated land. In the mid-Doab basin, the central tracts of Aligarh, Etah, Mathura, Mainpuri, Farukhabad, Etawah, Kanpur, Unnao and Fatehpur districts, the indices of soil disease intensify (Etah and Mainpuri alone have each between 200 000 and 300 000 saline-alkali acres) and the contrasts of rich against poor land become even more pronounced. Farukhabad, for example, boasts of the most intensively cultivated area in India — a market-gardening tract, on the lip of the Ganges uplands some two miles in radius from the cities of Farukhabad-Fategarh, which produces a minimum of three, frequently four and in some fields five, garden crops per year (rotations of potatoes, tobacco, vegetables, maize and wheat); beyond it lie vast grey expanses, dotted with clumps of cereal crops where irrigation by private tube-wells, installed on the security or with the profits of intensively cultivated parts of a holding, is making it increasingly possible to wash down the toxic accumulations of salts from the root-zone to an extent where paddy tolerant of moderate salinity can be cultivated. Such marginal reclamation is characteristic of land on the fringe of the central drainage basin. The vast saline tracts in the heart of the basin — moving east and south from Farukhabad — present a more complex problem. Vertical drainage is frequently impeded by the presence of an indurated layer or hardpan at varying depths (sometimes as close as two to three feet to the surface); the groundwater of upper aquifers may itself be alkaline, a fact which prevents its use as a reclamative (leaching) agent and restricts its irrigation utility to alkaline-tolerant crops — marginally, tobacco and certain varieties of paddy: Mathura district is singularly afflicted with a problem of brackish water. These complex problems proliferate in the eastern regions of the state, between the Ganges and the Gogra rivers. In addition, their supply of irrigation water is severely limited not merely by the intermittent occurrence of impervious strata in the soil profile, which can make well- and tube-well boring difficult (and therefore expensive) or even impossible, but also by the fact that these areas are served only by the tail ends of the Sarda Canal system and small-scale pump canals from the Ganges: these barely cope with the demands of the prosperous pockets, demands which are steadily rising as the new agricultural strategy progresses. In the central portion of this Ganges-Gogra Doab, alkalinity culminates not merely in vast expanses but also in intensity: pH readings of 11 to 12 (9-9.5 is already severely toxic) are recorded for parts of Azamgarh and Ghazipur districts. Beyond the Gogra, to the north, salinity is virtually absent. The problem of waterlogging occurs there as a consequence of heavy clay soils, of low permeability and high water-retention capacity (one-crop-per-year soils) and of inundations in areas adjacent to the great, shallow-bed, braided rivers of the north, the courses of which remain unfixed, altering according to the volume of monsoon precipitation. To the south of the state, comes the other extreme: as dry as the north-east is wet. The proverbial light soils and surface rock formations of Bundelkhand are also accompanied by impervious strata at intervals through the profile and irregularly distributed, often confined, aquifers which, if they can be tapped, yield very limited amounts of groundwater. Traditionally, agriculture in the region — a form of shifting cultivation for the most part — is fed in the cool season off rainwater stored in tanks or in pockets of thick black clay soil, sown once a year with a mixture of winter cereals and pulses when the rainwater has seeped below surface level.

In this environment, a pattern of both large-scale and minute disparities in fundamental soil and water conditions, ecological problems increase in frequency and magnitude as one descends from the northwest to the south-east. At the furthest extremities to the east and south of UP, these problems are seen in their most severe form, in sterile soil and unusable or inaccessible water. Vast tracts so affected — approximately two thirds of district Azamgarh, for example, is significantly to severely alkaline — are ringed by patchy cultivation, indicating that the condition is spreading, whilst resources in keeping with the state-level irrigation-intensive agricultural strategy must necessarily be concentrated on relatively confined pockets of prosperity — again, sugar-cane and wheat areas principally, followed by good, irrigated uplands soils sustaining millets or paddy and wheat rotations. Other, predominantly institutional problems have tended to follow the geomorphological pattern: the impact of population growth, for example, is most severely evident in the declining areas of east UP — densities of more than 1 100 persons per square mile being recorded in Ghazipur, Azamgarh and Ballia tehsils at the 1961 census. The combination of land reforms (the redefinition rather than redistribution of proprietary title) and mortgage laws have channelled recent investment in agriculture into immediately productive areas, from which a tiny minority of the land and the population dependent on it can benefit: disproportion in favour, on the one hand, of north/west as against south/east and, on the other, of productive as against problem areas within individual districts is striking even on the most casual observation.

This observation itself becomes more meaningful if we enquire into the cause of the physical disparities. They are not so much the indices of enterprise as against backwardness, but the result of geomorphological processes exacerbated by the introduction of public works in the 19th century — not a condition of stagnation, betraying a lack of capacity for change, but the dynamic consequences (for the processes set more rapidly on foot in the 19th century persist with their intensified momentum) of modernization. The deforestation which accompanied the construction of the railway networks throughout UP over the greater part of the century, intensifying from *ca* 1860 onwards, stripped off greater quantities of alkaline-tolerant, water-absorbent *dhak* jungle (*butea frondosa*) more rapidly than the slow expansion of agriculture. The increase in rates of evaporation and sub-soil capillarity which resulted provided sufficient pre-conditions for the accumulation of alkali salts in the upper layers of the soil. Erosion, particularly severe in undulating Bundelkhand and along the myriads of river catchments, minor tributaries of the Ganges, which intersect the eastern districts, was increased — a process which continues to strip off top-soil, exposing nobbly calcareous rubble in its place. Obstruction to natural drainage lines by road and railway embankments insufficiently provided with culverts increased the susceptibility of low-lying tracts to waterlogging. But the most complex and far-reaching distortions arose from the introduction of the essence of agricultural modernization, large-scale irrigation by canals.

The construction of the great canal systems tapping the Jumna and Ganges (on the model of smaller systems developed in Italy, France and to a much lesser extent, England) from the 1830's and 1840's was promoted according to the principle of maximization of production: areas of guaranteed, and potential, high productivity (that is to say, the north-west) suggested, by reason of their geographical advantages and celebrated agriculture, their selection as the recipients of large-scale investment promising an immediate return. The introduction of canal-irrigation dates the beginning of modern Indian agriculture. It brought in its wake northern India's first "green revolution". In the canal-tracts of the Meerut and Agra divisions, crop-patterns were substantially changed in the years immediately following the opening of canal branches: the old patterns of small-scale, well-irrigation "poly-culture" gave way to block-cropping of kharif (autumn) commercial crops (indigo and cotton, *e.g.*), sugar-cane and the rabi export staple, wheat. Millets and pulses were partially displaced and the wells themselves which had regulated, by labour intensive methods, the supply of water to the soil, were superseded and in many cases demolished by the inroad of the canals. The best tracts of central north-west uplands could withstand most of the pressures exerted by the sudden change, though the danger of overcropping was early manifest — in the 1860's — and the lack of restoration of nutriment to the hungry soil a matter of public debate in consequence. Further down, in the great central region we have described above, the consequences of canal-irrigation in terms of a radical distortion of the delicate mechanism of the hydrological cycle were early observed: embankment obstruction in low-lying areas combined both with lateral seepage through the (unlined) canal walls, while flush-irrigation at surface flooded the soil with more water than could be drained horizontally or vertically. Evaporation rates heightened by deforestation drew up subsoil water in which alkali salts, previously dispersed through the profile, rose in solution to accumulate in toxic quantities in the root zone and, in their dehydrated crystalline form, in the saline efflorescence on the surface, known as *reh.* In 1879, a year after the first governmental enquiry into salinity in the North-Western Provinces and Punjab and twenty years after the first detailed reports accompanied by chemical analyses of saline deteriorations on lands irrigated by the Western Jumna Canal, A.O.Hume spoke in no uncertain terms of the progressive problems of canal tracts:

"At first the result may be good, and marvellous are the crops that have been raised in the Doab on the first introduction of canal irrigation, owing to the first slender doses of potash and chloride of sodium [...].

Time passes on, some crops begin to be unprofitable; in the hottest time of the year, a glimmer as though of a hoar frost overspreads the land. The land grows worse and worse, but ever night and day nature works slowly on, and the time comes when, abandoned by the cultivator, the land glitters white and waste as though thickly strewn with crisp, new-fallen snow; never alas! to melt away, except under the rays of science.

Along the little old Western Jumna Canal, thousands of fields are to be seen thus sterilized. Along the course of the mighty Ganges Canal — a work as it were but of yesterday (opened, 1854) — the dreary wintry-looking rime is already in many places creeping over the soil.

Come it quickly or come it slowly, the ultimate result here is also certain; and, unless a radical change is effected in existing arrangements, we know, as definitely as we know that the sun will rise tomorrow, that the time must come when some of the richest arable tracts in Northern India will have become howling saline deserts." [6]

By 1891, the first agricultural chemist to tour India reported some 2 000 000-3 000 000 acres of saline soil in the north-west alone. Nothing more than the most peripheral experiments was done in the interests of organized reclamation. In 1926, the first branches of the Sarda Canal — a slight modification of the original 1872-1878 design — were opened, to serve eastern Rohilkhand, central, southern and "fringe"-eastern Oudh. Saline-alkali tracts throughout modern UP may be conservatively estimated to cover between 6 000 000 and 7 000 000 acres: the district of Unnao alone, where hundreds of thousands of low-lying acres are criss-crossed by the Sarda system, has already the maximum affected area, in proportion to irrigated acreage, for the state [7].

UP's second "green revolution" has proceeded on principles not dissimilar to the first; maximization of guaranteed and immediate productivity by means of irrigation-intensive techniques. One might interpolate here that the fertilizer factor, so prominent a part of the new agricultural strategy, surely marks a fundamental break with the past. Is this really so, however, if we consider that the recommended fertilizer inputs are those demanded by the new, high-

6. Hume, *op. cit.*, p. 25.

7. An account of technological innovation in agriculture, its physical, economic and legal consequences in late 19th century Uttar Pradesh (United Provinces) appears in E. Whitcombe, *Agrarian conditions in Northern India*, vol. 1 : *The United Provinces under British rule, 1860-1900*, Berkeley, Calif., 1971, chap. ii.

yielding varieties for immediate growth? One may query any long term benefit to the soil, especially when it is remembered that soils in high temperature zones have a chronic incapacity to store nitrogen. Substantial amendment of declining fertility in the soil — for example, in areas bordering on the intensely productive tracts and marginally affected by salt-accumulation or erosion — can hardly be achieved by inorganic fertilizer. Abandonment and, in many instances known to the present writer, official discouragement of the use of organic manures raises the question, how are the mechanical properties of alluvium to be sustained, and, for example, their water retentiveness strengthened? Further, the range of chemical treatments available through public supply channels includes no neutralizing amendments — for example calcium sulphate (gypsum) — for the rectification of salinity and alkalinity.

The crucial element of the new planned strategy, as of the old pattern of piecemeal modernization, is irrigation: the new, high-yielding varieties — exotic paddy and wheat, and the hybrid maizes and millets which form subsidiary programmes — are thirsty: the cost of their adaptation to the soils of the high-temperature zones of India is not merely to be measured in multiples of the recommended doses of nitrogen, phosphorus and potassium (NPK) fertilizer (at the current rate of 120-80-80 lb./acre) but in the amount of irrigation water required both to dissolve fertilizer for plant uptake and to sustain, by regular waterings at precise points in the life-cycle, the amount of vegetative growth of the high-yielding varieties. This, by virtue of their capacity to absorb at least twice the amount of nitrogen which local and improved indigenous strains can take, means a water-demand at least double that of indigenous and local improved cereals: in the case of wheat, five to six irrigations are recommended, as against two to three for local varieties.

The first fertilizer recommendations, calculated not on the basis of optimal requirement but of estimated available supply (in 1965-1966), were pitched at the modest level of 60-40-40 lb./acre NPK. By 1969-1970, this had doubled, as fertilizer manufacture has expanded to allow more precise tailoring of recommendations. But whilst it is generally admitted that the optimal doses in relation to varying soil conditions are still not established (either by the all-India coordinated fertilizer experiments on research farms and cultivators' fields or by the routine soil-sampling conducted by regional research stations on samples sent in by the National Extension Service village-level workers), it is clear that only the top-income group of "progressive farmers" (cultivators participating in the new strategy, selected initially on the basis of access to guaranteed irrigation facilities) apply fertilizer according to recommendation; a minority of large-scale farmers amongst these regularly exceed the recommendations, to the extent of 180 or even 200 lb./acre N (with proportionately increased PK basal dressings), in the interests especially of high-yielding seed production. Supposing, then, that top-productivity demands remain at this level, that the number of participants in high-yielding varieties (HYV) programmes increase — even to the extent of an additional .01 percent, bringing a few more thousand acres under increasingly intensive cultivation — and that the general level of fertilizer application rises whilst a greater acreage is brought under the programme as irrigation facilities are developed: the question then arises, can the water demands be met?

The net irrigated area of UP in 1966-1967 is officially recorded at 15 381 546 acres (the net area sown in that year being 41 247 853 acres). The development of, particularly, minor irrigation (chiefly private 4″-delivery tube-wells), to date has added several lakh acres to the total irrigated area: figures are not yet available. The total acreage represents an all-source aggregate, calculated in terms of command areas of the various installations. In 1966-1967, canals accounted for the largest irrigated acreage — 5 890 445 — with wells other than State or private tube-wells a close second, command 5 320 128 acres. The tube-well area was recorded at 2 755 462 acres in 1966-1967 and may well have passed the 3 000 000 mark to date. Assuming these figures to give an approximate estimate of command (that is, irrigable) area, questions arise as to the estimate of acreage actually irrigated, in the context of the new agricultural strategy.

In both the Ganges-Jumna and the Sarda canal systems, the water supply — drawn direct from the great rivers — is a function of annual monsoon precipitation: a shortfall means a reduction in irrigation water available for the following rabi season. As a consequence of the drought which coincided with the first two — and in the case of east UP, three — years of the new agricultural strategy, supply decreased at the same time as demand increased in accordance with the propagation of new techniques. A fundamental problem of regional distribution of irrigation water was aggravated: in the tail-ends of the canals, commanding central and south-western Doab districts, a persistently defective supply was reduced, in the drought, to nothing. In the upper reaches, sufficient water for a minimum of two, maximum three, irrigations has been mostly available — on main branches and distributaries: complaints of water shortage in minors even in Meerut and Bulandshahr divisions — was widespread. The maximum supply legally available does not however come up to full High-Yielding Varieties Programme (HVP) recommendations — cases are frequently reported locally of water-thefts, said to be committed by "progressive farmers" anxious to ensure maximum yields, whose only source of irrigation is the canal. Further, the traditional (since mid-19th century) roster system of distribution is not geared to the precise requirements of the HVP schedule: the new varieties' sensitivity demands irrigation at specific points in the life-cycle. Complaints, therefore, as to the uncertainty of canal-supply are increasing — and, predictably, water-thefts again on account of the inadequacies of the roster system. Beyond these immediate problems, arising from the subjection of an old irrigation network to new demands, the now historic manifestations of irrigation-induced hydrological imbalance — waterlogging and salinity — persist.

The groundwater reservoir seems to offer a more stable alternative for exploitation. Tube-wells, first developed by Sir William Stamp in the Meerut area in the early 1930's, are synonymous with "assured irrigation", the prime requirement for "progressive farming". State tube-wells are constructed and administered by a subsidiary office of the Canal Department, still the senior technical service of the State. They are generally of 6″ delivery, tapping aquifers at a depth of 180′ and below with a capacity of *ca* 36 000 gallons/hour. In accordance with the established (commercial) policy of the Canal Department, State tube-wells are sited in level uplands, readily irrigable areas, commanding a maximum rabi acreage (ensuring maximum revenue in water-rates). Initially, commands were fixed at 600 acres per tube-well — a figure which early proved impracticable, cultivators beyond the 200-acre periphery being provided with perhaps one irrigation in three or even four weeks. In 1969-1970, the command was finally reduced from a temporary 400-acres area to 200-acres. Policy has already led to a heavy concentration of State tube-wells in the immediately productive areas: as late as October 1969, Pratapgarh district, a predominantly kharif area, with at least 100 000 acres of highly salinized soil and much riverine erosion, had one State tube-well; Farukhabad tube-well division, on the other hand, numbered 311: by February 1969 a single sub-division of sandy-loam uplands accounted for 78 of these. The operation of State tube-wells has however proved frequently irregular: electricity cuts, mechanical faults and "mischief" by the operators themselves being the most general complaints. These, and the excessive areas fixed as commands, added to the stimulus provided by the inadequacies or absence of canal-irrigation allied with the demands — and prospects — of the IADP, the IAAP and now the HVP to exploit the upper aquifers (at varying depths of *ca* 20′-80′) by means of tube-wells of 3″-4″ delivery, privately owned and operated.

The degree of control which might be exercised by Government over private tube-well development in the interests of planned agriculture is, a priori, limited. No comprehensive hydrological survey of groundwater resources as yet exists, and therefore no detailed calculations of safe limit (for withdrawal) or of safe distance (for spacing between installations) to avoid excessive demand on the groundwater reservoir can be made: locally, approximate calculations are made on general analogies with neighbouring or apparently similar regions (in Pilibhit Tarai, figures from the partly similar area of Najibabad in Bijnour were used as the basis for safe-limit estimates). Even where such calculations have been made on the basis of pumping tests and hydrogeological investigations, no legislation exists which might be used to enforce them to assist planning. The only restriction on private-tube-well enterprise is the prohibition — amounting to an injunction against the infringement of departmental rights — against granting electric supply to tube-wells installed within 200 yards of a canal line: a measure designed to prevent the increase of lateral percolation by tube-well suction within such proximity and to protect canal department rights to water-sales. Diesel tube-wells can however be operated with impunity, though at greater cost in maintenance to the owner. General costs of tube-well installation are financed either by private capital (as predominantly in the Tarai) or, most commonly, by public credit distributed according to private creditworthiness: mortgageable title to land. Hydroelectric power provides the chief source of motor-power. In the interests of reducing costs of electrification on Government account, one furlong of free line is allowed per tube-well. The Hydel Department, which rules over energization independently from the minor irrigation department of the food and agriculture ministry (co-ordinated at district planning-office level), encourages clustering of tube-wells within the smallest feasible radius. A vegetable, wheat and sugar-cane producing village, for example, of 600 acres cultivated area some two and a half miles from Etawah commanded, in October 1969, no less than 44 minor irrigation installations, including 26 private tube-wells each with an irrigating capacity of *ca* 20 acres. Taking the existing developed areas, where clusters of tube-wells have been in operation at least since the introduction of HVP, as a model for present and future development, can we — bearing in mind the absence of a hydrological survey — make many deductions as regards groundwater supply from present manifestations? As far as these developed pockets may tell us, is it true, as a recent advertisement for an international drilling-rig firm would have it, that "India Has More Water Than She Knows What To Do With"?[8] The most overt effect of clustering leading to a regular withdrawal of more than 5-6 cusecs/sq. mile in coincidence — a vitally important factor — with recent drought has been to depress the water-table to a depth indicating at least a temporary excess of withdrawal over recharge. In the Rudrapur region of the Naini Tal Tarai, the water-table which was observed at depths of 2′-3′ in May-June as late as the early 1960s is now recorded at levels of 20′-25′. HVP developments in the Bhabar catchment north of the Tarai, through which hill-stream waters percolate rapidly to feed the Tarai groundwater reservoir, are at the same time reducing the available supply from one major source of recharge. Elsewhere, on the plains, extreme clustering is resulting in so rapid a depletion of upper aquifers that both old and new borings are being extended to deeper water-bearing strata: in the Farukhabad-Fategarh strip, tube-wells are lowered by 3′-5′ per year, to maintain the level of supply. Nearby, in Kasganj block, Etah district — a pocket of uplands prosperity (traditionally derived from indigo, wheat and sugar-cane) in stark contrast to the sprawling saline-alkali patches in the south-western two-thirds of the district, new tube-wells are built now to tap the second aquifer, the first being already on the point of exhaustion. Clustering, with such consequences for the water-table, can be beneficial. In a few low-lying pockets in Meerut and upper Rohilkhand divisions where later

8. Atlas Copco, *Financial Times*, 26 oct. 1970.

percolation from canals has led gradually to a rising water-table inducing root-zone water-logging, intensive tube-well development has achieved something similar to a hydrological equilibrium through the balance of withdrawal and recharge — a phenomenon cursorily observed in tehsil Jansath district Muzaffarnagar (in the Upper Ganges Canal command), of great significance but, again, one for which no precise measurements from the UP field are as yet available. Where no such artificial source of recharge such as canal-seepage supplements the regular (but fluctuating) supply from precipitation and from river-seepage, the effect of clustering seems less beneficial. Again, the co-incidence of drought heightens the effect: in Varanasi district, for example, widespread complaints have arisen against tube-well interference with the water-supply available — from upper aquifers — in masonry wells: in 1968-1969, the supply of drinking-water from wells in areas with pockets of tube-well development was severely reduced. The degree to which minor tube-well irrigation intensifies the demand on the groundwater reservoir and thus threatens to bring about new, or increased, hydrological disorder, becomes clearer if the relative discharge capacity of indigenous and of modern mechanical water-drawing systems are compared. The most sophisticated machinery known in indigenous agriculture is the Persian wheel — a ratchet-driven chain of buckets with a capacity of 1 500 to 2 000 gallons per hour. The regular discharge of the narrowest bore of minor tube-wells currently in operation (2 1/2''-3'') is set between 12 000 and 15 000 gallons per hour. Meanwhile, the rate of recharge of the prime source — annual precipitation — remains substantially unchanged from the time first rainfall estimates became available, *i.e.*, from the early 1890s. Can a modification of the new agricultural strategy be designed, on the basis of a sound and wide-ranging series of water-requirement experiments, to diminish the demand on groundwater to an optimal withdrawal-recharge ratio? This would necessitate a far more thorough survey of indigenous agricultural botany and an assessment of a wide range of strains capable of improvement without the loss of innate physiological advantages (such as low water requirement and drought resistance) than has yet been launched.

Further, the geomorphology itself of UP dictates regions where tube-well development is practicable. Problems of insufficient and of inaccessible aquifers abound both in the eastern districts and in Bundelkhand : resources available for both State tube-wells and for minor irrigation in these areas are necessarily concentrated on productive pockets, chiefly rabi (that is, wheat-growing) areas. Other problems arise from the quality of irrigation water in upper aquifers in regions severely affected by waterlogging and salinity-alkalinity: brackish, alkaline groundwater, with its high boron content, is inimical to plant growth — a problem which inhibits minor irrigation development in accordance with the HVP in alkaline tracts of eastern districts (Sultanpur-Pratapgarh, Azamgarh-Ghazipur, for example) and, widely, in Mathura district, where prolonged waterlogging in trans-Jumna basins has led to a serious deterioration in groundwater quality, making it impossible for the benefits of HVP to be extended to the major part of cultivation in the area.

Costs of intensified irrigation on the present lines of development are not merely to be measured in terms of patchy soil-water deterioration by water-logging and salinity, or in the depletion of aquifers by excessive tube-well demand; all irrigation installations permit at present, through the general lack of lined distribution channels, significant percentages of water-loss. Irrigation engineers generally admit of losses of up to 50 or even 60 percent from canal to field, of 10 to 20 percent from private tube-well to field, and from 5 to 10 percent from State tube-well to field: this last being regularly supplied, at government cost, with one mile of lined channel. It is clear from these estimates that a major economy is required in the form of a planned distribution network — financing of private tube-wells by public loans (at the rate of between Rs 6 000-10 000 per tube-well, according to drilling costs) rarely covers the cost of channel-lining at present. It is also clear that such a network should be developed by clay, or better, PVC (a type of plastic) or aluminium portable piping, a substantial amount of the cost being recoverable in the form of reduced water-loss (leading to reduced demand on aquifers).

The all-important question of the economic exploitation of water-resources, the consideration of old and new irrigation problems, and of the increasing demands of chemical treatment of the soil, dictates the need to assess the performance of the high-yielding varieties to date. Measurement of actual performance is as yet elusive: since gross output figures for the high-yielding varieties (as against total agricultural production, acreage expansion and acreage under improved local varieties) are not available, estimates are made on the basis of acreages reported sown and of estimated yield capacity — with selected crop-cutting experiments by way of corroboration. According to these estimates, the yield of a new variety of exotic parentage reaches a minimum of twice, frequently three times, and occasionally four or even five times the average indigenous yield, in the first and, if high inputs are sustained according to recommendation, second years of its life. Thereafter, genetic instability tends to manifest itself in the reversion of the dwarf characteristic, which straightaway inhibits high fertilizer uptake (through lodging), and a decline in yield to a level, over two succeeding seasons, of 40 or even 50 percent below its peak first year performance. "No one talks of S 64 (the breathtaking wonder-wheat which began the programme) any more", it was said as early as the rabi of 1968-1969. In the absence of progressive experimentation to establish yield-trends for several varieties over a period of years (the all-India co-ordinated experiments are conducted on selected varieties with differential fertilizer treatments for one year only), these general estimates — largely derived from substantiated local complaints — must suffice. We may safely conclude that the principal new varieties — for paddy as for wheat — have a clear superiority in yield, even under "control" conditions. Against this must be discounted the quality of the grain, which is not consumed locally but marketed where possible and fetches a price which may in the case of Mexican wheat, for example, reach a level of as much as Rs 20/quintal below that for local improved wheats. This consideration becomes the more significant when we remember that after the second season, if the original seed is maintained through local multiplication, the yield level drops: perhaps to 35-40 maunds (1 maund = 82 2/7 lb./acre), as against the average performance of local improved varieties' 30-35 maunds/acre. Costs also must be considered. The minimum all-in production costs for Mexican wheat current in 1969-1970 were generally quoted as Rs 250-300; for indigenous improved varieties, approximately one-half to two-thirds that figure. Add to this the rising costs of irrigation exploitation, in the case of over-developed aquifers, of fertilizer, and of constantly renewed seed to maintain high yield-levels. In view of the constant necessity for regular varietal changes, one must also estimate the wheat acreage — for example — regularly pre-empted for seed rather than food-grain production. The official demand for top-quality seed demands top-productivity conditions for its multiplication. Added to this is the stimulus provided by the pre-release seed market for the production of the latest in high-yielding strains, sold in the first instance — Triple Gene Dwarf, for instance, in 1968-1969 — for Rs 200-300/kg. Regular seed sales, on a yield of *ca* 50 maunds/acre of released varieties in their first season fetch Rs 20/kg minimum. Since the programmes began with next to no stock, the market is a rising one, and financing seed-production a safe risk. One might almost say that the fortunes of the Tarai are founded on genetic instability. Costs in technical and economic terms are, regrettably, matched by costs in disease. The high-yielding varieties have a notoriously low threshold of resistance. Inevitably, disease spreads — assuming on occasion epidemic form — where soil and water conditions are poorest. A classic example was provided by the paddy epidemic, chiefly due to Tungru virus (known in the Philippines, the home of "miracle" rice), in the eastern districts in the kharif of 1969-1970: some 22 districts were reported affected. The present writer saw vast areas typically affected with disease in the Ganges-Gogra Doab that season: estimates of 20 000 acres per district, for the most severely damaged regions, would seem reasonable. This becomes the more serious when it is remembered that, due to moderate to severe salinity and alkalinity being widespread in the east, paddy is for many areas the only crop which can be sown, and that due to recent drought, the last kharif saw areas sown for the first time for three or even four seasons. Losses of from 60 to 100 percent of the crop were generally reported from affected areas, disease tended to spread from the exotic into local varieties. Hybrid millets, the most costly of the new varieties forming part of the state programme, have proved similarly susceptible to diseases. These, however, have proved controllable with heavy doses of chemical pesticides and fungicides: the paddy virus could not be controlled, and the extinction of lesser paddy diseases proved to be beyond the logistics of the plant protection service. Unfortunately, it now seems probable that certain selections of Mexican wheat are not going to prove immune: outbreaks of *alternaria* blight, most commonly in S 227, were widely reported in Doab districts during rabi, 1969-1970. Some part of the increase in susceptibility to disease may prove to be due to what appears to be a decline in available trace elements in the soil: in all probability, a consequence of intensive fertilization with ammonium sulphate has led to a Zn deficiency in some highly productive areas: cases are reported from the Government Rice Research Farm at Masodha, Faizabad district and, widely, in the Tarai. The paddy disease, *khaira,* is believed to be symptomatic of such deficiency. Problems of increased propensity to and incidence of plant diseases must also be examined in relation to a deficiency of major nutrients. Outbreaks of *alternaria* blight, severe in irrigated areas of many districts during the wheat season of 1969-1970, may be partially caused or at least aggravated by insufficient applications of nitrogen. Once again it is clear that the high-yielding varieties demand, for their successful cultivation at least risk, a precision in adherence to recommendations which, in the physical as well as the economic context of modern Uttar Pradesh, is prodigiously difficult to attain.

The recent agricultural history of northern India is characterized by the pursuit of maximum yields per acre — a policy of highest economic return at lowest economic cost; in short, maximization through major technological innovation of the productive potential of the most promising alluvial areas. In tracing the intensification of agriculture from the early 19th century, the liabilities as well as the assets are clearly evident; arising in the first instance from the introduction of irrigation, in the context of public works development, without accompanying measures to provide the necessary supply of fertilizer and alkaline amendments to the soil, and in the second, from the introduction of exotic strains of cereals and chemical treatments together with intensive exploitation of new irrigation sources, chiefly groundwater, in an ecosystem already distorted through the cumulative effects of an earlier "green revolution". In sum, these liabilities, inherent in the precedent on which current agricultural policy is based, consciously or unconsciously, and apparent in the present condition of large areas of the north Indian alluvial plains, constitute an effective restraint on the capacity of the maximization policy to achieve its stated aims. The nature and degree of this restraint need to be assessed in economic terms; alternative methods must be designed to raise per acre yields on a broader nutritional basis than concentration merely on cereals can allow and in the interests of optimum rather than maximum intensification of productivity of a wider classification of arable tracts than the prevailing "oasis development" admits. For this, a form of cost-benefit analysis is required which can estimate costs, within a reasonable range of variation, in relation to ecological disequilibrium and hazard, manifest and latent.

Before such estimates can be made, in terms of an order of economic priority, the physical processes themselves must be defined, a task which belongs primarily to the natural sciences. The physical laws of the biosphere, geological, hydrological, meteorological and biological, are for the present defined in terms of generalized change over a time-scale of geological age corroborated at certain, often arbitrary, points by small-scale experimentation designed to reveal the processes at work in achieving equilibrium or disequilibrium at a given instant in a given set of conditions, to determine the factors of significance in such processes and to establish the nature and extent of their interrelation. The major problems of agricultural ecosystems in the modern world, however, and particularly in the so-called "developing countries", are the product of accelerated change, of a sudden and often radical alteration in the course of natural laws leading to the disruption of delicate soil-water mechanisms and to depletion of resources hitherto accumulating over millenia. Conventional earth-sciences analysis is both too general in its formulations and too minute in its experimentation to account precisely for such phenomena as for example the recent agricultural history of UP outlined above exhibits. Photo-interpretation and remote sensing can only survey more precisely the product of processes of distortion arrested in observation at a given instant over a wider area than is possible on the ground, whereas what is required for cost estimates is for that range of spatial observations to be matched, in part at least, by a comparable degree of precision over time — recent historical time, since the accelerated changes which concern us are largely man-made, and of greatest importance from the time of introduction of large-scale technology.

It would be difficult to find a more complex or more representative "natural laboratory", of geomorphological processes — both primary genesis and secondary distortion — than north India. The range of natural and "unnatural" — distorted — variation is at the same time matched by a collection of technical records of observation and analysis of agricultural conditions over the past hundred or so years. This "natural laboratory" is to be found in uniquely concentrated form in the state of UP, the administrative boundaries of which have remained almost constant since the accession of Crown Government in 1858. Its complex geomorphology has already been analysed above. With the aid of the technical documentation of the 19th and early 20th centuries preserved for the most part in the proceedings and reports of the revenue, agriculture and irrigation departments of the local government, month by month and year by year, we can reconstruct the basis for a quantitative approximation not merely of the principles of polyculture underlying the small-scale cultivation patterns of the alluvial plains prior to the introduction of the canal systems — the first great canals of the modern world — but also of the ecological consequences of technological innovations from the point of time marking their introduction: in short, a reconstruction of the partial transformation of a polycultural agrarian scene and the definition in detail of chains of major and minor consequences of public works is possible. This historical analysis of physical processes cannot be made uniformly for a complete time-series: no continuous set of observations exists in the records. Further, instruments of the period could measure only in terms of a greater degree of approximation than modern scientific technology customarily tolerates and much of the conceptual structure underlying modern physical science had yet to be formulated in concise and especially in mathematical terms. But already by the end of the 19th century, the collection of observations, in the field and under experimental conditions, was both comprehensive in the range of its representation of outstanding ecological problems of the time and precise within the limits of contemporary method; further, the very lack of sophisticated scientific technology seems to have sharpened the quality of field observation (which prior to the development of complex instrumentation and experiment had to stand as the premises of scientific argument) and to have allowed for analytical formulations, in terms of qualitative description, of the various processes at work in the manifestation of ecological imbalance. Pieced together from the voluminous technical archives of the British Indian government — several thousand volumes for UP alone — a time-series allowing for gaps in the records arbitrarily arising from insufficient observation can be constructed and the descriptive data on processes translated into more concise formulation. Something of the degree of temporal precision obtainable, from the point of view of causation, may become clear when we realize, for example, that the completion of every section of the thousands of miles of road and railway embankments, the construction and opening for irrigation of every branch (down to each mile) of the canal system, can be dated to a month of a year — and, in consequence, the ecological effects of each innovation traced to a precise point of origin in time as well as in space.

The focal point of this analysis of distortion is the focal point of both 19th and 20th century agricultural policy: irrigation. The ecological disruption brought about by public works construction, the combined effects of deforestation provoked both by local agricultural expansion and by the railway's large-scale demands for wood-fuel together with the obstruction of natural drainage lines by embankments can be seen in its most complex form in the canal-irrigated tracts of UP, where lateral percolation from the high-level unlined channels traversing low-lying areas added a further cause of hydrological imbalance. The analysis of the soil-water processes at work in such an environment made by H.B. Medlicott, FRS, in the 1870s, for example, anticipated the geochemical formulae of Hilgard and Gedroitz by twenty years and still stands as the best framework against which to design experimentation. A classification of the inter- and intra-regional progression from simple to complex distortion (from obstructed surface drainage, for example, to subsoil lateral seepage combined with disturbed surface flow) can be made over the area of the state and on the historical time-scale, using the records to mark out areas and phases of the aggravation (measured now in terms of pH) of the sodic-alkali hazard. Data available for irrigation wells in the

1860s and again in the second decade of this century enable us to estimate hydrological "budgets" for the alluvial plains, in terms of withdrawal and recharge ratios, from discharge figures collected by field observation, paired with approximate rainfall figures with theoretical calculations made for rates of infiltration, runoff and evaporation. Against this framework, analyses of the hydrological effects of canals for selected areas and differential spring-level measurements can be set. Finally, a set of chemical analyses made in 1912 of fifty-eight salt-affected sites (twenty-nine within the command area of the Lower Ganges Canal plus twenty-nine control sites), with detailed profile examinations and laboratory analyses of samples provides a unique point of departure for establishing spread and intensity factors over sixty years: the focus of a survey programme to be taken up in 1972.

All this is essentially preliminary. Such analysis as is scientifically acceptable and can be made from the UP records can establish the historical perspective of one of the most severe problems of arable regions in the "developing" world, to a remarkable degree of precision : *séparé du passé, le présent est muet sur le futur*. The next stage is to design surveys and experiments to tie the historical time-scale with the geological and to provide a bridge from the recent historical manifestations of ecological disruption of north India to the geomorphological processes occurring over a greater span of time in the Americas, Central Asia and the Middle East which have resulted in the same present condition of imbalances, analysed on geochemical and geophysical scales. This done, the path to complex simulation of distortion processes by means of computer modelling is open and the possibilities of precise prediction of definitive processes of deterioration and their quantification in terms of economic cost clearly established.

APPENDIX

Table 1. *Oudh (Population: 11 500 000): comparative table of major heads of public account, 1870*

	Rupees
Civil administration	6 155 100
Military establishment	2 650 546
Imperial public works	1 233 848
Agriculture	492

Table 2. *North-Western Provinces: annual expenditure on agriculture 1887 (representative year)*

	Rupees
	—
Director and staff, Department of Agriculture	62 000
Experimental farms (chiefly for export staples)	12 400
Well-sinking	7 000
Reclamations of saline-alkali experiments in indigo-cultivation tract	20 000

Table 3. *Uttar Pradesh: annual expenditure on agriculture from 1951-1952 to 1960-1961 (thousands of rupees)*

	Development and research	Engineering and colonization
	—	—
1951-1952	15 051	18 771
1952-1953	16 385	16 258
1953-1954	14 895	28 805
1954-1955	16 380	22 136
1955-1956	17 170	21 405
1956-1957	22 965	52 970
1957-1958	26 369	52 690
1958-1959	28 593	47 070
1959-1960	33 042	48 940
1960-1961	36 711	48 200

Source: Finance Department, UP.

Table 4. *Uttar Pradesh: agricultural development loans: minor irrigation (private tube-wells) (hundreds of thousands of rupees)*

1960-1961	2.89
1961-1962	15.40
1962-1963	44.00
1963-1964	73.00
1964-1965	126.00
1965-1966	597.00
1966-1967	698.00
1967-1968	1 030.00
1968-1969 (to 15 January)	10 000.00

Source: Land Development Bank, UP (1960-1966: Land Mortgage Bank).

MARSHALL I. GOLDMAN

Ecological facelifting in the USSR or improving on nature*

Introduction

From the earliest of recorded time, man has sought to reshape nature in order to suit his purposes. The magnitude of his surgery has been limited only by the extent of his technical competence. This competence has not increased in linear fashion. Frequently, earlier generations were capable of efforts beyond the reach of their descendants. But whatever the engineering or planning skills of a particular generation, the intent was generally to make life more comfortable or more profitable. All too often, however, difficulties would arise when one man's definition of comfort and profit differed from another's. Sometimes such differences would develop between contemporaries and sometimes between sons and fathers or grandfathers. Moreover, the attempt to improve on nature in one sector, more often than not set in motion other forces which sometimes have brought an even greater need for remedial action than there was in the first place.

Although we are primarily concerned here with how the Soviets have sought to rearrange nature, it is readily conceded that such schemes are not a monopoly of the communist countries. For example, we in the United States almost succeeded in severing Florida from the mainland with a canal. The so-called North American Water and Power Alliance had a grandiose plan to reroute numerous rivers from the northern part of our hemisphere. And without any plan, we managed to create a dustbowl out of our midwest by overcultivation and a dying lake out of Lake Erie by over-industrialization. Redoing nature, intentionally or unintentionally is an age-old process and generally it plays an important part in the process of economic development. Unfortunately, after an initial project is completed, a subsequent reordering of nature

* Portions of this article are taken from the author's forthcoming study, *The spoils of progress: Environmental pollution in the Soviet Union*, Cambrige, Mass., MIT Press, 1972.

is often felt to be necessary in order to compensate for the destruction the planners and builders generated with their first project.

No matter how simple it may appear to be at first, man's efforts to improve on nature often turn out to be a complex undertaking with unexpected ramifications. It is like tampering with the free market. When you make an adjustment in one sector, somehow or other, there are after-effects in another sector. Engels saw the essence of the matter with clarity in the 19th century.

"Let us not, however, be very hopeful about our human conquest over nature. For each such victory, nature manages to take her revenge. Each of these victories, it is true, has a first order of consequences which we can anticipate. But in the second and third orders (secondary and tertiary effects) there are quite different, unforeseen effects which only too often cancel out the significance of the first. The people who in Mesopotamia, Greece, Asia Minor, and elsewhere destroyed the forests to obtain cultivable land, never dreamed that they were laying the basis for the present devastated condition of these countries, by removing along with the forest the collecting centres and reservoirs of moisture. When, on the southern slopes of the mountains, the Italians of the Alps used up the pine forests so carefully cherished on the northern slopes, they had no inkling that by doing so they were cutting at the foots of dairy industry in their region: they had still less inkling that by doing so they were thereby depriving their mountain springs of water for the greater part of the year, with the effect that these would be able to pour still more furious flood torrents on the plains during the rainy seasons." [1]

Engels' statement has come to have particular meaning today. First of all, some of the same incidents described by Engels' in the 1880's are reoccurring in the world, including, as we shall see, the USSR. Second, as serious as the secondary and tertiary effects were several decades ago, with our vastly more powerful technology, the potential for damage is even greater now. Given Engels' concern over this question, it is ironic that the highest potential for increased destructiveness comes when the state monopolizes all the productive powers of the country into a single decision maker's hands as often happens in a communist country. To some extent the drive to redo nature is no different in a communist country from what it is in non-communist countries, especially those that are underdeveloped. In a communist country, however, the opposition or resistance to the restructuring power of the state is likely to be considerably less because of the absence of private property or opposition parties. With such concentrated power at its command, the potential a communist state has for reordering nature is unprecedented.

Finally, as important as the economic, political and corrective factors may be for explaining why man attacks nature in such a vigorous way, there may also be a psychological element, especially in the case of Russia. Citi-

1. Frederick Engels, *Dialectics of nature*, New York, International Publishers, 1940, pp. 291-292.

zens in large land masses as well as planners in developing countries generally seem to have an undue fascination for large water bodies. In the first instance this may be an attempt to make up for the absence of large ocean bodies which most other countries of the world are able to enjoy and in the second instance, it may just be that unharnessed water power constitutes a mocking reminder about a country's impotence. Alternatively as Peter Wiles has put it, this excessive concern for water may be nothing more than a Freudian response. Whatever the precise explanation, the interplay of these economic, political and psychological forces is especially well illustrated by a study of what the Russians have been doing to the Caspian and Aral Seas.

1. In the beginning

The Caspian and Aral Seas are unusual water bodies. Unlike most seas or lakes in the world, the flow of water is one way — in. Water is not carried out of either of these major seas to other rivers or seas or oceans. Both water bodies are located in very dry regions of the world where the evaporation rate is exceptionally high. The rapid evaporation absorbs the incoming water which explains why even though there is no outlet, the seas do not overflow. In the case of the Caspian Sea, the rapid evaporation rate also makes possible a valuable mineral recovery operation. Water is drawn off the Caspian into the Gulf of Kara-Bogaz-Gol where evaporation is especially rapid and the residue is converted into valuable minerals and salts. The general characteristics of both seas are presented in Table 1.

Table 1. *Characteristics of the Caspian and Aral Seas*

	Caspian Sea	*Aral Sea*
Elevation	- 28 m	53 m
Area		
low water	372,000 km²	64 to 66,458 km²
high water	424,000 km²	
Maximum depth	1,020 m	68 m
Average depth		16,4 m
Volume		1 023 km

Sources : Soviet geography : Review and translation 5, May 1965, p. 325; *ibid.* 6, June 1965, p. 328; V.L. Shul'ts, "The Aral Sea problem", *Soviet hydrology : Selected papers* 5, 1968, p. 489; L.B. Malinkevič, B.A. Beljanov, "Kaspij glubže kilometra", *Priroda*, Aug. 1966.

Even more intriguing, both the Caspian and Aral Seas have had rather erratic geological lives. Researchers feel that the Aral Sea was dry only 30,000 years ago. Subsequently, a sea was formed and then several centuries ago around the 12th century, the Aral Sea contracted only to expand again during the 13th and 15th centuries [2]. In somewhat the same way, the water level of the Caspian has changed markedly over the last few centuries. In the 2nd century B.C., the shoreline was at 32 meters below sea level [3]. Villages were built along the edge of the sea only to be submerged as the Caspian rose in the centuries that followed. By 1400 A.D., the sea depth increased to 22 meters below sea level which it is believed was similar to the depth that existed in 2000 B.C. [4] Except for a slight dip in the 16th century, the level of the Caspian was fairly stable until the mid-19th century [5].

The changes in the level of the Caspian and Aral Seas up until the mid-19th century are explained primarily by variation in rainfall and temperature in the watersheds of both seas [6]. Beginning in 1929, the level of the Caspian Sea and in 1960 the level of the Aral Sea, began to fall rapidly at rates that were clearly due to more than just changes in rainfall [7]. Whereas between 1847 and 1928, the level of the Caspian fell by 56 centimeters or 6 millimeters a year from 1939 to 1965, it fell by 2.47 meters (8.2 feet) or 67 millimeters a year [8]. By 1970 it had fallen another .1 of a meter so that the total drop was 2.6 meters (8 1/3 feet) [9].

The recent history of the Aral Sea is similar. From 1960 to 1967, the water level fell by 1.76 meters (5.5 feet) or 24 millimeters a year [10]. The drop is expected to continue so that by 1980, the sea will have fallen a total of 4 to 4.5 meters [11]. Since the average depth of the Aral Sea is 16.4 meters (50 feet) and its maximum depth is only 68 meters, it is estimated that by the year 2000, the Aral Sea will have turned into a salt marsh [12]. Even by 1980, it is expected that the area of the sea will have been reduced from the 64-66,000 square kilometers it was in 1960 to 15-25,000 [13] square kilometers and its volume from 1,023 cubic kilometers to 180-190 cubic kilometers [14].

2. A.V. Šnitnikov, "Verojatnye tendencii kolebanij vognosti territorii SSR", *Voprosy geografii* 73, 1968, p. 168.

3. *Ibid.*, p. 76.

4. L.N. Gumilev, "Khazaria and the Caspian", *Soviet geography : Review and translation* 6, June 1964, p. 60; Šnitnikov, *op. cit.*, p. 76.

5. A.D. Dobrovol'skij, A.N. Kosarev, O.K. Leont'ev (eds.), *Kaspijskoe more*, Moscow, Izdatel'stvo Moskovskogo Universiteta, 1969, p. 135.

6. B.A. Apollov, "Značenie ekonomičeskih nauk: Problemy Kaspijskogo morja", *Voprosy geografii* 57, 1962, p. 80; *Komsomol'skaja pravda*, Nov. 1968, p. 2.

7. B.A. Apollov, S.N. Bobrov, "Kaspijskoe more budet žit", *Priroda*, Feb. 1963, p. 72.

8. Dobrovol'skij, Kosarev, Leont'ev (eds.), *op. cit.*, p. 128.

9. A. Iordanskij, "The Caspian calls for help", *Soviet geography : Review and translation* 6, June 1964, p. 37.

10. *Soviet geography : Review and translation* 3, 1969, p. 146.

11. *Pravda*, Nov. 7, 1968, p. 2.

12. V.L. Shul'ts, "The Aral Sea problem", *Soviet hydrology : Selected papers* 5, 1968, p. 489; A. Kosarev, "The diminishing Southern Seas", *Soviet life*, July 1970, p. 13.

13. The conversion of the metric scale into the linear system is sometimes rounded off since so many of the original figures are approximate sums anyway.

14. Shul'ts, *op. cit.*, p. 490.

2. Economic development and environmental disruption

Whatever natural explanation there may have been for fluctuations in the level of the Caspian and Aral Seas, by early 1930 in the case of the Caspian and 1960 in the Aral, man made factors became more important. As shown in Table 2[15], the area of the Caspian Sea was fairly steady from the years 1917 to 1933. Except for a brief respite during World War II, from 1933 on, the Caspian fell sharply. This coincides with the spread of industrialization and urbanization and the attempt to increase agricultural output.

Table 2. *Area of the Caspian Sea (square kilometers)*

Year	*Area*	*Year*	*Area*
1906	403 250	1936	394 340
1907	402 680	1937	392 360
1908	402 680	1938	387 710
1909	403 250	1939	382 940
1910	401 640	1940	379 440
1911	399 470	1941	377 950
1912	399 560	1942	380 230
1913	398 570	1943	380 710
1914	399 380	1944	380 230
1915	401 180	1945	377 370
1916	402 000	1946	378 480
1917	402 460	1947	380 080
1918	401 000	1948	381 030
1919	400 820	1949	379 760
1920	399 650	1950	376 900
1921	398 390	1951	374 760
1922	397 490	1952	374 570
1923	396 950	1953	373 240
1924	396 950	1954	372 660
1925	395 860	1955	371 710
1926	396 770	1956	370 940
1927	398 480	1957	372 470
1928	400 100	1958	375 150
1929	401 640	1959	375 910
1930	400 550	1960	374 760
1931	399 380	1961	371 520
1932	400 190	1962	369 700
1933	399 920	1963	371 520
1934	397 940	1964	382 850
1935	396 230	1965	372 100

Source: A.D. Dobrovols'kij, A.N. Kosarev, O.K. Leont'ev (eds.), *Kaspijskoe more*, Moscow, Izdatel'stvo Moskovskogo Universiteta, 1969, p. 132.

15. Dobrovol'skij, Kosarev, Leont'ev (eds.), *op. cit.*, p. 132.

The role of man as the prime mover becomes apparent when we examine what happened to the sources that supplied the sea. Just as a pinched air hose can cause a deep sea diver to suffocate, so a blocked or diverted river can cause a sea to shrink. Evaporation in Central Asia is intense and in the absence of cool weather or unusually heavy precipitation, any diversion of water has a marked effect. This is an especially acute situation in Central Asia since both the Caspian and Aral Seas are heavily dependent on only a few rivers. For example the Aral Sea is fed by only the Syr Darya and the Amu Darya Rivers which originate in the mountain ranges which separate the USSR from Afghanistan and China. A larger number of rivers flow into the Caspian, but except for the Volga and its tributaries, none of them amount to much. Rivers provide 80 % of all the water added to the Caspian each year and the Volga makes up 80 % of the river flow[16]. So just the diversion of the Volga, Syr Darya and Amu Darya could and did have disastrous consequences for the Caspian and Aral Seas. Why did these diversions take place?

Even though capital can be put to many alternative uses in a developing country, all too often the project with a high and immediate payback takes a back seat to projects with a longer payback period. This is particularly so if the slow return project also provides the planners with a chance to reshape their country's water courses. In fairness, it must be acknowledged that massive water projects are a means of utilizing readily available quantities of unskilled labor in order to build up a country's infrastructure. But as mentioned earlier, of equal if not greater importance in commissioning water projects is the primeval or mystical urge in men that unutilized streams and water bodies apparently brings out. Although planners in almost all countries are affected with this peculiar passion for power planning, the reaction is perhaps strongest in the developing countries. To a poor country, idle rivers serve to remind it of its backwardness. Some planners may view the river as a source of fertility and power. Others may simply conclude that since other countries have developed that way, they too must dam up their own rivers.

In addition to whatever else he may be known for, Stalin will go down in history as the greatest rearranger of men and nature the world had ever seen, at least as of 1953. Other rulers have had the dictatorial power to give the orders and divert the manpower and equipment, but until Stalin, no one had the technology as well as the power to carry out such huge undertakings over such a vast expanse. Whether or not such action was economically warranted was inconsequential to Stalin. Given Stalin's severe case of what we can call aquaphilia, the results were inevitable.

Once it was decided to redo the rivers of the Soviet Union, it was natural that the Volga would be singled out for special attention. Not only did the Volga slice through the center of the country, but it was the longest river flow-

16. S.N. Bobrov, "The transformation of the Caspian Sea", *Soviet geography: Review and translation* 7, 1961, p. 49; Dobrovol'skij, Kosarev, Leont'ev (eds.), *op. cit.*, p. 133.

ing south in the country and the longest Soviet river west of the Urals. Naturally Stalin saw the Volga as the centerpiece in his overall design. In the early 1930's, it was announced that 13 big dams would be built along the Volga. These dams and the reservoirs that were to form behind them would make possible a variety of projects. The most obvious were electrical power and water for irrigation. In addition canals were to be dug and river channels enlarged. By March, 1937, Stalin had managed to link Moscow to the Volga and the Caspian Sea. Given the connections between the Volga and the White and Baltic Seas which had been completed in June, 1933, this meant that Moscow was also joined by water with the north. When Stalin completed a canal linking the Volga and the Don River in July, 1952, ships from Moscow could also sail to the Azov and Black Seas. In this way, water from the Volga not only transformed Moscow into a port of five seas, but it provided Moscow and Central Russia with direct access to an increased water supply for industry and municipal needs.

While these projects provided some important benefits to the country, they also brought with them serious shortcomings. In addition to the often valuable land lost behind the newly erected dams and reservoirs, a good deal of water was lost. Some of it disappeared into underground channels; but large quantities simply evaporated into the air. When combined with the increasingly large quantites of water diverted from the rivers to the irrigation canals, the river flows had diminished sharply by the time they reached the sea.

Diversion of the Aral's arteries began after World War II with the siphoning off of water from the Syr Darya for irrigation in the Fergana Valley, an oasis in Uzbekistan, Tadzhikstan and Kirgizija [17]. By 1965, almost all the water from the Syr Darya had been tapped for irrigation so that it was virtually dry by the time it reached the Aral [18]. Only the Amu Darya River had any water left to feed the Aral and it too was shrinking rapidly. In 1962 a canal was built from the Amu Darya to the Karkill Oasis [19]. By 1968, 37 canals were already feeding on the Amu Darya and plans had been announced for the construction of 18 more in the years to come [20]. For example in 1969, construction began on a major dam at Tyuyamuyan on the Amu Darya in order to provide more water for irrigation. In 1970, additional work was performed on the Amu-Bukhara Canal for the same purpose [21]. With the main sources of their supply diverted, the Aral and Caspian naturally suffered.

To many Soviet economists, much of what was done was regarded as needless waste. Although economists are no more immune from the passion for power

17. Shul'ts, *op. cit.*, p. 489.
18. *Komsomol'skaja pravda*, Sep. 16, 1965, p. 2; *Soviet news*, Apr. 7, 1970, p. 6.
19. *Soviet geography: Review and translation* 6, 1970, p. 511.
20. *Komsomol'skaja pravda*, Aug. 11, 1968, p. 2.
21. *Soviet geography: Review and translation* 1, 1970, p. 60; *ibid.* 6, 1970, p. 511.

planning than anyone else, it is possible that if a system of more meaningful prices and economic valuations had been used as they suggested, the ecological damage would have been less. The fact that no payment had to be made for the land that flooded made it easier for the engineers to engulf large quantities of formerly valuable land. Several Russian economists estimate that in Central Asia, as much land has been lost through flooding and salination as has been added through irrigation and drainage [22]. Presumably more efficient use of the land would have increased productivity enough to offset the need to invest so heavily in irrigation and flooding. Despite these criticisms of the economists, Soviet engineers envision irrigating another 8. 3 million hectares in addition to the 4.6 million hectares already under irrigation in 1967 [23].

Similar questions were also raised about the value of making Moscow into a port of five seas. The Volga-Don Canal reportedly has not been heavily utilized and apparently will never justify its cost. Again if more appropriate cost estimates had prevailed and if Stalin had allowed someone to pay attention to such matters, there is the slimmest of chances the canal would not have been built thereby lessening the drain on the Volga. (Realistically, however, as long as Stalin was in charge, no cost system would probably have made much difference.)

3. A cause for concern

Whether or not a fall in the Caspian and the Aral Seas could have been averted or alleviated, the fact remains that the water levels of the two seas fell. When it became clear what was happening, many scientists expressed alarm. Why were they so concerned? [24]

Any sudden change in one's environment is unsettling. Not only is it psychologically disturbing, it may also be physically inconvenient and financially costly. Usually, man is able to adapt himself gradually to new sets of conditions. Should these conditions change again, then a new process of adjustment must take place. But when the change is not just seasonal but long run in nature, with no indication of where it may end, the effect can be particularly unstabilizing.

22. D. Armand, *Nam i vnukam*, Moscow, Mysl', 1966, pp. 40 and 81; I.P. Gerasimov, "Basic problems of the transformation of nature", *Soviet geography: Review and translation* 6, 1968, p. 448.

23. A.S. Kes', "Problemy preobrazovanija prirody sredjnej Azii", *Izvestija Akademii Nauk, serija geografičeskaja* 6, 1967, p. 87.

24. B.A. Apollov, K.K. Gjul', V.G. Zavrev (eds.), *Materialy vsesojuznogo soveščanija po probleme Kaspijskogo morja*, Baku, Izdatel'stvo Akademii Nauk Azerbajdžanskoj SSR, 1963, p. 10.

The reduction in the flow of water ot the Caspian and Aral Seas had an immediate effect and was quickly noticed. The reason for this is that a portion of the Caspian and all of the Aral Sea is very shallow. Consequently any reduction of water immediately shows up as exposed land. By 1966, the area of the Aral Sea had diminished by 10 % from what it had been in 1960 and was shrinking rapidly. Since the southern part of the Caspian had depths of up to 3,280 feet, contraction in this area is not much of an issue. However it is a substantial matter in the northwest, north and northeast [25]. Frequently, maximum depths of only 15-30 feet are reported and it is here that the sea has retreated the furthest. Whereas for every drop of one meter there is only a reduction of .5 % in the total volume of the sea in the south, 17 % of the volume disappears in the north [26]. The retreating sea has also affected mineral operations in the Gulf of Kara-Bogaz-Gol. For years as the sea water evaporates, the shallow gulf has been a major source of valuable minerals and salts such a sulfur nitrate, bromides, chlorides and sulfur magnesium. But as the Caspian has fallen, the channel into the Gulf has shriveled up. The flow of water into the Gulf has been reduced from 20 to 9-9.5 cubic kilometers a year. As a result the maximum depth of the Gulf has fallen from 13 to 3 meters [27]. Moreover some authorities who are concerned with the Caspian argue that the flow of water into the Gulf should be further reduced or eliminated completely to prevent needless evaporation and loss of water from the sea [28]. They are opposed by those whose main interest focusses on the Gulf and who argue that a valuable source of minerals is being lost [29].

What else has happened as a result of the drop in water levels? The damages include pollution of the seas, a drop in the fish catch, an increase in disease, loss of seaports and reduction in farm land.

One way to reduce or eliminate some types of water pollution is to dilute the effluent until it reaches nontoxic levels. Naturally if the water flow is reduced, there is much less dilution so that the DO_2 (dissolved oxygen) in the water falls rapidly. In the same way the relative concentration of pollutants rises. The problem of water pollution is particularly serious in the Caspian Basin where there is more industrial activity than in the area around the Aral. It is probable that even if the flow of water into the Caspian had not been reduced it would still have become polluted. The pollutants originate from emissions on the sea itself and from its tributaries.

25. Apollov, *op. cit.*, p. 81.
26. Bobrov, *op. cit.*
27. I.I. Stas', "Kompleksnoe osvoenie Kara-Bogaz-Gola", *Priroda*, Sep. 1968, pp. 108-109, p. 33.
28. Z.L. Vendrov, G.G. Gangardt, Y. Yu. Geller, L.V. Korenistov and G.L. Sarukhanov, "The problem of transformation and utilization of the water resources of the Volga River and the Caspian Sea", *Soviet geography: Review and translation* 7, Sep. 1964, p. 32.
29. D.V. Bujnevič, "Perspekitvy Kara-Bogaz-Gola", *Priroda* 5, 1969, p. 32.

The Caspian is a major source of oil. An entire city has been constructed several miles offshore and numerous oil wells have been drilled beneath the sea. Nowhere in the world is this done without oil spills. Nor has the Caspian been spared blowouts and leaks at its wells. At one time an oil spill stretching 2 000 square miles was reported on the Caspian [30]. In January, 1971, a major fire raged out of control for almost a month at one of the rigs. After the fire was extinguished, debris and oil slicks covered vast areas of the sea [31]. Oil discharges also emanate from several of the refineries along the banks of the Caspian. For years virtually no effort was made to treat the waste of the refineries. It was reported in 1966 that 47,000 metric tons of oil were dumped into the Caspian from the Republic of Azerbaidzhan itself [32]. Nor is the natural state of the sea improved by the blasting and seismic explosions that have been used since 1941 in the search for more oil [33].

Conditions deteriorated so that in October 1968, a special resolution of the Council of Ministers was adopted in order to prevent further pollution. Entitled *On measures to avert the pollution of the Caspian Sea*, the resolution sought to accelerate introduction of preventive measures and the construction of treatment plants at 100 refineries and factories along the sea as well as at 14 cities. All of these installations had been dumping their waste into the water for years without any restraint [34]. The new law also sought to stop oil tankers from discharging their ballast into the sea [35]. Special discharge and treatment receptacles were built at selected cities along the coast in order to provide some place other than the sea for the tankers to dump their ballast [36]. While there has been some improvement, there are indications that as yet all these efforts have not been completely successful and that oil and sewage discharge into the Caspian continues to be a hazard [37]. As recently as late 1971, there were reports that major cities like Baku, Makhachkal, Krasnovodsk and Gousan were still dumping untreated raw sewage into the sea [38].

If and when the emission of oil and other pollutants along the sea is brought under control, the battle will have only begun. Oil also flows into the sea from several of the major rivers which feed the sea. Thus in March 1971, *Pravda* reported that an oil pipeline broke along the Ural River [39]. This pipe-

30. A. Simonov, "Cleaning up the sea", *Soviet life*, Jan. 1970, p. 59.
31. *Pravda*, Jan. 2, 1971, p. 31; *Socialističeskaja industrija*, Feb. 6, 1971, p. 4.
32. *Priroda*, Jan. 1968, p. 115.
33. *Literaturnaja gazeta*, Sep. 27, 1966, p. 2.
34. *Pravda*, Oct. 3, 1968, p. 2.
35. *Bakinskij rabočij*, June 12, 1868, p. 2.
36. *Pravda*, Oct. 3, 1968, p. 2; Simonov, *op. cit.*
37. A. Iordanskij, "The Caspian calls for help", *Himija i Žizn'* 1, p. 41.
38. *Pravda*, Oct. 3, 1968, p. 2; Sep. 20, 1969, p. 2; *Turkmenskaja iskra*, Sep. 20, 1970, p. 2; *Literaturnaja gazeta*, Mar. 3, 1971, p. 11.
39. *Pravda*, Mar. 20, 1971, p. 2.

line carries oil from the Mangyshlak Peninsula alongside the Caspian to oil refineries near Kuibyshev along the Volga River. *Pravda* reported that barriers had been erected to contain the oil but that oil was nonetheless seeping into the river which in turn would carry it down to the Caspian.

Until this incident, the main flow of oil into the Caspian came from the Volga. For years only feeble efforts were exerted to force factories and municipalities to treat their waste. Since the banks of the Volga are heavily industrialized, this meant that a variety of industrial effluents, particularly oil, were sent off in enormous quantities to the Caspian. In 1966, factories and cities along the Volga discharged over 300,000 cubic meters of untreated sewage into the river each hour [40]. One authority estimates that the Volga carries about one half of all the discharged effluent in the USSR [41]. Particularly bothersome were the several refineries which either had no or frequently inoperative facilities [42]. The concentration of oil has reportedly been so great that on one occasion at least, the Volga caught fire. As one newspaper put it: "The children set the Volga on fire and the firemen came and put out the river!" [43]. Volga steamers now carry signs forbidding passengers to toss cigarettes and lighted matches overboard [44]. One writer explained such signs as evidence of the concern about litter prevention; but given the river's incendiary past, it is more likely a sign of fire prevention.

The reduced flow of water and an increased discharge of oil and other industrial and municipal wastes combined to create an environment that can hardly be considered hospitable for water life. Fish kills along the Volga and its tributaries are a common calamity. The Volga along with the Ural, the second largest supplier of the Caspian, are both periodically classified as dead rivers [45]. Today because of the pollution and dam construction along the Ural, it no longer carries fish to the Caspian [46]. Inevitably this affects fish life in the Caspian itself. That this entails a significant economic cost becomes apparent when it is realized that prior to 1929 and the fall of the water level, the Caspian yielded up to 40 % of the fish catch in the USSR [47]. Furthermore, the cost of catching fish in the Caspian was 40-50 % of what it was in the Pacific [48]. The decline in the fish haul in the mid-1930's can be seen in Table 3.

In 1967, the total fish catch was less than one half of what it was in 1936. The figures are drawn from different sources, but the sturgeon catch by 1970 was about one quarter of what it was before the revolution. In some areas,

40. N.D. Kazancev, *Pravovaja ohrana prtrody v SSR*, Moscow, Znanie, 1967 (series 17).
41. *Literaturnaja gazeta*, Mar. 3, 1971, p. 11.
42. *Turkmenskaja iskra*, Mar. 3, 1971, p. 3.
43. *Socialističeskaja industrija*, July 4, 1970, p. 2.
44. *Krokodil* 24, Aug. 1970, p. 4.
45. *Bakinskij rabočij*, June 12, 1968, p. 2.
46. *Pravda*, July 12, 1967, p. 3.
47. Bobrov, *op. cit.*, p. 47.
48. Apollov, Gjul', Zavrev (eds.), *op. cit.*, p. 11.

Table 3. *Fish catch in the Caspian (in 1 000 metric tons)*

Year	*Total*	*Sturgeon*	*Sudak*	*Sprat*
—	—	—	—	—
1900		30-40		
1936	500	21.5	55.2	5.3
1950	332	13.5	31.4	21.6
1960	387	10.1	14.6	176
1967	230			

Sources: B.A. Apollov, K.K. Gjul', V.G. Zavrev (eds.), *Materialy vsesojuznogo soveščanija po probleme Kaspijskogo morja*, Baku, Izdatel'stvo Akademii Nauk Azerbajdžhanskoj SSR, 1963, p. 10; A.D. Dobrovol'skij, A.N. Kosarev, O.K. Leont'ev (eds.), *Kaspijskoe more*, Moscow, Izdatel'stvo Moskovskogo Universiteta, 1969, p. 254; *Ekonomičeskaja gazeta*, Feb. 27, 1968, p. 19.

fishing for sturgeon has been banned [49]. Because of the shortage, the price of caviar has risen so high that one Soviet paper complains that some Soviet citizens have taken to caviar rustling. The poachers sneak out illegally in speedy motor boats and sell their catches at speculative prices [50].

The fall in the catch of the more valuable fish has been partially offset by an increased haul of cheaper fish such as sprat. Still intensive efforts have been made to restock and regenerate the more valuable fish stocks. The poorer fish species, however, are often an important link in the food chain of the richer species. Consequently, the increased depletion of the less desirable fish is likely to handicap even more the recovery and return of fish like the sturgeon which will only thrive when there is an abundant base for them to feed upon, This is not an unimportant question. The sturgeon after all is the source of caviar and caviar has provided a valuable supply of foreign exchange. Since the Caspian is the source of 80-90 % of all world's sturgeon and 90-95 % of the world's black caviar, the maintenance of the Caspian as a fertile ground for the sturgeon is a priority matter [51].

The catch of fish has been affected not only by a deterioration in the quality of the water but by a disruption of the fish breeding habits. The erection of dams has severed the migratory and spawning habits of the fish which breed in the fresh water streams and then move into the seas. Some dams on both the Volga and Ural have been equipped with fish gates but there is considerable debate about their effectiveness. Moreover the dams which were designed to prevent the annual spring floods simultaneously prevent the nourishing of traditional breeding grounds in the deltas of the various rivers. Thus new sites have had to be found as some of the old sites have been left high and sometimes dry or swampy. Even the new lower lying breeding areas are sometimes affected by inadequate supplies of water. This happens when the

49. *Literaturnaja gazeta*, Mar. 3, 1971, p. 11.
50. *Zarja vostoka*, Feb. 2, 1970, p. 2.
51. *Bakinskij rabočij*, June 12, 1968, p. 2; Bobrov, *op. cit.*

dam operators violate their operating instructions and release less water than stipulated. The dam engineers are likely to do this whenever the spring flow is somewhat less than normal [52]. The overall effect of the curtailed flow of fresh (?) water into the Caspian from the Volga and Ural has also caused the saline content of the water to increase to what the Russians describe as 13 %. (It is not clear what the 13 % is a percentage of.) In some areas, levels as high as 20 % have been reported [53]. The impact on fish life can be deduced when it is realized that the same authorities report that a saline content of 4-10 % is appropriate for fish while 4-7 % is considered to be the optimum. It is not only the lack of water that affects aquatic life in the Caspian. Just like the Aswam Dam in Egypt, dams on the Volga also hold back the flow of silt and nutrient which is an essential source of food for the water life population in the Caspian [54].

Although the quality of the fish native to the Aral Sea was not as high as it was in the Caspian, the impact of polluting and shrinking the Aral has been even greater. From a typical haul of 40 metric tons in 1962, the catch dropped to 20 metric tons in 1967 [55]. Apparently by 1970, it had fallen to 6-8 metric tons or to 20 % of what it had been [56]. And as the salt content of the sea rises, the expectations is that the remaining fish in the Aral will rapidly be annihilated [57].

This disruption of the environment can also have other unexpected and undesirable effects on the regions's ecology. One of the fish that flourished along the Karakum Canal which was fed by the Amu Darya was the Belyi Amur. Its breeding grounds were adversely affected when water was drawn off for irrigation and contaminated with pollutants. This eliminated most of the fish but not the mosquito larvae which the fish used to consume. As a consequence there was a sharp rise in the mosquito population including some that transmitted malaria. As a result the disease has returned to Ashkhabad after having been gone for many years [58]. The drop in the quantity and quality of water in the Volga is also an important factor in explaining why Astrakhan, a major city at the mouth of the Volga, was one of the first cities in the USSR to report the outbreak of cholera during the epidemic of 1970 [59].

52. *Ekonomičeskaja gazeta*, Feb. 27, 1968, p. 19; O.S. Kolbasov, *Legislation on water use in the USSR*, Moscow, Iurizdat, 1965, pp. 145-149; *Literaturnaja gazeta*, June 17, 1970, p. 11; *Current digest of the Soviet press*, Oct. 12, 1966, p. 15.

53. For a contrary view see Dobrovol'skij, Kosarev, Leont'ev (eds.), *op. cit.*, pp. 185-188.

54. *Ekonomičeskaja gazeta*, Feb. 27, 1968, p. 19; "Ocenka prirodnyh resursov", *Voprosy geografii*, Moscow, Mysl', July 1966, p. 21.

55. *Soviet geography: Review and translation* 3, 1969, p. 146.

56. *Socialističeskaja industrija*, Aug. 15, 1970, p. 2.

57. *Kazahstanskaja pravda*, Feb. 6, 1969, p. 2.

58. *Turkmenskaja iskra*, Sep. 16, 1969, p. 3.

59. *The New York Times*, Aug. 7, 1970, p. 10; *Socialističeskaja industrija*, Aug. 22, 1970, p. 3.

The deterioration of the Caspian and Aral Seas has had other less severe consequence as well. Several fishing villages once located on the shores of the Caspian now find themselves located as far as 30 miles from the shore [60]. One-time steamship ports such as Ilychik and Astara have had the same experience. Access to Muinak and Aral'sk in the Aral Sea has also been blocked [61]. This has necessitated extra expense for dredging and in some cases the relocation of the ports [62]. There is now only one navigable channel in the Volga delta [63].

The falling Caspian has also created turmoil for the oil drillers. They must decide whether to locate close to the water on the assumption that the level of the sea will fall another meter or two (3 to 6 feet) by 1980 and perhaps by a comparable amount by the year 2 000. Alternatively, some might decide to locate a respectable distance above the water in case the sea should return to its previous heights [64].

The Caspian has been subjected to so many forces that it is sometimes difficult to interpret their impact. For instance in 1965, a report appeared in the scientific journal *Priroda* (Nature) about the discovery in the Caspian of an unusually high recording of what was called natural strontium [65]. Because of ambiguities in the article, it is unclear if the reference is to strontium 90 and if this implies the sea is radio-active. V. I. Timoščghuk, the author of the article implies that the recorded levels are higher than those recorded in other seas of the world and that the strontium content is particularly high on the eastern shore. According to the article, strontium concentrations range from 4.24 milligrams per liter on the western shore to 17.10 milligrams per liter on the eastern shore. In some places readings as high as 25 milligrams per liter have been reported. According to one estimate made by officials in the Division of Radiological Control in the Massachusetts Department of Natural Resources, this amount indicates doses of radioactivity several hundred million times higher than anything ever recorded in water bodies in this country. The only exception would be water directly affected by atomic testing, processing or disposal. If such readings have been correctly interpreted (the Massachusetts officials find it hard to believe that such high readings are indeed correct) this suggests that the Caspian is an unusually "hot" sea.

Less spectacular yet of equal concern is the uncertainty over what effect the shrinking seas will have on the weather. Evaporation patterns are being changed as new water bodies are being created and old ones dissipated. This in turn affects wind circulation and surface water accumulation. Water

60. Bobrov, *op. cit.*, p. 50.
61. *Soviet geography: Review and translation* 3, 1969, p. 146.
62. Bobrov, *op. cit.*, p. 51.
63. Apollov, Bobrov, *op. cit.*, p. 69.
64. Kosarev, *op. cit.*, p. 13; *Pravda*, Oct. 7, 1968, p. 3.
65. V.I. Timoščuk, "Prirodnyj stroncij v Kaspijskom more", *Priroda*, Jan. 1968, p. 90.

bodies tend to temper the continentality of the climate. Already there are reports that due to the contraction of the Caspian Sea, the climate around Mangyshlak has become more continental with longer winters and shorter summers [66]. Although some specialists have argued that only the temperature around the narrow strip will be affected, the same changes are occurring around the Aral Sea [67]. Moreover since the disappearance of the Aral is much more imminent, there is also concern about the impact on humans of the disappearance of this water body. In all likelihood, the area will become a desert with salt and dust storms [68]. There is considerable fear that the existing population will find it too difficult to live in such surroundings without the tempering presence of a large body of water. As a result there may well be a large-scale migration as the water disappears.

Given the damage the shrinkage of the Caspian and Aral was causing, it was natural that several Soviet scholars would suggest proposals to restore the health of the seas. In other words, now that man has had his negative impact, what could he do to offset thisda mage? If enough money is available, solutions can always be found. Nature takes its revenge, however, because invariably these new corrections tend to generate their own negative consequences which require yet additional rectifications. It is to these proposals that we now turn.

4. Reshaping the Earth

In the literal sense, some of the cures which have been proposed for the Caspian and Aral Seas have earth-shaking implications. The "solutions" range from doing nothing to altering the makeup of the rivers, and seas in Siberia. Some of the plans are new and some are almost 100 years old. All of them, however, involve an attempt to improve on nature which usually turns out to be expensive and not always wise.

5. No problem

Because of the expense involved in executing some of the more grandiose plans, some specialists have argued that nothing be done. In other words, they see nothing wrong with allowing the Caspian Sea to shrivel up and the Aral Sea to shrink into a salt marsh. Since almost all the other plans proposed involve expenditures of hundreds of millions of rubles, those who are prepared to see the seas contract or disappear, question whether such sums are warranted. In other words, what harm will there be if water for the seas

66. Apollov, Bobrov, *op. cit.*, p. 70.
67. Shul'ts, *op. cit.*, p. 490.
68. *Ibid.*; *Komsomol'skaja pravda*, Aug. 11, 1968, p. 2.

is cut off and used instead for irrigation or industry? The geographers V.L. Shul'ts and S. Iu. Geller make just such calculations [69]. In their view the harmful effects of letting the Aral disappear would be:

1. A slight impact on the climate
2. Fishing will decrease
3. Muskrats which provide valuable furs will disappear
4. Reed growth in the river deltas will disappear
5. The Aral Sea will no longer be used as a waterway
6. There may be dust and salt storms.

By their calculations, the loss entailed would not be large. Shul'ts and Geller have calculated that the loss suffered by the disappearance of fish from the Aral Sea will amount to 40-60 million rubles ($ 44-67 million) a year [70]. The inability to use the Aral Sea for transportation will cost about 10 million rubles ($ 11 million). Presumably this is the maximum loss that will be entailed and since there are still some fish being caught the loss figure is not yet that high.

Somewhat more extensive calculations have been prepared for the Caspian. Based on the estimate prepared in 1959 by the Oceanographical Commission of the Academy of Sciences of the USSR, the cost of relocating ports and channels in the Caspian costs at least 100 million rubles ($ 111 million) a year [71]. At the same time, the revenue of the fishing industry was also estimated to have fallen by 100 million rubles a year [72]. No one knows precisely how many other costs have been incurred. The geographer, S.N. Bobrov, estimates, however, that every time the Caspian drops one meter, it costs 400 million rubles ($ 444 million). As opposed to the loss of the seas, the gains that would follow from diverting the water flowing into it are:

1. Instead of the useless evaporation of two thirds of the flow of the Amu Darya and Syr Darya which would otherwise take place in the Aral Sea, 8 million hectares of cotton land could be irrigated [73]. If in addition, Lake Balkhash is drained and its Ili River harnessed for irrigation, another 5-6 million hectares of land could be put under cultivation [74]. Some specialists calculate that since the yield from one hectare (2.47 acres) of irrigated land is about 1,000 rubles ($ 1,110) a year, this could add revenues of another 8 to 14 billion rubles ($ 9 to 15.5 billion) a year, of which about two fifths would be profit [75].

69. Shul'ts, *op. cit.*, pp. 490-491; S. Iu. Geller, "Problema Aral'skogo morja", *Izvestija Akademii Nauk, serija geografičeskaja* 6, 1967, p. 90.

70. Geller, *op. cit.* This is at the old rate of exchange before devaluation.

71. Apollov, Gjul', Zavrev (eds.), *op. cit.*, p. 11.

72. *Ibid.*, p. 336; Geller, *op. cit.*, p. 61.

73. Kes', *op. cit.*, p. 88.

74. *Ibid.*; Shul'ts, *op. cit.*, p. 491.

75. Geller, *op. cit.*, p. 90; *Komsomol'skaja pravda*, Nov. 22, 1968, p. 2.

2. The dried-out bed of the Aral, like the Gulf of Kara-Bogaz-Gol, could serve as a valuable source of salt and other minerals.

Adding this all up, Shul'ts and Geller conclude that it would be wiser to let the Aral and Caspian dry up or shrink and use the water elsewhere. As they see it, diverting the water for irrigation would benefit the total economy by several billion rubles whereas the loss of the Aral and the shrinking of the Caspian would cost less than one billion rubles. Accordingly, they see no immediate or convincing need to replenish these seas.

6. Localized solutions

Most specialists, however, feel that the Caspian and to a lesser extent the Aral are worth preserving. Reconstituting a sea is obviously not simple or cheap. Where does one find more water when the existing stock of water is already in short supply and the surrounding area is very dry? Logically the solution is to find an area with a surplus of water and bring some of this surplus in. As we shall see, this is in fact what many have proposed even though "bringing it in" may mean transporting it several thousand kilometers. But recognizing the cost and ecological consequences of such a massive operation, others have suggested approaches that are more localized in character and which focus on redirecting the water use patterns in the immediate area.

The most readily agreed upon solution is to concentrate on reducing pollution. That after all was a basic purpose of the October 1968 Resolution on the Caspian Sea. Implementation of pollution controls would probably do little to halt the fall in the level of the sea, but it would prevent the further destruction of sea life to the extent that it stems from deteriorating water quality. To do this, water treatment installations would have to be built along the Ural and especially the Volga Rivers. Similar steps would have to be taken by the cities and installations along the Caspian. Improved treatment control by oil drillers, refineries and shippers would be particularly important. But as everywhere else in the world, the Soviets have found that improved treatment does not come cheaply or without resistance. Yet no matter which solution is finally adopted, pollution control seems to be an essential prerequisite. In any case, improved water treatment would generate less ecological disruption than the other plans.

In a similar vein, suggestions have been made to offset the fall in the flow of nutrient to the sea. As mentioned previously, this is caused by the erection of dams which block the movement of silt. One report shows that the phosphorus content of the Caspian which used to be 100 milligrams per cubic meter of water has fallen to 13 milligrams. The plankton, therefore, have less to grow on, which, in turn, hurts fish and plant life. To make up for this deficiency, one specialist suggested pouring 3 000 tons of superphosphate into the

Caspian [76]. Ironically, the production of this fertilizer would use up some of the electrical power created by the dams which blocked off the silt-flow in the first place.

Since the loss of the Caspian fish is a major cause for the concern about preserving the Caspian, another localized solution is to increase the volume of artificial breeding. Many fish farms and artificial ponds have already been built and more have been called for. Hopefully this will compensate for the loss of the natural breeding areas [77]. But it is likely that the artificial breeding of fish and the feeding of the sea will never suffice to compensate for what used to happen naturally. Probably Russia's production of caviar will continue to diminish. One solution to this has been to develop synthetic caviar. In fact some initial success has been reported with a milk protein [78]. As long as nothing happens to Soviet cows, this may suffice.

Some planners have proposed "a more imaginative scheme" construction of a dam through the entire middle of the Caspian [79]. According to the geographer, S.N. Bobrov, this would make it possible to maintain the shallow northern part of the sea even though less water flows into the Caspian. The southern part of the sea which is deeper and suffers less from a fall in water inflow will then be allowed to drop by one to two meters. A fish gate of some sort would be included to provide for the movement of fish across the Caspian. Assuming the money would be available for such a massive project, there would certainly be a question of how Iran would react to such an undertaking. Iran also relies on the Caspian for a good portion of its fish and caviar. To the extent that the dam hampered the flow of fish from the breeding grounds of the north and to the extent that the southern part of the sea was made to bear the full burden of the diminished inflow of water, the Iranians presumably would oppose such efforts.

Since a dam across the Caspian is sure to create international if not ecological, complications, the scientist I.I. Stass has argued instead for bringing in water from the Black Sea [80]. At one time, the two seas were linked together, so presumably this would not involve too much of an ecological disruption. It would also spare the fresh water of the Volga for irrigation. Stass suggested that the link-up could be carried out by utilizing the Kum-Manych trough which once served as a strait connecting the Sea of Azov to the Caspian.

Critics of this plan fear that the inflow of Black Sea water would throw off the ecological balance of the Caspian. Because the Black Sea is saltier than the Caspian, the inflow of this water might adversely affect fish life in the Caspian, which after all is the main purpose of the whole exercise [81]. Moreover

76. *Sovetskaja Rossija*, July 14, 1970, p. 4.
77. *Socialističeskaja industrija*, July 26, 1970, p. 2.
78. *Ibid.*, Nov. 15, 1960, p. 3.
79. Bobrov, *op. cit.*, p. 56.
80. I.I. Stass, "Saving the Caspian from drying up", *Sputnik*, May 1970.
81. Bobrov, *op. cit.*, p. 54.

through the years, the Caspian has fallen 28 meters (92 feet) below the Azov so that the engineering requirements of this venture would be complicatedt Assuming that everything could be worked out, some conservationists fea. that plan may save the Caspian at the expense of the Azov. The high salr content of Black Sea water would be hard enough on the Caspian, but it would be devastating for the Azov which has also been severely damaged in recent years. Due to a reduced inflow of water into the Azov, causing a higher salt content, the fish catch is only 5-10 % of what it was a few decades ago [8] Some have even argued that 5 cubic kilometers of Volga River water be divert[2] ed from the Caspian to the Azov and that a dam be built between the Azov and Black Seas to prevent the further inflow of Black Sea water with its higher salt content into the Azov [83].

As far reaching as some of these proposals may sound, they are modest in comparison to the projects which have been given the greatest support and which to some degree have already been partially implemented. In their search for more fresh water for the area, some planners in some of the scientific institutes have decided to go where water is actually in surplus. Under such circumstances, they were naturally attracted to the Arctic Ocean. As noted earlier, the purposeless discharge of all that potentially productive water into the inaccessible wastes of the Arctic tantalizes and frustrates government officials in the water short areas of the south. Presently 80-85 % of the river flows of the USSR move north into the Arctic or Pacific Ocean where seemingly they serve only 20 % of the population [84]. Under the circumstances, what could make more sense than to utilize some of the water surplus of the north in order to eliminate the water shortages of the south. One part of this plan involves rerouting the Pechora and Vychegda Rivers in the northwest of the country while a similar proposal involves the Ob and Enisei in Siberia.

7. The rivers of Siberia

The thought that it might be possible to "improve" on nature and reverse the flow of these mighty rivers did not originate entirely with Soviet planners. Prerevolutionary writers like Ia. Demchenko advanced the idea of rerouting the Ob and Enisei as early as 1880 [85]. Soviet planners have updated such proposals to take account of more advanced technology and geology, but the basic approach is the same [86].

82. *Socialističeskaja industrija*, Aug. 15, 1970, p. 2; *Literaturnaja gazeta*, May 17, 1966, p. 2; *ibid.*, Mar. 5, 1969, p. 10.
83. *Trud*, Feb. 11, 1970, p. 4; *Soviet news*, Feb. 16, 1969, p. 140.
84. *Pravda*, Dec. 11, 1970, p. 3.
85. Shul'ts, *op. cit.*, p. 491.
86. *Kazahstanskaja pravda*, Feb. 6, 1969, p. 2.

The project was to begin with the construction of a dam and storage reservoir at Tobolsk. Here the Irtysh and Tobol Rivers converge just before they go on to flow into the Ob [87]. In time the feeder area may be extended eastward by constructing a 1 500 kilometer (900 miles) canal. This would make possible to add the waters of the Angara (which drain Lake Baikal) via the Enisei to the reservoir at Tobolsk. Ultimately, about 20 % of the waters of the Ob and Enisei could be diverted to this reservoir [88]. A chain of twelve pumping stations will force the water from the reservoir southward toward the north-flowing Tobol River, making it flow backward. The water carried by the Tobol River will then move through the Golovnoi Canal ultimately to the city of Kazalinsk, located slightly east of the Aral Sea and near the Syr Darya River. From Tobolsk to Kazalinsk is 1 500 kilometers (900 miles). More important than the distance, this link necessitates a breakthrough into the 800 kilometer long (560 miles) Turgai Gates, the water divide between West Siberia and the Aral-Caspian Basin. When the canal is built, it will have involved a route of over 3 000 kilometers (1 800 miles) via canals and river beds through which 45 to 70 cubic kilometers of water a year is to be moved [89]. The engineering work is equivalent to raising the Missouri River and forcing it to flow backwards *over* the continental divide so that it empties into the Pacific instead of the Gulf of Mexico.

Once the Turgai Gates have been breeched, the rest of the trip is almost all downhill. The water will move into the Turgai River and on to the Upper Minbulak Depression. There part of the water will be diverted to a 4 500 square kilometer reservoir which will be formed northeast of Kazalinsk and part of it will be moved another 1 000 kilometers (600 miles) to the Caspian. The Upper Minbulak Reservoir will then feed into a vast irrigation system which will be designed to encompass almost all of Central Asia. This irrigation system will include the 110 kilometer (66 miles) Kazalinsk Canal which will feed into the Syr Darya and the 870 kilometer (500 miles) Turkestan Canal which will provide water for the irrigation of the lower Syr Darya. The Amu Darya and Turkmenia Canals will also be linked to carry water to the area between the Amu Darya and Syr Darya as well as parts of Turkmenistan. Several other smaller canals fill in the system and theoretically should make it possible to irrigate almost 25 million hectares (75 million acres) more than is being done at present and without any further drain on the Aral Sea [90].

An alternative to the Tobolsk, Golovnoi, Kazalinsk route is the diversion of the water from the Irtysh through the Karanganda Canal. Under either approach, however, the Aral Sea is unlikely to rise to its former level since most

87. *Soviet news*, Apr. 7, 1970, p. 6; *Business week*, June 13, 1970, p. 43; *Krasnaja zvezda*, Jan. 17, 1971, p. 4; *Pravda vostoka*, Jan. 9, 1968, p. 2; *Soviet geography: Review and translation* 3, 1969, p. 146.

88. *Kazahstanskaja pravda*, Feb. 6, 1969, p. 2.

89. *Pravda vostoka*, Jan. 9, 1968, p. 2; *Soviet news*, Feb. 17, 1970, p. 79.

90. *Soviet news*, Feb. 17, 1970, p. 79; *Trud*, Feb. 11, 1970, p. 4.

of the Siberian water will be used for irrigation which promises a much higher economic return than water used to fill the seas [91].

The Caspian Sea will be brought into this project through the 650 kilometer (400 miles) Ust-Urt Canal. The Ust-Urt will run between the Golovnoi Canal and the Mangyshlak Peninsula on the east bank of the Caspian. Once the water from Siberia arrives, the Caspian Sea will not shrink as rapidly. With some of the urgency removed, 5 cubic kilometers of the nonsalt water of the Volga River can be diverted through the Don River to the Sea of Azov in order to save it from the encroaching salt water of the Black Sea.

8. The rivers of the northwest

While the diversion of some of the Siberian water to the Caspian Sea may help, to most Soviet planners the fate of the Caspian is also dependent on another grandiose scheme — the rerouting of water from the northwestern part of the country. Although it now seems to have a somewhat lower priority than the Siberian rivers diversion, the benefits which it is claimed will arise out of it are virtually as far-reaching.

Like the Ob, Enisei, Irtysh and Tobol Rivers, the Pechora and Vychegda Rivers also carry their waters north to the polar regions where they serve "no useful purpose". As in Siberia, the inability to utilize such vast resources to many engineers and geographers only underlines the under-utilization of Russian natural resources. It is not surprising, therefore, that the northwest, just like the Siberian project, has a prerevolutionary history. Admiral Ribas suggested rerouting the Pechora and Vychegda to the Kama and then the Volga Rivers as early as 1789 [93]. The current interest in reversing the rivers dates from 1933-34 [94]. Survey and design work continued periodically since that time. Several versions have been offered and a widely accepted plan was completed in March 1961 [95]. It was reworked and presented to Gosstroi (ministry of State Construction) of the USSR in March 1967 [96]. This variation was actually surveyed and plotted by demobilized servicemen during the 1960's but apparently the signal to begin a massive construction program has not been forthcoming [97].

The general scheme that is now under consideration calls for the construc-

91. *Soviet news*, Apr. 7, 1970, p. 7.

92. *Pravda vostoka*, Jan. 9, 1968, p. 2; *Trud*, Feb. 11, 1970, p. 4.

93. N.I. Shishkin, "On the diversion of the Vychegda and Pechora rivers to the basin of the Volga", *Soviet geography: Review and translation* 5, 1962, p. 46.

94. Apollov, Gjul', Zavrev (eds.), *op. cit.*, pp. 36-37.

95. *Krasnaja zvezda*, Nov. 4, 1970, p. 4; Appollov, Gjul', Zavrev (eds.), *op. cit.*, p. 37.

96. *Trud*, Mar. 19, 1967, p. 2.

97. *Krasnaja zvezda*, Nov. 4, 1970, p. 4; *The New York Times*, Mar. 28, 1971, p. 1.

tion of a series of dams. Behind these dams, reservoirs would be formed which would raise the level of the rivers so that as in Siberia, the rivers would flow backward. Thus the first of a series of dam were to be built at Yaksha on the Pechora. The Pechora River would then move south via the Pechora-Kolva Canal to the Kama and then the Volga [98]. Further north, the Pechora would again be diverted to the Kama, this time by way of the Vychegda River. This would require a dam at Pokcha and Nivel Izhem which would cut off the Pechora from its northern course [99]. A canal would then carry the backed-up Pechora to the Vychegda River at Ust Kulom [100]. Another dam at Ust Kulom would raise the combined waters of the Pechora and Vychegda and direct them into the Vychegda-Kama Canal which presumably would carry almost 40 cubic kilometers of water each year to the Kama [101].

In addition to the construction of the dams, there were also plans for a series of supplementary complexes which would provide water for hydroelectric power and irrigation [102]. Future possibilities provided for the diversion of additional water from the Kubinskoe Vozha and Laga Lakes as well as the Sukhona and Onega Rivers [103]. Another variant would reverse the flow of Lake Lagoda and divert its water from the Baltic Sea in the north to the Caspian. The backers of this project argued that it might obviate the need for rerouting the Pechora and Vychegda [104].

As with the Siberian project, the construction costs of these various alternatives would reach into the billions of dollars and would involve construction of 800 kilometers (500 miles) of new waterways and the movement of 680 million cubic meters of dirt [105]. It was claimed that such expenses were warranted, however, because of an anticipated payback period of four years [106]. After several postponements and revisions, including one that eliminates the link up with the Vychedga River so that only the Pechora, Kolva and Kama

98. For a longer description of the alternatives, see P.P. Micklin's article, "Soviet plans to reverse the flow of rivers: the Kama-Vychegda-Pechora Project", *The Canadian geographer* 3, 1969, p. 199; *Krasnaja zvezda*, Nov. 4, 1970, p. 4.

99. Apollov, Gjul', Zavrev (eds.), *op. cit.*, p. 40.

100. *Krasnaja zvezda*, Nov. 4, 1970, p. 4.

101. Not everyone agrees on just how much water will be diverted. Bazenkov says it will be 37 km^3 whereas the report in *Krasnaja zvezda* says it will only be 8 km^3. See F.A. Bazenkov, "Sud'ba vody v naših rukah", *Geografija v škole* 5, 1968, p. 18; *Krasnaja zvezda*, Nov. 4, 1970, p. 4; I.V. Bestužev-Lada, "Rekonstrukcija planety: Proekty i prognozy", *Junost'*, Dec. 1969, p. 91; *Krasnaja zvezda*, Nov. 4, 1970, p. 4.

102. Micklin, *op. cit.*, p. 199.

103. *Soviet news*, Apr. 7, 1970, p. 8.

104. I.A. Kuznecov, F.K. Tihomirov, "Ladozesko-Kaspijskij vodnij trakt", *Priroda*, Jan. 1965, p. 88.

105. *Ekonomičeskaja gazeta*, Feb. 21, 1961, p. 3; Micklin, *op. cit.*, p. 213; G.L. Saruhanoe, "Pečora-Kaspij", *Priroda*, July 1961, p. 57; Apollov, Gjul', Zavrev (eds.), *op. cit.*, p. 42.

106. *Krasnaja zvezda*, Nov. 4, 1970, p. 4.

are joined together, expectations were in 1970 that the project would be completed by the late 1970's [107].

With the publication of the 9th Five Year Plan for 1971-75, it seemed unlikely, however, that the northwest and Siberian projects would be completed as soon as some planners would like. The Five Year Plan contained no evidence that full funding had been authorized as at one time it was thought it would [108]. In fact, an initial version of the 9th Five Year Plan provided for the construction of a dam on the lower Kama River [109]. Authorization for this dam was omitted from a subsequent version of the plan [110]. Nevertheless as is frequently the case, the planners and engineers on the projects have long time horizons and are normally content to move piece by piece.

Major portions of both projects have already been completed. That at least is how the numerous dams which have been built along the Volga and Kama have been treated [111]. Similar work is progressing gradually in Western Siberia as we saw along the 500 kilometers, Irtysh-Karaganda Canal [112]. Instead of flowing north, water from the Irtysh now goes to Kazakstan [113]. This canal breeches the Irtysh River near its origins at Yermak and will soon provide additional water for the area around Karaganda [114]. Ultimately the river is again to be tapped at Tobolsk just before it flows into the Ob. The Irtysh-Karaganda Canal at Yermak goes a distance of almost 500 kilometers (300 miles) and is designed to carry 2.5 cubic kilometers of water a year. Twenty pumping stations are to be built so that the water can be raised a height of almost one-and-half kilometers (1 mile) [115]. Work has also begun on a system of feeder canals. The Amu-Bukhara Canal is being expanded and more of the Amu Darya water is being diverted from the Aral Sea on the assumption that ultimately the water will be supplemented with supplies brought in from Siberia [116].

Despite the completion of a considerable portion of the design and survey work, actual construction has moved erratically. In at least one case, this turned out to be most fortunate. Vast quantities of oil were discovered near Ukhata, one of the areas that was slated for flooding as a reservoir [117].

107. *Ibid.; Soviet news*, Apr. 7, 1970, p. 8; T.R. Detwyler, *Man's impact on environment*, New York, 1971, p. 303.

108. *Socialističeskaja industrija*, Feb. 14, 1971; *The New York Times*, Mar. 28, 1971, p. 11.

109. *Pravda*, Feb. 14, 1971, p. 4.

110. *Pravda*, Apr. 11, 1971, p. 4.

111. Bestužev-Lada, *op. cit.*, p. 89.

112. *Ibid.; Kazahstanskaja pravda*, Feb. 19, 1971, p. 2; Armand, *op. cit.*, p. 79.

113. Bazenkov, *op. cit.*, p. 17.

114. T. Shabad, *Basic industrial resources of the USSR*, New York, 1969, p. 293; *Socialističeskaja industrija*, Apr. 29, 1971, p. 4.

115. Bestužev-Lada, *op. cit.*, p. 89.

116. *Soviet geography: Review and translation* 6, 1970, p. 11.

117. Shabad, *op. cit.*, pp. 20-22.

9. The wayward engineers

The flooding of some of the Soviet Union's most valuable oil reserves is a concrete instance of how improving on nature may generate costs that are greater than the benefits. Yet as some of the more imaginative planners have noted, even if the area had been flooded, the oil ministry could always drill over the water. As it turns out, this may have been one of the least complex effects of the proposed rerouting of the rivers.

Though some of oil land has been spared, vast quantities of other expansive property are likely to be destroyed. This includes not only farm land, but towns and promising deposits of raw materials. According to most Soviet critics of flooding, destruction of vast quantities of land in the USSR has been a problem in the past and is likely to continue as one as long as land and raw materials are undervalued. Until the July 1967, price reforms, land and underground raw materials were treated virtually as free goods. A price is now charged but usually it does not adequately reflect the economic values involved [118]. Similarly since 1966, dam builders have been obligated to see that new lands are put into use to replace any land flooded in the process of construction. But without an appropriate charge for land such laws are not likely to generate much response [119]. Thus reservoirs or dam storage areas in the USSR in 1970 covered 12 million hectares of which 6 million hectares consisted of land that had been or could have been utilized for agricultural crops [120]. Valuable timber and sometimes oil land has been flooded and sacrificed in the same way [121]. As of 1965, 5.7 million hectares had been flooded due to dam construction and other activities of man.

Some proponents of the river reversal program argue that even though flooding does occur, diversion of the Siberian rivers may still result in a net increase in arable land. Since many of the river basins in Siberia are already severely water logged or marshy, these specialists feel that removal of this surplus to the south will help drain 40-60 million hectares of Siberian land [122]. To other Soviet critics such estimates seem unduly high. These skeptics insist that the building of these dams and reservoirs, particularly along the lower Ob "would have a disastrous effect on the general water regimen of the West Siberian plain" by causing an increase on the soil that is water logged [123].

118. *Trud*, June 28, 1970, p. 2; Iu. Sukhotin, "Concerning evaluation of natural resources", *Problems of economics*, July 1968, p. 29.

119. "Ocenka prirodnyh resursov", *Voprosy geografii*, Moscow, Mysl', 1968, p. 51; *The New York Times*, Apr. 9, 1971, p. 2.

120. *Sel'skaja žizn'*, July 14, 1970, p. 3; *Current digest of the Soviet press*, Dec. 22, 1970, p. 12.

121. Ju.I. Gordeev, "Opravdano li sozdanie niže-obskogo morja?", *Priroda*, June 1963, p. 51; Armand, *op. cit.*, p. 81.

122. *Soviet news*, Feb. 17, 1970; p. 79; *ibid.*, Apr. 7, 1970, p. 7.

123. *Ibid.*, Mar. 11, 1969, p. 103.

Another byproduct of the dam building and irrigation process is salination of the soil[124]. This is a particularly severe problem in dry Central Asia, especially where there is no suitable drainage of irrigated fields. According to academician Gerasimov, salination "has now spread to a substantial part of our irrigated land"[125]. He goes on to point out that not only does salination lower the productivity of the land, sometimes it makes irrigated land completely useless. According to his data, the total area of land abandoned due to salination in Central Asia exceeds the area of newly irrigated land[126].

Concerned by what he feels to be excessive flooding, water logging and salination, the respected Soviet ecologist, D. Armand, argues that it might be wise in some instances to sacrifice a bigger dam and greater electrical generating capacity for less flooded land and several low dams with smaller individual electrical capacity[127]. He, too, blames the failure to adopt a less destructive alternative on the absence of an adequate charge for land. With virtually no charge for land, planners have little need to make opportunity cost calculations to see if alternative projects which destroy less land would be cheaper. As evidence, Armand points out that in contrast to practice in noncommunist countries, Russian planners and engineers seldom build their dams in mountain valleys where there is less good land to be engulfed[128]. The reason for this is that dam construction in the mountains is usually more complicated and dangerous and therefore more expensive. Consequently, as long as any land lost through flooding is considered a free good and not an element to be included in any cost estimate of alternative dam sites, it is natural that the engineers will select those sites which are the most accessible and where construction costs will be lower even though this usually means the flooding of many more acres of land.

More realistic pricing of water would also reduce the flooding and soil salination that takes place. If water were more expensive, less of it would be squandered or wasted. Peasants would also use it more sparingly on their fields and more effort would be put into insuring that irrigation canals were well constructed to prevent leaks[129]. Because water is so cheap it does not pay to spend much on the construction or the maintenance of the irrigation canals. As a result there is extensive evaporation and seepage. According to one estimate, 7 million cubic meters of water a year are lost through leaks

124. I.Iu. Dolgushin, "The effect of climatic fluctuations on the physical environment and conditions of economic development of the middle Ob district", *Soviet geography: Review and translation* 6, June 1969, p. 302; *Komsomol'skaja pravda*, Sep. 16, 1965, p. 2.

125. *Soviet geography: Review and translation*, Mar. 11, 1969, p. 103.

126. *Ibid.*, 6, 1968, p. 448; Armand, *op. cit.*, p. 40.

127. *Ibid.*, pp. 81-83.

128. *Ibid.*, p. 83.

129. "Ocenka prirodnyh resursov", *Voprosy geografii*, Moscow, Mysl', 1968, p. 81; *Komsomols'kaja pravda*, Sep. 16, 1965, p. 2.

and evaporation just from the Karakum Canal[130]. Such seepage is also a significant cause of salination. The combined effect of a price on water and a higher price on land might make it economically advantageous to cover and line irrigation canals so as to prevent evaporation and salination. If it is still decided to bring in water from Siberia, a proper price on water might make it worthwhile to bring it in through a system of pumps and pipes rather than through open ditches, canals and dams with flooded reservoirs[131].

Another way to reduce evaporation would be to follow the advice of those who argue that the flow of water into the Gulf of Kara-Bogaz-Gol should be curbed. By blocking off the passage way into the gulf, some geographers claim that there would be a saving of 10 cubic kilometers of water a year in reduced evaporation[132]. This suggestion is opposed by industrial ministries which fear the closing off of the inflow of water and the resulting cessation of operations at Kara-Bogaz Gol will make it more difficult and costly for them to obtain needed raw materials.

Juggling the natural environment around by reversing rivers and building dams often sets off other unanticipated reactions. It is not always easy to pinpoint, but dam construction down to bedrock and stream diversion seem to disrupt underground water flow. This could create chaos for regions hundreds of miles away that suddenly find their underground wells have dried up[133]. Similar side effects are likely to follow the building of vast new reservoirs throughout Siberia and Central Asia. New and larger water surfaces are now exposed to evaporation. Several ecologists feel this could give rise to entirely new weather and rain patterns not to mention what changes it might have on the flora and fauna of the area[134]. Among other possibilities, the creation of broad unobstructed spaces on the surface of the new lakes and reservoirs could easily lead to severe wind storms[135]. This is already a problem in many parts of the USSR. Much effort of Soviet conservationists has been directed to the creation of barriers such as trees. Flooding and creation of new water bodies is a step in the opposite direction.

Equally uncertain is the effect of this geographic facelifting on the Arctic Ocean. Only a few ecologists have dared to question what might happen if

130. *Ibid.*, Sep. 16, 1965, p. 2.

131. *Literaturnaja gazeta*, June 17, 1970, p. 11.

132. Vendrov, Gangardt, Geller, Korenistov and Sarukhanov, *op. cit.*, p. 32.

133. *Soviet news*, Mar. 11, 1969, p. 102; *Literaturnaja gazeta*, June 17, 1970, p. 11; *Komsomol'skaja pravda*, Aug. 11, 1968, p. 2.

134. *Kazahstanskaja pravda*, Feb. 6, 1969, p. 2; *Soviet news*, Mar. 11, 1969, p. 102; I.P. Gerasimov, "Reducing the dependence of the Soviet agriculture on natural elements to a minimum", *Soviet geography: Review and translation* 2, 1962, p. 5; *Soviet geography: Review and translation* 3, 1964, p. 60; V.S. Mezentsev, "The natural moisture balance of the West Siberian plain and the lower Ob problem", *Soviet geography: Review and translation* 5, May, 1964, p. 24.

135. *Soviet geography: Review and translation* 10, 1965, p. 3.

the flow of these large rivers were to be cut off. Although their conclusions are sometimes contradictory, the one thing they agree on is that enormous forces may be set in motion that could affect the whole earth [136].

According to one school of thought, the diversion of all that warm water from the Arctic would deprive the region of a major portion of what little moderating influence it now receives [137]. Without water from these warmer regions of the country, the Arctic ice cap will spread. At worst this could mean a return to the ice age [138]. An opposite but no less happy theory has been advanced by Hubert Lamb, a British climatologist [139]. He fears that the diversion of the Ob, Enisei and Pechora would deprive the Arctic Ocean of about one half of its fresh water supply. In his view, this water "keeps the top layer of the ocean comparatively fresh, so that it freezes more easily. If the supply was reduced or cut off, there would be large scale melting". Lamb contends that this could lead to a warming of the northern hemisphere. The Mediterranean climate would move northward and those areas that now have a Mediterranean climate would probably warm up so that they had a North African-type climate. Going on from here, one can speculate that such a warming effort would cause a melting of the ice cap and the subsequent flooding of vast regions of the earth.

Equally upsetting is the hypothesis of Dr. Raymond L. Nace of the United States Geological Survey. He asserts that such massive river reversal projects, be they in the USSR or the USA, could affect the rotation of the earth [140]. By shifting such a vast weight from the North Pole to the Equator, the spin of the earth could be retarded, Furthermore, just as the rotation of a wheel is affected by moving a small weight around the rim, so the earth might develop a wobble. Baseball pitchers and umpires have long known that by roughing the seams of the ball or a large enough section of the surface, the flight of the ball can be affected significantly. Altering the earth in such a profound way, however, can hardly be considered a game.

River reversing and dam construction have ramifications not only upon nature but upon our social and economic activity. Initially the prospects and often the results seem to be positive. Automatically, increased utilization of the area is of course desirable, especially if the full social costs are not reflected in the costs of operation. More often than not, however, the time quickly arrives when the resources have become overtaxed again so that even greater expenditures are required to remedy the newest exigency. This is

136. I.P. Gerasimov, "Futurology in Soviet geography", *Soviet geography: Review and translation* 7, Sep. 1970, p. 523.

137. *Soviet geography: Review and translation*, Mar. 11, 1969, p. 105.

138. *The New York Times*, July 18, 1970, p. 36; I.P. Gerasimov, "Reducing the dependence of Soviet agriculture on natural elements to a minimum", *Soviet geography: Review and translation* 2, 1962, p. 37.

139. *Sea secrets* 6, 1970, p. 6.

140. *The New York Times*, Feb. 13, 1970, p. 61.

comparable to what we can in the United States call the "build another highway" syndrome. The more highways that we build, the more cars crowd onto those highways. In the case of water usage, the misdirection of resources is intensified because the newly available water is usually heavily subsidized either as an outright gift or as a byproduct of electricity generation. Moreover once such projects become part of a hydroelectric complex, electricity generation usually take precedence over the other water needs. Thus as we have seen, instead of being released at times most appropriate for fish breeding, water is conserved behind the Volga dams to insure the uninterrupted flow in electrical generation[141].

The misuse of water resources is not unique to the USSR. Exactly the same kind of action and reaction takes place in the southwestern part of the United States. Because of the shortage of water, states like Arizona apply enormous political and other pressure to bring in more water from the north. Dams are built. Cheap water comes in which in turn attracts more industrial and agricultural activity so that water becomes scarce again. Thus just as in Arizona, the diversion of water in the Soviet Union from the Dnepr River to the water-short Donbass Region 550 kilometers away has proven to be only a short run solution. New industry in the Donbass has more than absorbed all the extra water that was brought in by this canal which has cost $ 600 million[142]. Of more immediate relevance here, the same criticism has been made about the Irtysh-Karaganda Canal[143]. In fact, the whole river reversal effort is likely to lead to even greater misallocation of resources. There are many economist and geographers who charge that as long as the rivers are increasingly diverted for irrigation and industrial use, the Aral and Caspian Seas will never return to their normal levels[144]. New and cheap water supplies attract new and thirsty users and like highway construction, it is seemingly impossible to keep ahead of demand.

Despite such ominous warnings, there are still many engineers and economists who feel that these water diversion projects should move ahead and indeed they support the construction which is already underway. Since the natural consequences of their activities are rather frightening, the river movers often try to find economic arguments to substantiate their cause. They calculate how much agricultural production can be increased through irrigation but not how much land will be removed from agricultural use. As we have seen, cost/benefit analysis can be used to prove most anything, including the conclusion that the seas should be allowed to dry up. Moreover no matter how many billions of rubles a particular project may cost, not only

141. *Trud*, Mar. 19, 1967, p. 2.

142. *Trud*, Nov. 12, 1966, p. 2; *Vodosnabženie i sanitarnaja tehnika* 2, 1971, p. 3.

143. *Trud*, Nov. 12, 1966, p. 2.

144. L.A. Žuvkovič, "Skorost' zapolnenija Kamsko-Pečorsko-Vyčegodskogo vodohranilišča", *Vestnik moskovskogo universiteta, Geografija* 2, 1967, p. 110.

is the economic benefit usually shown to be higher, but the calculations are made to show that the project has a very short pay back period[145]. In fact it sometimes seems that the project can be made to pay for itself almost before the work is even completed.

Calculations of this sort should be as suspect in the USSR as they have become in the USA. In addition, in the USSR, as in the USA, actual construction expenditures somehow almost always end up exceeding the original estimates. Furthermore even where calculations are conducted with an extraordinarily conservative perspective, the cost/benefit analysis is misleading because social or external costs are so hard to quantify. Some critics of these grandiose plans have come to recognize the handicap they are working against and that they cannot include the psychic cost of losing the water for recreation and other nontangible use, but there is little they can do to counter such reasoning[146]. One of the few acceptable arguments the critics can muster is that while river reversal may benefit the Central Asian regions, it will do so only at the expense of Western Siberia[147]. This accusation is one national officials if not planners must heed just as they listen when the San Franciscans complain about the water-napping proclivities of the Los Angeleanos. Regional price and self-interest is one of the few forces that is an acceptable challenge to "progress". Unfortunately for Siberian rivers, even regional rivalry does not appear to be a potent-enough barrier.

10. Conclusion

Nature is not always a perfectly balanced mechanism. Periodically, it brings forth its own disasters which have nothing to do with man. What concerns us here, however, are those instances where because of man, disruptive or destructive tendencies are created or accelerated where otherwise there would be no difficulty. As Engels implied, once the initial damage has been done, the iterative effects do not always dampen down. Diverting the Volga, Syr Darya and Amu Darya has given rise to problems that seemingly can only be solved by generating new difficulties.

Critics of such efforts should not be regarded as Luddites who are opposed to all technological change or experimentation. Nor are they necessarily against "progress" nor do they seek a return to the "good ole days". What they are concerned about is that technological prowess is so often embraced without skepticism. They are especially wary of engineers who insist that no matter how serious the trouble, they can provide a solution. In a world

145. *Ekonomičeskaja gazeta*, Feb. 21, 1961, p. 3.

146. *Trud*, Nov. 12, 1966, p. 2.

147. S.L. Vendrov, "Water management problems of Western Siberia", *Soviet geography: Review and translation* 5, May 1964, p. 23; *Literaturnaja gazeta*, June 17, 1970, p. 11.

which dashes from one technological revolution and solution to another, some conservationists now feel that placing blind trust in science and technology is too dangerous a policy to follow.

Some of these dangers could be reduced if somehow social costs could be more accurately reflected. The hazards are further aggravated in the USSR where all costs, not just social costs are misrepresented. Together this intensifies what we can call Tsuru's complaint. Shigeto Tsuru of Hitsubashi University in Tokyo is perplexed by the tendency of man to spend large sums of money in order to create new facilities when often existing resources are available and could be used just as well. It seems especially irrational when environmental disruption is generated in the process [148]. Thus he wonders why new land must be reclaimed when existing land is underutilized or unutilized a few miles away. In the Soviet context, Tsuru would presumably ask why new lands must be irrigated when present lands are being used inefficiently or unproductively especially when good land is flooded in the process of building the reservoir. If the existing resources were used properly, productivity would increase so that presumably such a massive redesign of nature might be unnecessary.

The propensity to authorize enormous public works schemes is likely to increase in the future for a least two reasons. First, each day new and more advanced machinery is invented which increases the scope of man's capabilities. His potential for change becomes greater each day. Second, the desire of the developing countries to catch up with the ever-moving developed countries becomes greater as the distance between the developed and developing increases. When massive public works projects are presented as one-jump solutions for closing the gap, the temptation becomes irresistible.

Decisions of this sort often have ramifications beyond the borders of one individual country. The example of what could happen to the ice cap of the Arctic or the change in the weather pattern of Asia are some examples. The fall of the fish catch in the Caspian which also affects Iran is another instance. Some planners simply do not care if other people suffer while they fulfill their self-assigned destiny. Two scientists, I.A. Kuznecov and F.K. Tihomirov suggest that it would be far wiser to reroute the water from Lake Lagoda from its present destination *outside* of the country so that it would flow instead south to the Caspian *within* the USSR [149]. According to Kuznecov and Tihomirov, it seems unfair that the water, which, after all originates in the USSR, should be allowed to flow outside the country where it does the USSR no good. The impact this could have on the White Sea and Scandinavia of such a change does not concern them.

National selfishness, however, does not mean that international coopera-

148. S. Tsuru, "In place of GNP", *supra*, pp. 11-25.

149. I.A. Kuznecov, F.K. Tihomirov, "Ladozesko-Kaspijskij vodnij trakt", *Priroda*, Jan. 1965, p. 88.

tion will necessarily obviate all the problems. On the contrary, if several large countries in the world started to cooperate on such projects, the hazards could be just that much greater. For example the Japanese are already worried that the United States and the Soviet Union will decide between themselves to build a dam between Alaska and Siberia across the Bering Strait. Colder Pacific Ocean water would then be blocked which should then induce a larger inflow into the Arctic of warmer water from the Atlantic Ocean. To the Japanese, this threatens to throw off their whole ecological and environmental balance. Nonetheless not only does the Russian scientist Bestužev-Laga urge the construction of such a dam across the Bering Strait, he also dreams excitedly of building another 400 kilometer (250 miles) dam along the northern shore of the Black Sea from the Danube to the Perekop River [150]. The water which normally flows into the Black Sea could then be used for irrigation while water from the Mediterranean Sea would flow into the Black Sea. In this way, the Black Sea would also become warmer. The warming effect of the dams across the Bering Strait and the Black Sea would be supplemented by another dam Bestužev-Laga proposes for the Baltic Sea. Together these projects would cause the ice cap to melt. Bestužev-Laga feels these projects will provide countless benefits for mankind, all at a cost of only 11 billion rubles ($ 12 billion) [151]. Unfortunately Bestužev-Laga sees one major obstacle to the implementation of such a grandiose scheme.

"To carry out these dreams at the present time, there are no other obstacles except the politics of the imperialist powers which keep up international tensions."

This is probably the first time that anyone has come up with a convincing argument for maintaining imperialism and continuing the cold war!

Postcript

On March 17, 1972, the Soviet government announced a billion dollar program that is intended to clean up pollution in the Volga and Ural Rivers by the end of 1975. Such a program is to be commended. If carried out successfully, it should do much to improve the quality of the water flowing into the Caspian. It will not however, do anything to augment the flow of water into the Caspian since the dams and diversions for agricultural use will be unaffected.

150. Bestužev-Lada, *op. cit.*, p. 93.
151. *Ibid.*, p. 95.

Appendix

This first international symposium on the political economy of environment was convened jointly by the École Pratique des Hautes Études and the Maison des Sciences de l'Homme under the auspices of the International Social Science Council, in July 1971, in Paris. About thirty scholars of eleven different countries participated at the four-day meeting. The agenda centered around the following fields of interest:

1. National income accounting and measurement of social costs.
2. The limitations of the cost-benefit approach to environmental problems.
3. Environment, externalities and economic theory.
4. Environment and development planning in rich and poor countries.

Out of the discussions emerged the need for further detailed studies and subsequent reunions. It therefore was decided by the participants to create an *International Research Group for the Political Economy of Environment*. Meetings of the Group are to be held at regular intervals around topics of particular interest. The next meeting will be organized by the Institut de Recherche Économique et de Planification and the Université des Sciences Sociales de Grenoble during winter 1972 in Grenoble.

Maison des Sciences de l'Homme

FREDA M. BLAU

IMPRIMERIE NATIONALE (2 565 061 6)

FSC
www.fsc.org
MIX
Papier | Fördert
gute Waldnutzung
FSC® C083411

Kolibri 360 GmbH
Ferdinand-Jühlke-Straße 7
99095 Erfurt, Deutschland
produktsicherheit@kolibri360.de